Possible Experience

Understanding Kant's
Critique of Pure Reason

Arthur W. Collins

UNIVERSITY OF CALIFORNIA PRESS
Berkeley · *Los Angeles* · *London*

University of California Press
Berkeley and Los Angeles, California

University of California Press, Ltd.
London, England

© 1999 by
The Regents of the University of California

Library of Congress Cataloging-in-Publication Data

Collins, Arthur W.
    Possible experience : understanding Kant's Critique of pure reason / by Arthur W. Collins.
       p. cm.
    Includes bibliographical references and index.
    ISBN 0-520-21498-6 (alk. paper).—
  ISBN 0-520-21499-4 (pbk. : alk. paper)
     1. Kant, Immanuel, 1724–1804.
    Kritik der reinen Vernunft.
     2. Knowledge, Theory of. 3. Causation.
     4. Reason. I. Title.
  B2779.C54   1999
    121—dc21   98-33670
                                 CIP

Printed in the United States of America

9 8 7 6 5 4 3 2 1

for Rufus and Jacob

Contents

Preface

This book identifies and tries to remove the greatest single obstacle faced by students and teachers in their attempts to understand Kant's theoretical philosophy. We can approach this obstacle through the phrase *transcendental idealism,* which is one of the titles Kant gives his philosophy as a whole. These words naturally suggest that Kant is presenting some form of idealism, but in fact he is not. An idealist philosophy is any conception of consciousness and knowledge according to which the things we immediately apprehend in experience are realities that exist in our own minds. If there are nonmental realities at all, they are posited realities or, if we can know things outside our minds, they are known mediately and by inference from our unmediated experience of mental things. Apart from a few voices to the contrary, most readers of Kant, from well before the appearance of the *Critique of Pure Reason* up to the present, have assumed that transcendental idealism is, first of all, idealism, and that the relevant problem of interpretation is that of finding the difference, if any, between Kant's idealism and that of other idealist philosophers. I say that this view is incorrect and that its dominance has been extremely harmful to thinking about Kant. Although I approach Kant through only one issue, the discussion involves the main contentions and features of Kant's theoretical philosophy. I am convinced that a sound understanding of this issue is crucial to comprehension of the *Critique of Pure Reason* as a whole.

Readers frequently find some version of phenomenalism in Kant's account of experience and knowledge. For our purposes, we can treat phenomenalism as a form of idealism because phenomenalism is reductive, and it is nonmental things that are reduced. By including phenomenalism as a variety of idealist interpretation, I am willing to disregard distinctions some philosophers want to respect.[1] A putative contrast between phenomenalism and idealism is supported by the thought that phenomenalism does not deny the existence of nonmental objects but instead presents an explanation of just what such objects are. For example, they are "logical constructs out of sense data." A common objective of the reduction attempted by a phenomenalist logical construction is ontological parsimony. The same parsimony is intended by any phenomenalist translation of statements about physical objects into a language the referring terms of which are confined to sense data and other mental existents. While we ordinarily allow for the existence of mental realities such as thoughts and perceptual experiences and also allow for the existence of outer nonmental objects as entities in addition to and other than mental things, the logical construction, or the translation program, proposes the deletion of the nonmental objects from our ontology. Advocates of phenomenalism speak of outer physical objects but do not thereby go beyond an ontology of mental things, and thus an idealistic ontology.

I have also included under the broad umbrella of idealism views sometimes ascribed to Kant that are not reductive and that merely confine the evidence for the existence of nonmental things to mental representations. Such theories are not phenomenalist, but they do belong to the class of views that Kant brings together under the heading "problematic idealism." They do not close the door to skepticism but virtually invite the skeptical thought, "Any amount of such 'evidence' is compatible with the nonexistence of outer objects," and the skeptical question, "With what right do we regard mental states as evidence for nonmental realities at all?"

Again, many readers think that, in the face of critical reactions to the obviously idealistic tenets of the first edition of the *Critique of Pure Reason,* Kant contradicted those tenets in the second edition, or exacerbated contradictions that were already present in the first edition.

The understandable thought that Kant's transcendental idealism is a genuine form of idealism is conveyed, for example, by the definition of the term *idealism* in Simon Blackburn's 1994 *Oxford Dictionary of Phi-*

losophy: "Any doctrine holding that reality is fundamentally mental in nature . . ." and "major forms of idealism include subjective idealism, or the position better called immaterialism and associated with Berkeley, according to which to exist is to be perceived, *transcendental idealism,* and absolute idealism" [emphasis added].[2] If we judge in the light of two hundred years of idealist interpretation of Kant, this dictionary entry seems to be in good order. If, on the other hand, that interpretation is fundamentally wrong, as I mean to argue, the explanation for such a widespread misunderstanding must lie not merely with this army of readers but just as much with Kant himself. Indeed, the supposition that Kant's philosophy is a form of idealism is by no means a simple prejudice read out of the words "transcendental idealism." The *Critique of Pure Reason* abounds in apparent confirmations of that supposition. Many confirmations take the form of what sound like flat statements of an idealistic thesis. There are also fundamental and large-scale developments in Kant's system that seem to require idealism if they are to make any sense at all. For illustration of the flat statements, consider Kant's repeated contention that we can apprehend only appearances and that appearances are "representations" and can exist only in *our faculty of representation.* Surely all the things that exist in our faculty of representation are mental things. As an illustration of the fundamental developments, consider Kant's grand effort to show that objects of experience are products of a *synthesis* we perform, that is, of a mental combinatorial activity operating on mental representations.

In light of these Kantian assertions and doctrines, it would be surprising if most students of Kant did not find an idealism in his work, since the appearance of idealism could not be much more prominent than it is. In the last chapter of this book, I discuss a number of interpretations of Kant by first-rate philosophers, past and present, in order to convey something of the history, the persistence, and the variety of idealistic readings, and I also take note of the work of several recent nonidealistic commentators. For the main body of this book, I do not talk about the interpretations of other writers on Kant. In order to understand the widespread incorrect interpretation, I use only Kant's writing as the source for the seeming idealism of his work. One of the features that make the present study distinctive is the attention it gives to the problem of reconciling the most prominent and misleading idealistic-sounding assertions and themes in Kant with a wholly nonidealistic outlook. I will also locate the interpretation of Kant that I defend here with respect to the small minority of recent commentators who do not present Kant as an idealist.

———

This book is neither a brief general commentary on the *Critique of Pure Reason* nor an introductory text. I address only one topic, albeit a pervasive topic, and I try to make only one point, albeit a point of fundamental importance. The book discusses prominent themes in Kant's theoretical philosophy, with the single objective of making it possible to see apparently idealistic passages without the idealism. It is a commonplace that Descartes's introduction of the egocentric skeptical perspective in philosophy has had and continues to have a decisive role in modern thinking. In what follows, I try to show how the broadly Cartesian outlook of readers of Kant enables them to see in his writings assertions that are quite the opposite in meaning of the assertions he takes himself to be making. Of course, his vocabulary and rhetoric are partly to blame for misunderstandings. The term *transcendental idealism* is only the most obvious example. In spite of such difficulties in Kant's texts, the great preponderance of the misreading of Kant arises from Cartesian presuppositions on the part of the reader that make it hard or impossible to recognize the very many clear indications of Kant's opposition to idealism, root and branch.

The present work concentrates on Kant's conception of "representations," on his conception of space and time, on the nonfoundationalist stance of his famous "How-possible?" questions, and on his deep argument against the very possibility of a Cartesian subject enduring in time while surveying the contents of its own consciousness. I do not find a single discussion in the *Critique* or in any other of Kant's works where he presents this last argument in full. I draw on diverse materials on this point, most prominently on the Paralogisms and the Refutation of Idealism but also on Kant's repeated discussions of the need to represent the unity of time spatially. Where the precise wording of the text seems important for my single objective, I have not hesitated to present very detailed analyses of it. In these explications, I believe that the structure of Kant's arguments can be used to more or less *prove* his entirely anti-idealist intentions.

The sections of the *Critique* to which I have devoted the most detailed examination are the Transcendental Aesthetic and parts of the Transcendental Deduction of the Categories, as well as the above-mentioned Refutation and Paralogisms. In order to profit from the reflections that are presented here, it seems to me that a reader must have made, or be in the process of making, a substantial effort to understand Kant through hard study of the *Critique*. Undergraduate and graduate students are certainly to be found among such readers of Kant, and I intend this work to be of interest and of use to students at all levels, as well as to professional philosophers and Kant scholars. I came to most of the ideas presented here in the context of efforts to help students in numerous seminars on the *Critique*. I hope that their understanding was helped, and since I am sure that mine was, I am grateful to those students. I have translated all of the quoted passages myself with consultation and help from other translations. At the same time, I have been careful not to let an appearance of support for my understanding of a passage rest on *my* translation. Where I find that options available to a translator impinge significantly on the issue of idealism, I discuss the translation explicitly and I include the German text in the notes.

My interests in this topic are not merely historical. The skeptical moves that lead to one or another form of idealism in metaphysics are part of a widely shared philosophical inheritance. A broadly Cartesian outlook still dominates the preliminary "set" from which philosophical theorizing takes it start. The tenacity of this preliminary outlook derives from its apparent fit with obvious facts about experience. For the most part, if not in all cases, we know what our beliefs are even if they turn out to be false beliefs. We know how things appear to us, even if appearances prove to be radically misleading. What is the subject matter of the knowledge that survives erroneous beliefs and illusory appearances? Most philosophers accept the idea that the subject matter belongs, in some sense, to the contents of our consciousness. This much of the Cartesian method of doubt and its idealist resolution is retained, even by philosophers who repudiate Descartes's dualism and conception of mental substance. Our states of belief and other "mental representations," together with our perceptual experiences, are inner realities of some kind, although there is no consensus whatever about the kind of realities these mental things are. Debates flourish about the nature of these inner mental representations, while the idea that immediate experience involves such realities, whatever their nature, is subjected to little critical reflection. Many contemporary philosophers of mind propose a physical constitution for mental realities. In a programmatic spirit, it is imagined that, with the advance of science, the inner states will prove to be neural states or, perhaps, causally defined functional states that are realized in the form of states of the brain. This prevailing, allegedly anti-Cartesian, materialism does not reject the Cartesian assumption that it is *inner* mental things with which we are first acquainted.

Kant's repudiation of the fundamental Cartesian outlook supports another way of thinking about experience and the mind, and in my opinion can yield real understanding that replaces the perennial quandaries of idealism. Kant brings into focus the conceptual deficiencies of the very idea of the Cartesian subject of experience, and he is not distracted by the issue of the metaphysical substance to which mental realities are assigned by Descartes. When it is liberated from idealistic interpretation, Kant's thinking needs no modernization and has immediate application to our own philosophical problems.

In three different ways, the prevalence of this Cartesian strand of thought in contemporary epistemology and the philosophy of mind is responsible for the widespread and mistaken view that Kant's philosophy is a form of idealism. First, the assumption that this starting point is broadly unavoidable encourages the associated assumption that Kant, in his wisdom, did not try to avoid it. Second, even those philosophers working today who might espouse an alternative to this idealist preliminary outlook are likely to ascribe the outlook to Kant because of the tradition of idealist reading of Kant stretching back to the first reviews of the *Critique of Pure Reason*. After all, Kant did not succeed in his efforts to correct the misinterpretations of his contemporaries, and their understanding, or misunderstanding, of him engendered the whole German idealist school. Third, Kant himself does not sufficiently appreciate the idealist bias with which his work will be greeted. He therefore contributes to misunderstandings by expressing himself in ways that philosophers of Cartesian orientation will take to imply a Cartesian starting point.

The influence of Cartesian thinking on the understanding of Kant is the topic of chapter 1. The pattern of the discussion thereafter is determined by the roster of themes that readily engender mistaken idealistic understandings of Kant's philosophy. In chapter 2, I consider Kant's conception of subjective conditions for the possibility of experience. The point is that Kant's radical subjectivism is not a commitment to the mental status of objects of apprehension, although it is easy to conflate subjectivism and the mental status of objects within the framework of empiricist thinking with which we are all too familiar. There is no justification for passing from the contention that all of our knowledge of objects is subjective to the very different claim that the objects we apprehend and of which we have knowledge are mental realities. Chapter 3 anticipates the response "Even if one cannot equate subjectivism and the mental status of objects, doesn't Kant explicitly assert that his subjectivism is a *subjective idealism,* namely, transcendental idealism?" The chapter examines just what Kant means by "idealism" versus "realism." To this end I focus on the contrasts he employs—material versus formal, and empirical versus transcendental—to make it clear that transcendental idealism is only formal idealism. As such, transcendental idealism implies nothing about the mental or nonmental status of the realities we experience. Kant holds that real objects of experience have matter as well as form. True objects, the objects of outer sense, the objects that paradigmatically exemplify reality with both matter and form, are not mental objects. The same dialectical procedure links the successive chapters of the rest of the book. Chapter 4 corresponds to the question "Even if 'transcendental idealism' is a doctrine about forms that contains no idealistic claim about the objects of conscious experience, doesn't the contrast of things-in-themselves and appearances entail an idealistic conception of the latter?" In the course of this discussion, I consider the relationship of Kant's contrast of phenomena and noumena to the quite different dichotomy of appearances and things in themselves. By clarifying the difference between these often identified contrasts, one is able to see beyond the usual idealist interpretation.

Kant states emphatically and often that appearances are representations and, as such, not things that exist outside of our minds. In chapter 5, I examine Kant's conception of representations and his use of the term *Vorstellung* in order to dispel the impression that he espouses an unambiguous idealist philosophy in his prominent passages about representations and the nature of objects of experience. Since so very much hinges on the concept of representation, and since many idealist readings turn on misunderstandings of it, the chapter is long and detailed. In a similar spirit, chapter 6 deals with those passages in which Kant seems, in one stroke, to bring the "outer" itself into the mind via the assertion that "space is in us." An examination of Kant's concept of space suffices to dispel the idealistic impression that Kant's language often creates. Kant plainly rejects the idea that space is itself a container-like entity, and as a consequence, his characterization of space does not by any means imply the mental character of outer things apprehended as occupants of space.

Chapter 7 focuses on the Paralogisms in examining the Kantian thesis that seems most stubbornly idealistic. In a passage of thought that is very close to the spirit of Cartesian skeptical epistemology, Kant considers the fact that representations never guarantee the existence of any of the outer objects that are assumed to cause them. He seems to espouse the very "problematic idealism" he purports to reject elsewhere, and he seems to leave us with the traditional problem of the external world. This line of thinking, by itself, threatens to rule out the immediacy of our apprehension of outer things and to undermine any nonidealistic reading of Kant's overall view. The full investigation of this issue is undertaken in chapter 8, where, with the help of a digression concerning Leibniz, it is urged that Kant is not a foundationalist in epistemology and that the idealist interpretation of his skepticism requires foundationalist assumptions; and in chapter 9, where the stance of the Kantian "How-possible?" questions is examined in order to show that Kant endorses and tries to justify both scientific and everyday conceptions of reality without trying to place those conceptions on a foundation of absolutely secure premises.

The same stance of acceptance of everyday experience is revealed in the "clue" for the identification of the Categories by means of forms of judgment in chapter 10, and this is linked, in chapter 11, to the difference between Kant's attitude toward the parallelism of inner and outer sense and the radical repudiation of ordinary thinking about the outer by Cartesian and empiricist epistemology. This chapter articulates a fundamental asymmetry between the inner and outer intuition that has large implications for Kant's conception of the mental and is mostly ignored by Kant himself. The fundamental concept of the self or subject of experience is examined in chapter 12. Kant's Refutation of Idealism is located with respect to the absence of intuitive apprehension of the self. In Kant's thinking, both inner intuition and self-knowledge are conceptually dependent on the accessibility of enduring spatial objects. He elucidates the doctrine of the unity of apperception and the conditions for such unity by relating it to the views of Berkeley and Hume on the absence of consciousness of a self as subject of experience. Kant's justification of the ordinary and the theoretical presumption that subjects are enduring entities explains how the representation of an enduring self is possible in the absence of any intuitive apprehension of an enduring subject.

The realistic outlook ascribed to Kant throughout this study is confirmed in a discussion in chapter 13 of the sense in which Kant holds that "representations make objects possible." Using Kant's handling of the spatial representation of the unity of time as a paradigm, this chapter shows that Kant does not try to *argue for* the existence of external things or of an enduring subject, which he takes to be understood in everyday thought and which must be presupposed by all philosophical speculation. Chapter 14 discusses the sense in which lawlike connections among representations mark the empirical reality of objects. Chapter 15 is devoted, for the most part, to the views of others who have written about Kant's philosophy. It attempts to relate a number of variants of idealist interpretation to the themes developed in this study and to explain why the misunderstanding of such a fundamental aspect of Kant's thinking is as widespread as it is. Finally I discuss recent, more realistic, writings about Kant. I compare some of these with my account, and I acknowledge their influence on and confirmation of my ideas.

It goes without saying that I am deeply sympathetic with Kant's general views, although I also find the details of his theories frequently unconvincing and regrettably dominated by organizational and methodological principles that make up the Kantian architectonic. For the most part, I confine myself here to the exposition of fundamental positions that I take to be essentially defensible. In the last few chapters, I raise serious criticisms of Kant's claims concerning the parallelism of inner and outer sense. In chapter 5, I find decisive defects in his contrast of judgments of perception and judgments of experience. These criticisms are offered because they are immediately relevant and helpful to the exposition of Kant's intentions. I do not mean to imply that apart from these matters I find everything else in the *Critique* to be in good order. There are of course endless difficulties, inconsistencies that I do not pretend to be able to resolve, passages that I cannot understand at all, and so forth. I cannot say, by any means, that Kant *never* slides into claims that are contrary to the basic anti-idealistic philosophy that he develops. In spite of very numerous and serious defects, I believe the overall thesis of the *Critique of Pure Reason,* at least concerning the theme of idealism, is correct and is an enormous philosophical accomplishment. This short book is an effort to explain only that much of Kant's philosophy.

Note on Texts and Abbreviations

Quotations from the *Critique of Pure Reason* are taken or translated from *Kritik der Reinen Vernunft,* edited by Raymund Schmidt (Hamburg: Felix Meiner Verlag, 1956). For other writings by Kant I have used the edition of the Königlichen Preußische Akademie der Wissenschaften (Berlin: Walter de Gruyter, 1968). References to this edition are abbreviated "Akad.," followed by volume and page number. References to the *Critique* employ the standard "A" and "B" followed by page numbers indicating the pagination of the first and second editions, respectively.

CHAPTER I

Kant and the Cartesian Philosophy of Mind

The crucial topic for understanding the *Critique of Pure Reason* is Kant's conception of the objects of empirical knowledge. It is only because our experience is of *objects* that the synthetic *a priori* knowledge Kant wants to account for in the *Critique* is accessible to us. Objects, in the relevant sense, are perceivable spatiotemporal entities that exist in a shared empirical world.[1] These objects exist in one space and endure in one time, and as such, they exist during intervals between mental episodes of perception of them, and in places where no one is able to perceive them. When outer things do exist unperceived, they are *real* objects of *possible* experience. In affirming the uniqueness of space and of time, Kant is expressing the thought that the very spatiotemporal region that one person can observe can also be observed by another. The very object that one perceiver detects can be detected by another. These are unremarkable opinions except for the fact that so many philosophers have denied them. Kant does not deny them, and for him objects cannot possibly be items that exist only in the mind of a perceiver. Perceived spatial objects do not reduce to perceptions or to any other mental reality.

To readers of the first edition of the *Critique* who understood Kant otherwise and supposed that his "objects" are realities that are created by the mind and that can be found by inspecting the contents of consciousness, Kant replied that, inspecting the contents of his consciousness,

> all of the foundations of my own existence that I find within are representations and, as such, they presuppose a permanent thing distinct from them-

selves. For the very idea of my own existence in time requires outer permanent things and their changes. Only in the setting of such realities can I locate
my own existence in the time in which they [outer things] change.[2]

Kant goes on to stress that our relation to this permanent outer reality
(not to be confused with any inner mental subject matter) is "perception." The outer perceived reality, the existence of which Kant says he
proves, is not posited or inferred or believed in or imagined. Nor do we
apprehend merely representations of outer nonmental realities. Rather,
Kant means us to understand that our experience of them is immediate
apprehension of outer objects. Inner experience is the mode of access that
is here said to be "mediated." Kant says, "Here, however, it will be established that outer experience is actually immediate . . . ," and ". . . inner
experience is itself mediated and only possible through outer."[3]

Thus Kant is not an idealist, and "transcendental idealism" is a misleading title for Kant's philosophy in so far as it seems to advertise a thesis that merely corrects the errors of the defective versions of idealism
Kant expressly refutes. In an appendix to the *Prolegomena,* expressing
his disappointment with Garve's review, which saw idealism everywhere
("*allenthalben*") in the *Critique,* Kant himself voices regret about his
own use of "transcendental idealism" and the wish that he could "give
my concept a different name" in order to avoid just this misunderstanding. "Even the most zealous realists" would not be able to defend
the objectivity of geometry without the doctrine of the ideality of space
and time as Kant intends it. He says that his is merely "critical" idealism, and it would be reasonable to take this as implying a contrast with
what we might call a "constitutive" idealism that his reviewer mistakenly ascribes to him.[4] Kant contrasts his confusingly named "idealism"
with the views historically known under this designation thus:

> The principle of all *genuine* idealists from the Eleatic school to Bishop Berke-
> ley is contained in the following formula: "All knowledge through sense and
> experience is nothing but mere illusion, and truth lies only in the ideas of the
> pure understanding and reason." In contrast, the fundamental principle that
> rules and determines my idealism is: "All knowledge of things out of pure
> understanding or pure reason is nothing but mere illusion, and truth lies only
> in experience."[5]

Of course, Kant was not misled by his own terminology, and his "Refutation of Idealism" does not include an exemption for a correct idealism
that Kant puts forward, for he puts forward no genuine idealism at all.

This broad characterization of his philosophy plainly coheres with the few passages and global comments that I have quoted, but it surely goes against many things that Kant himself says clearly and frequently in the *Critique of Pure Reason* and elsewhere—things that are not matters of peripheral detail but central themes of the first importance for him. As we have said, the great majority of able readers of Kant, guided by prominent passages that seem easy to interpret, find a very different outlook according to which we know at first hand only our own mental representations and we need a system of complex theoretical commitments and posits in order to defend claims to know anything outside our own minds. I am convinced that the explanation for this startling discrepancy is to be found in the relationship many readers see between Kant's theoretical philosophy and a roughly Cartesian outlook in the philosophy of mind and epistemology. Kant's own statements are commonly misunderstood when they are interpreted by readers who think that a Cartesian outlook is viable if not inescapable and who, as a consequence, suppose that Kant has accepted such an outlook. When this presumption is set aside, a great many of the things that suggest idealism can be better understood in ways that do not carry this suggestion at all. The repudiation of the Cartesian conception of consciousness, the very conception that many commentators adopt and assume that Kant adopts, is one of the great objectives of the *Critique,* and I think that much of what Kant says cannot be rightly grasped unless this objective is understood.

I am not able to see the contrast of the understanding I will defend and an idealist reading of Kant as a question of two opposed interpretations of the difficult writings of an important thinker of the past. An interpretation that finds a kind of idealism in Kant, that ascribes to him a reduction of objects to mental representations, and that sees him confronted by the familiar agenda of solipsistic problems also fails to capture the originality, profundity, and merit of his thought. To see Kant as proposing that the "outer" objects with which we are familiar in experience are really only mental constructions, and thus to see his philosophy as akin to the idealism of the British empiricists, is to ascribe to him a stale doctrine, already exhausted by his predecessors, and a philosophy that bears all the marks of a dead end. Such a reading makes Kant's characteristic concepts merely a system of difficult abstractions that makes no noteworthy progress with the quandaries faced by his predecessors. If such were Kant's philosophy, it would be a tiring exercise that ends by bringing us to the very problems by which we were stumped in the first place.

Kant does say, and sometimes he says very clearly, that empirical objects are extra-mental realities that are accessible to our immediate apprehension. But he also says that appearances are merely representations. And appearances are the constituents of nature and the subject matter of science and of all our knowledge of reality. So it sounds as if the only reason he is able to say that empirical objects are directly apprehended is that he subscribes to some form of phenomenalism. If empirical objects are reduced to mental representations, then we can apprehend them directly only in the unsatisfying sense that we apprehend our mental representations directly. It is no wonder that so many find phenomenalism in Kant!

Let us go over this interpretative maneuver more closely. Assuming that inner representations of outer objects figure in our perception, and assuming that outer objects are somehow constructed out of inner representations, or that talk about outer objects is equivalent to talk about inner representations, then *my* objects must be constructed out of *my* representations. You, after all, are just one of the outer objects that needs constructing as far as I am concerned. If you have your own mental representations, they are of no help to me, and mine are of no help to you. If, with the help of your mental powers, your "synthesizing" abilities, you make an object of some of your representations, my universe is not thereby enriched by the object you have constructed. This is the familiar—can't we say the over-familiar?—privacy of the mental. If the ontology of objects really comes down to mental things, objects of perceptual consciousness cannot very well be shared or public objects. But let's not be dogmatic. Who knows for sure? Maybe there is some unsuspected, clever, and extraordinary account that gives sense to discourse about public objects on a foundation of private constructions. I am willing to assert dogmatically that there is nothing in Kant's philosophy that looks in any way like an attempt at such an extraordinary account. Considering how very popular this picture of Kant's outlook is, we ought to be surprised about the absence of textual support for it. There are no discussions of the problems of privacy and solipsism in Kant. He writes the *Critique of Pure Reason* as though problems of privacy simply do not arise with his principles. Some commentators have gone so far as to assign to him, at least metaphorically, an Averroist conception of a single *human mind in general* in order to retain the mental character of the realities we apprehend while accommodating Kant's evident commitment to a public world.[6] Since few are attracted by such a spectacular expedient, many readers have to think that Kant does not really give footing to public objects, although he may imagine that he can get out of the grip of his private foundations for all knowledge in some way that he curiously fails to state. Thus P. F. Strawson says that transcendental idealism must slide at once into "transcendental solipsism."[7] In one way or another, as a consequence of our inability to understand Kant's thinking about knowledge of the ordinary public world, we are tempted to ascribe views to him about private objects of consciousness that raise very large and obvious problems that he either neglects to address at all or doesn't even notice. At the same time, the vexed opinions that are imposed on Kant are less original, less coherent, and less valuable than those he really holds. Kant is hard to understand and sometimes he is inconsistent, but the idealist interpretations make him harder to understand and more obscure and inconsistent than he is.

I am saying that many readers of Kant have been led astray by the faulty assumption that Kant adopts a preliminary Cartesian stance that is itself very popular and that has dominated philosophical thinking throughout the period since Kant wrote. This is not really a conjecture about the unstated thought processes of commentators and readers of Kant. The assumption is manifest in the idealist interpretation itself. Unless a reader supposes that Kant holds that people are acquainted only with the contents of their own minds, he cannot propose an idealist interpretation of Kant's philosophy. Almost everyone endorses such an interpretation, but then almost everyone thinks it obvious that Kant confines our immediate apprehension to mental representations.

We all know that modern philosophy has been profoundly shaped by the Cartesian philosophy of mind. The Cartesian egocentric, subjective, skeptical starting point was absorbed by and gave decisive shape to British empiricism. This philosophical stance created the modern epistemological turn in philosophy and set the schedule of central skeptical problems that have continued to exercise a decisive influence. The general idealist propensity of modern thought is directly traceable to this Cartesian root. Its more recent manifestations include the idealistic foundationalism of the positivist movement; the many empiricist epistemological programs like those of Mill, Lewis, Russell, Moore, Price, Goodman, Jackson, Armstrong, and Chisholm; the rehabilitated "methodological" solipsism of Putnam and Fodor; Quine's contention that physical objects are merely posited and are elements of an explanatory "myth"; and the authentication of Cartesian dualism as an unrefuted philosophy by Kripke. Cartesian assumptions, hardly subjected to critical reflection, profoundly affect and shape even those philosophies that are expressly designed to be anti-Cartesian—for example, behaviorism and the materialist philosophy of mind that flourishes in so many variants at present.[8]

To be sure, there are many philosophers who do not think that we face solipsistic problems and who suppose that things in the outer world are somehow the immediate objects of our conscious apprehension. The old solipsistic agenda is rather tired, and a good many thinkers, quite rightly, simply ignore it. But for the most part, this is not a consequence of a philosophical development that has thought through and beyond the Cartesian stance. On the whole, even those who do not involve themselves in the quagmire of egocentric epistemology do not know just why they should not do so, and they are quite willing to suppose that Kant must have adopted this familiar stance.

The Cartesian egocentric and skeptical starting point envisions a conscious subject who apprehends, in the first instance, merely the passing contents of his own mind. This self-knowledge is offered as the ground floor for philosophical reflection. The triumph of this conception is well expressed by Hume when he says,

> 'tis universally allowed by philosophers and pretty obvious in itself, that the only objects present with the mind are impressions and ideas, and that external objects become known to us only by the perceptions they occasion.[9]

Hume exaggerates, but in the modern European and American traditions, the acceptance of this starting point for philosophy is not far short of the universality Hume claims. Even more important, Hume is right that an enormous number of thinkers suppose that once the egocentric solipsistic conception is brought to our attention, it is "pretty obvious in itself." This conviction has the effect of stifling further reflection that might radically re-evaluate the egocentric starting point that is imagined to be obvious.

In sum, many interpreters of Kant would be willing to fall in with Russell's supposition that the Cartesian solipsistic perspective is inescapable and that solipsism itself is irrefutable, although unrewarding, as a philosophy.[10] They *assume* that Kant accepts this view and that it informs his complex theoretical windings. Every minimally educated student knows that Kant explicitly rejects and refutes a lot of what Hume and Locke asserted, and that Kant also identifies Descartes as the proponent of defective idealistic and metaphysical views. But this is consistent with my contention that most readers of Kant are themselves persuaded that Descartes did quite properly call attention to the solipsistic subjectivity of our *immediate perspective on things*. They see in Kant's philosophy an acceptance of this limited Cartesian message, which is, by itself, of immense significance. Having made this assumption, it becomes easy to construe much of what Kant says in terms of the Cartesian starting point he is imagined to share. This assumption is sufficiently strong that it survives in the assessment of Kant's thought, even though he does not explicitly confirm the adoption of a Cartesian starting point in his writings and makes a great many assertions that seem to indicate unambiguously that he does not adopt it.

Kant does not merely fail to make prominent a solipsistic outlook; he argues that such a starting point cannot possibly exist. We are conscious at all, Kant holds, only because we are conscious of things outside our minds. We can be aware of private, transient, merely mental contents (not mental objects), but this potentiality requires conscious acquaintance with objects, and as I said at the outset, these objects have to be public, enduring, nonmental things.

CHAPTER 2

Subjectivism versus Idealism

Kant has to invent the terms for his own rejection of the traditional Cartesian starting point. In the process, his distinction between the subjective and the objective, and his uses of the words *object, objective,* and *representation,* become flexible to a fault. He takes over many thoughts and concepts that have grown out of the tradition he means to overthrow. He says a great many things that sound like commitments to the old starting point. His transcendental arguments, the shifting viewpoints of his regressive investigations of conditions, his recapitulations "from below," his contrasting synthetic and analytic modes of exposition, and his endless, mostly unannounced, fresh starts on difficult points all contribute to the possibility of misunderstandings.[1] To this one must add the fact that he conducts his discourse, for the most part, at a celestial level of abstraction from which he seldom descends for the sake of illustration. The resulting text seems to have numerous flat contradictions in it, so it is not surprising that readers can take his point to be the opposite of what he intends. Concerning the theme of idealism in particular, Kant seems to be remarkably unappreciative of the ease with which his words lend themselves to idealistic interpretation, and his apparent surprise at such interpretations is itself surprising.

The single point at the core that is most easily misunderstood is that Kant's philosophy is indeed, like Descartes's, a "subjectivism." In the case of Kant's thinking, to call his view a subjectivism is to draw attention to the thesis that all of our experiences of reality, and all characterizations of reality of which we are capable, are necessarily framed in terms that relate what exists to our cognitive powers. No conception of reality accessible to us yields descriptions of things in mind-independent terms. Kant purports to solve the main problems he addresses by finding subjective roots for what others might have taken to be objective matters independent of us and our thinking. Descartes and other idealists also present a thoroughgoing subjectivism. But for idealists, subjectivism entails not the mind-dependence of our descriptions of outer reality but the relocation of objects of immediate consciousness from outer to inner reality, from the material to the mental realm. Both philosophies are subjective, but their salient conceptions of subjectivity are strikingly different.

Kant develops his subjectivism in the course of his investigations of conditions for the possibility of experience. The emphasis on experience is itself an important piece of philosophical ground shared by Kant, Cartesian idealists, and empiricists and skeptics who adopt the Cartesian philosophy of mind. This circumstance encourages an exaggerated assessment of the similarity of the doctrines. In order to bring out similarities and differences more precisely, let us reflect in a Kantian spirit on the very idea of experience and of conditions for the possibility of experience.

Inanimate objects do not have experience. They cannot have experience because they are not constituted in whatever way it is that makes experience possible. Let us call the constitutional prerequisites that something must satisfy if it is to have experience at all the *subjective conditions* for possible experience. Whatever these subjective conditions are, it is clear enough that the constitution of a normal human being satisfies them. An individual subject might satisfy the subjective conditions and, nonetheless, never have any experience because its constitutional potentialities are never brought into operation in the course of its existence. That is not what happens to rocks and molecules of water, for they have no capacity for experience for which occasioning circumstances might fail. Human beings might never have any experience if they were cruelly kept alive but not exposed to any stimulation at all. Such unfortunate creatures, endowed with the potential for experience, would not have any because other external conditions that have nothing to do with the constitution of the subject of experience are not met. So there are *objective conditions* for the possibility of experience as well as subjective conditions.

But what is *experience?* What is it to *have experience?* What is a *subject* of experience? We cannot think to much purpose about conditions for the possibility of experience unless we can respond to these questions with reasonable definiteness. Ultimately, I want to do my best to say what Kant thinks are the right answers to these questions. What we ought to say about these large and general questions depends on other issues and problems that must first be brought to light and patiently investigated.

Informal reflection on experience will quickly suggest perceptual examples. If we add the qualification "conscious" to perceptual experience, we will naturally call to mind contexts in which subjects recognize and are able to describe what they perceive. Conscious perceptual experience generally operates in the background in Kant's discussions of experience and the possibility of experience. For the long run, however, the appeal to perception is presumably too narrow, because nonperceptual processes of introspection or self-consciousness also seem suitable examples of conscious experience, and these are also intended to be covered by Kant's thinking. "Introspection" and "self-consciousness" are familiar ideas, but here too we do not start with an ability to say exactly what these things are. I am willing to let legitimate questions go unanswered for the present and to depend on rough intimations and our shared confidence that, whatever conscious experience is, we do have conscious experience and that *we are subjects* of such experience. Even in the absence of further clarity, the idea of subjective and objective conditions for the possibility of experience makes reasonably good sense. Let us reflect a bit more on this idea.

Rocks are bombarded by the same *stimuli* that fall on the body of a human being and figure in the development of conscious perceptual experience. Of course, it makes sense to call things the rocks are bombarded with "stimuli" only because they also fall on creatures that are *sensitive* to them. It is easy to agree that being sensitive to stimulation is a necessary condition for having conscious experience of the world. This plausible conviction is not inhibited by lack of specificity as to just what being sensitive amounts to. Whatever we eventually come to spell out under this heading, sensitivity is one subjective condition for the possibility of conscious experience of things in the environment of the subject.

We would get off to a bad start in thinking about Kant if we were to construe subjective conditions as merely empirical matters that might be clarified and articulated in detail by scientists studying just what it is about the constitution of a subject that is required for bodily sensitivity to stimuli. Kant's viewpoint is a major departure from either commonsense or scientific reflection. But his sophisticated outlook is reached by a few steps starting from naive speculation.

Empirical knowledge, by definition, depends upon perceptual experience as the indispensable source of evidence. As soon as we agree that the attainment of experience is not just a question of input into the creature that has experience, but that it also depends upon constitutional features that make a subject fit for experience, a puzzling theoretical question comes into view. Experience is a product to which the satisfaction of subjective and objective conditions contributes. The puzzling theoretical question is this: In the *content* of our experience, what is traceable to the objective conditions or input and what to the constitution of the subject?

As a theoretical question, this is forbiddingly abstract. Nonetheless, everyone familiar with the most modest philosophical reflection can recognize a deep and difficult issue here through contemplation of illustrations. Everyone knows, for example, that colors are imputed to the outer world of material objects at a commonsense level of thought and talk, but that many philosophers think that colors exist only in the subject. Visual input comes from a colorless reality, these philosophers say, and colors come into existence in the experience of a subject as a consequence of stimulation by a noncolored environment.

I do not mean to take a stand on this philosophical view about the nature of color, or to agree that it is an improvement over common sense. The question preoccupied Descartes and empiricists of both the seventeenth and the twentieth centuries, but Kant shows no special interest in it, though he certainly does think that color is subjective. I draw on the theme as an illustration only because everyone is familiar with this philosophical passage of thought. For the theoretical question about objectivity and subjectivity in experience, the thesis of the subjectivity of color provides a useful illustrative context.

We have empirical knowledge of colored things. Naively, we ascribe the existence of colored things as objects of experience to the world. We think of the constitution needed to apprehend such objects in experience as merely a sensitivity *to the colors of things*. But on reflection, some philosophers rearrange these conceptions in ways that alter the role of constitutional contributions to conscious experience. Experience of colors is not to be explained by the simple formula "Apprehension of a feature requires suitable sensitivity." This won't apply if the feature is generated by, and not *revealed* in, experience.

As a preliminary characterization, we can say that Kant's conception of the significance of the subjective contribution to experience is a

generalized instance of the same kind of thinking that prompts philosophers to assert that colors are subjective. What about other aspects of
the domain of ordinary experience, and which of them does Kant allo-
cate to subjective foundations? In order to address this question, we have
to sketch the contents of the domain of ordinary experience as ordinarily conceived. As we shall see in chapter 9, Kant appeals freely to our
familiarity with the world of everyday experience, and he expects that
we will assess some of his principles favorably when we do no more than
contemplate them in the context of untechnical and prephilosophical
thought about experience.

Experience, at the level of common sense, reveals a spatiotemporal
world of relatively durable bodies. The bodies have various properties
such as size and shape, color and heat. Such bodies move around, col-
lide with one another, combine, fragment, grow, collapse, coalesce and
evaporate. We discover that what happens in the world of experienced
bodily things generally conforms to regular causal principles. At least,
let us assume that we discover that. Ultimately, when we succeed in a
scientific representation of this world, we recognize that the objects and
properties it manifests fit mathematical characterizations and these characterizations are the basis of causal theories that generate detailed and
penetrating explanations of what happens in the physical world. Furthermore, conscious experience includes a reflexive *self-consciousness*.
Subjects of experience appreciate that they are themselves enduring
beings, and their consciousness reveals their own transient experiential
states and other mental things, as well as the extra-mental world of bodies and the features and relations of bodies. Let us make do with this
rough account of physical and mental subject matters as a tentative roster of the contents of experience.

The thought that color is not revealed in experience but is instead created by processes belonging to the subject when that subject is stimu-
lated by a colorless reality is a modest adjustment of this general commonsense picture. Kant's "transcendental" or "critical" idealism is a
radical adjustment. He ascribes *everything* in the roster of contents of
experience I have just sketched to subjective sources, and *nothing* in it
is simply revealed by experience. Space and time are not apprehended
via the input that generates experience. According to Kant, space and
time themselves, and all the mathematical characterizations that apply
to things by virtue of their spatiotemporality, are traced to subjective
conditions for the possibility of experience. Space and time do not characterize the reality that first stimulates or, as Kant says, *affects* the sub-

ject. Thus the structural integrity and durability of bodies are subjective features. Moreover, the fact that experience is of *objects* at all is traced to subjective conditions for experience. The causal structure of reality is generated from subjective sources, and it, too, is not a revealed feature of the realm from which original stimulations come. Finally, even the subject, as itself a locus of self-conscious experience, is not revealed but, rather, appearances of the subject arise in our experience, like other contents, as a consequence of processes that satisfy subjective conditions for the possibility of experience.

Kant's understanding still leaves room for a contrast between aberrant perception that engenders false opinions about what is perceived and normal perception that provides a basis for valid perceptual beliefs. In other words, Kant deploys a second contrast of objective and subjective within the overall subjective domain. This is not a particularly difficult aspect of Kant's thinking, and it has many precedents. The example of color that I have already spelled out will naturally give rise to just the further distinction between how things seem and how they really are that Kant employs. Even if we regard color as a subjective feature of things, we will still be able to distinguish color blindness and normal vision, and to identify false opinions about color traceable to the influence of drugs or illness. We will say, "It looked red but it was actually blue," even though we do not think that colors are simply revealed features of reality. Such a contrast depends on an ability to compare cases with one another. The judgment that something is not really the color that it seems to be cannot be made simply on the basis of one episode. There is an appeal to the organization of experiences behind any such judgment.

Kant provides a complex theory about the organization of elementary sensory input as the setting for the contrast between subjective and objective at a second level. This is the theory of mental activity elaborated in the Transcendental Analytic. Within the organized system, the term *objective* is irreducibly bound up with the concept of an *object*. The intuited elements are organized by our constitutional combinatory powers, and this is another subjective contribution to possible experience. By virtue of this combinatory mental activity, our experience is not merely apprehension of a flow of transient sensations but instead rises to the level of representation of complex stable objects. Combinatory unification culminates in the achievement of a representation of nature as a single system of such objects constituted of permanent substance and standing in a network of causal relations with one another. Against the background of this systematic organization of our representations, those representations that do not fit into the resulting scheme of things are not perceptions of objects but merely illusions.

This characterization of the constructive performance of the mind in creating the representation of nature provides more opportunities for idealistic interpretation. For it seems that the objects that ground the Kantian conception of objectivity are creations of the mind and reside only in the mind. The mind-imposed, law-covered organization of elements that constitutes Kant's concept of objects seems to imply that, speaking without artifice, there are no objects *out there*. For example, Hume explains that our conception of outer objects has no foundation except for the systematic organization of our impressions and ideas that he explicates with the theory of "constancy and coherence." Hume concludes that although we have an ineluctable belief that we apprehend outer things, there is no rationally defensible reason for thinking that there are any such objects. Kant seems to allow talk of outer objects on the basis of an account of the organization of mental representations that is much more complex than Hume's but offers no better reason for thinking that objects are really outside the mind. This apparent similarity to Hume's doctrines does not survive detailed reflection on Kant's conception of experience.

In the thinking of Galileo and Descartes, the subjectivity of color is essentially connected with the idea that we are able to understand the motions of bodies in the physical universe objectively in terms of concepts such as position, shape, mass, and velocity. The colors of moving bodies are irrelevant to this understanding. This circumstance, together with a rough appreciation of the physical basis of perception,[2] leads more or less directly to the conclusion that color belongs only to the realm of our mental representation of bodies and not to bodies *per se*. In sum, color and other sensuous "secondary" qualities do not enter into the mathematical-causal characterizations of physical reality in terms of which scientific understanding develops.

It is not this kind of consideration that marks aspects of perceived reality as subjective for Kant. Rather, he takes the mathematically characterizable features of bodies (position, shape, and so on) to be themselves subjectively generated and not revealed features of reality. The contrast between colors and other sensuous qualities, on the one hand, and mathematically representable characteristics, on the other, is a contrast *within* a domain all of whose features are ascribed to subjective sources by Kant. Ultimately, as we shall see, Kant's system makes color and other sensible features *more objective* than spatial and temporal characteristics. In this, Kant differs in a striking way from the Galilean-Cartesian conception of the subjectivity of the sensuous, which is still widely accepted. Habituation to the standard line of thinking about secondary qualities is an obstacle that exists in the system of philosophical ideas of most readers, and it has to be set aside if Kant's conception of subjectivity is to be properly grasped.

Subjective registrations of simple sensuous qualities are *sensations* according to Kant. Realities *outside* affect the subject of experience, and the sensitivity of the subject is constituted by the fact that being affected brings about sensations. These are the *immediate* input for conscious experience, and as such, they constitute the whole of the objective contribution to possible experience. Nonetheless, according to Kant, we cannot regard the sensory qualities that are familiar to us in sensations as revealed features of the reality that stimulates our subjective faculties and thus occasions sensations. In fact, within Kant's understanding, immediate experience and scientific investigation based upon it do not reveal the intrinsic nature of the affecting reality at all. We never do attain any such knowledge of the reality that originally affects us.

If only revealed features of the "outer" reality that affects us were to count as objective features, then, for Kant, there would be nothing objective in experience. This looms as a wholly disappointing conception of experience. Do we get to know nothing about the world we inhabit? Does experience give us no access at all to the real universe? In one sense, the disappointing answer to these questions is Kant's answer. He thinks that in experience and in scientific thought built on experience, we never learn anything about the reality that, in impinging on us, is responsible for the satisfaction of what we have called objective conditions for the possibility of experience. The notion of the reality that affects us in the first place is, for Kant, the notion of *things as they are in themselves.* Considered as they are in themselves, we know nothing about them, and we can never characterize them except through appearances of them that are accessible to us. Such appearances are the sole input and subject matter of our experience and knowledge of the world. In Kant's exposition, a willingness to use the plural "things" in referring to the affecting reality can improperly suggest that we have some conception of reality as it is in itself to support characterizing it in terms of a multiplicity of entities, and it thereby also suggests some conception of the individuation of such entities. For Kant, the individuation of things belongs entirely to the realm of subject-dependent appearances.

At the same time, there is also a sense in which the confinement of our knowledge to the domain of appearance is not a disappointment at all. Kant always stresses that his "appearances" are not illusions. They make up the subject matter of science, which is not a domain of dreams or imaginings. Appearances constitute reality as it appears to us. Representation of reality should not be regarded as an insuperable obstacle to knowledge of it. Representation always leaves open the possibility of revision and reconstruction of our picture of how things are, but at the same time it constitutes our picture of *how things are*. The negative conception of representation as an obstacle derives mostly from comparison with Kant's idea of a nonsensible intellectual intuition that would apprehend realities as God does and without need of representation at all. Since we do not really understand, much less believe in, such a way of getting at reality, subjective representations can be regarded as the avenue to, and not the barrier to, knowledge of reality.

Most important, in the comparison with Cartesian idealism for the sake of which we began this survey, appearances as conceived by Kant are not all mental realities. "Inner things" that are mental and private are among appearances. Appearances also include bodies in space, which are physical and public. An overall objective of our discussion will be to clarify the "degree" of reality Kant ascribes to appearances and the significance of the contrast between empirical reality and the reality of things-in-themselves. Further, we have to distinguish between the enduring objects of outer sense, which are spatiotemporal objects, and the things accessible to inner sense, which are neither spatial nor enduring objects. For the present, let us reflect on the concept of primary qualities in order to form a provisional idea of the contrast between Cartesian and Kantian subjectivity.

The theory of secondary qualities detaches sensuous characteristics from the outer object in space and assigns to them a wholly inner and mental existence. Nothing out there is literally colored. But there are square things and, generally, things that fit mathematical description. This is, at any rate, the understanding of Descartes, Locke, and the problematic idealists. Colors are only found in the inner mental world, whereas shapes characterize things in the outer physical world. Thus, the subjectivity of color is wrapped up with its mental status, and the objectivity of shape with the fact that outer physical things really do have shapes.

As I have said, Kant clearly includes the accessibility to mathematical description that is exemplified by bodily things among the subjective and mind-imposed features of them. If we followed the pattern of Cartesian thinking, this would mean that Kant brings the whole spatial world into the mind. He often sounds as if he means to do precisely that. Deferring, for the present, just what he does mean, note that color and mathematical characteristics are united again on the basis of Kant's subjective account of space. The very thing that is square can be red, too. Once color and shape can inhere in one and the same object, we can appreciate that the subjectivity of color does not *necessarily* entail mental status. Colors are ways that things look to us and, more generally, to creatures that can see. Colors are subjective in that, for example, creatures with differently structured eyes might see the same things differently. Be this as it may, in the first instance, it is *things that can be seen* that have color, and those things have to be outside the perceiver at some distance in space, in the direction in which the perceiver is looking, if their color is to be seen. The subjectivity of color is not, by itself, a ground for an inner locus. Color is a perceivable feature of outer things. It is a feature *of those things,* even if it is subjective. This line is at least intelligible, while the same cannot necessarily be said about the denial of it. How can we see things at all if they are not outside us, in the right direction, reasonably lighted, and so on?

If we adopt this conception of color, we will have to say, for instance, that a thing can have more than one color at the same time. If tomatoes look red to subjects with one kind of eye and blue to subjects with another kind of eye, there will be no reason to insist that tomatoes are really one color rather than the other. To subjects, colors are ways of looking, and things can have more than one way of looking. It will still be the case that a subject cannot apprehend more than one color in a thing at the same time. The point I stress is that we can allow for the subjectivity of color without making color a feature of something inner and mental.[3]

I am not presenting this discussion of color as an exposition of Kant's explicit thinking about sensuous properties. The idea of color as both a feature of a visible object and as a subjective feature can be used as a model for grasping Kantian subjectivity in general. If we ask, "Would there be any colors without us?" divergent answers suggest themselves. If there were no perceivers at all, then nothing would look any way to any subject, and no ways of looking would be realized. For ways of looking are only manifest *in experiences*. We can understand expressing this connection between color and perceivers by saying that there would be no colors if there were no perceivers. On the other hand, even if there were no perceivers, the existence of perceivers would be possible. Maybe, a few million years ago, there were no perceivers on our planet, and none elsewhere. But things had colors then in that they were already so constituted that they would have looked a certain way had some perceivers turned up. Once we think of color as a feature of an outer object, the object can be said to have it even if it is never manifested in any experience. This stance is already in place in that we do not suppose that things lose their color in the absence of light. Light makes the colors visible, it does not create them. In an analogous spirit, we understand that perceivers are able to apprehend the colors of things and that they do not create colors when they look at things. So we can also justify the view that things would have color whether or not there were any perceivers.

Both of these thoughts, which tend in opposite directions, are exploited by Kant from time to time when he is speaking of appearances. He says that space would be "nothing" were it not for us and our receptivity, and this is like saying that there would be no colors if there were no subjects of experience. And he also says that spatial things endure as such through intervals in which they are not perceived, and this is like saying that things would have color even if there were no perceivers. The idea that spatiality, like color, is a subjective, mind-dependent feature of objective, mind-independent reality makes room for both thoughts.

Within the framework of the concept of secondary qualities, the features of an object that are said to be subjective are understood to have that status in comparison with other features that are objective. Kant's subjectivity abandons this contrast, for, as we have said, everything that we get to know about things is more or less patterned on "how things look to us." This contrastless subjectivity is one of the difficulties in Kant's thinking. The absence of contrast does not, however, imply mental status. It is surfaces that are colored, and mental things don't have surfaces. The subjectivity of color does not change this circumstance at all. If color need not be mental in being subjective, then the other features of things we can get to know may also be subjective without being mental. At least, we would need arguments to show that this understanding is not feasible. In fact, it is Kant's intention that we understand the subjective character of the knowable features of outer objects in this way. Only this understanding makes sense of the basic contrast and parallelism of inner and outer appearances. Outer appearances are so called because they are not mental realities. We will return to this theme in chapter 5.

To sum up, when we apprehend a colored thing, we get to know how it looks to us but not how it is in itself. It is physical things outside our minds whose colors we perceive. Things inside the mind are not naturally thought of as visible at all. In itself, the thought that color is subjective is not equivalent to the thought that what is colored exists in the mind. A special quandary arises if it is space rather than color that we take as illustrative of a subjective feature of spatial things. The case is special because spatiality is frequently taken by philosophers to be the very thing that contrasts with sensuous features like color in being objective and outside the influence of the apprehending subject. Kant does, indeed, mean that nonmental realities are spatial only "to us," much as things are red only to subjects with the appropriate perceptual organs. This thesis about space, however, does not cancel the nonmental status of the things that fit spatial characterization.

I raised a puzzling theoretical question when I first introduced the contrast of subjective and objective elements in experience: what features of the things we experience are simply revealed in experiencing them, and what features are traceable to conditions that have to do with the constitution of the experiencing subject? The theory of secondary qualities amounts to one answer to this question: spatiality is revealed, while color is traceable to subjective conditions. Kant's answer is that nothing is simply revealed. But even this radical answer does not convert the reality experienced into something that exists in the mind. There may be reasons for making the further step, but it *is* certainly a further step, and it is not a step that Kant takes. He thinks that the empirical objects we perceive in space are not mental realities. This thought relies, to begin with, on the fact that it is not a mental reality that first affects us and generates the appearance of spatial things. Mental reality is the realm of temporal and not spatial representations. Nonmental realities appear to us as spatial things. The fact that Kant makes space subjective does not mean that he relocates spatial things in the mind.

CHAPTER 3

Idealism and
Transcendental Idealism

To any reader of Kant who accepts the Cartesian picture of a conscious subject surveying only his own mental contents, the term "transcendental idealism" will seem to be an apt designation in that it suggests that Kant's explicit subjectivism also identifies subjectively characterized reality with a mental realm of representations existing only in the subject. All of the idealist projects of empiricists, up to and including the twentieth century, have been just so many subjective accounts of the objects of consciousness, in the Cartesian sense. For all these projects, the recognition of the subjectivity of things can rightly be read as an allocation of the things deemed subjective to a mental existence. In the context of Kant's transcendental idealism, I want to develop the theme that, for him, "subjective" cannot be equated with "mental."

I have already stressed that spatially located things are not mental. Kant reminds us, in the context of his refutations of idealism, that this is his conception of outer sense.[1] Outer sense apprehends things outside the mind, and it is this that distinguishes outer from inner sense. Of course, there are mental episodes in which we seem to apprehend outer entities but actually do not do so. Thus,

> The existence of outer things is required for the possibility of a specific consciousness of the self, but it does not follow that every intuitive representation of an outer thing establishes the existence of the thing in question, since some representations can be merely the effect of imagination (for example, in dreams and illusions). These cases involve the (imaginative) reproduction

of earlier outer perceptions, which were themselves only possible as a consequence of the reality of outer objects.[2]

In cases of seeming perception where there is no apprehension of something that exists outside the mind, the episode is just an illusion and not
an apprehension of a spatial reality that is somehow also an inner reality. The aberration consists in the absence (nonexistence) of the outer spatial thing that seems to be present and not in the presence of an inner spatial thing. Since there are no inner spatial things, we cannot advert to such
things in order to explain what happens in aberrant perception. It is desirable to keep in focus Kant's conception of imagination as "thought of an
object that is not present." This contrasts with the idea that the object in
imagination is really present but is also a merely inner and mental object.

The idealist, according to Kant, understands that in normal perception what is really present is always an inner mental object and not the
outer reality that we naturally take ourselves to apprehend. For this reason, says Kant, idealists maintain that no seeming apprehension of an
outer thing is really such. All perception of outer reality is illusion. Thus
Kant says that idealists admit only one form of intuitive receptivity,
namely, inner sense. It is this doctrine that he opposes emphatically.

Many readers of Kant do not believe that he is entitled to contrast his
view with traditional idealism in these terms. Whatever else "transcendental idealism" might be supposed to mean, it is thought to assert that
we are, in the first instance, apprised of our own mental representations.
Kant is said to hold that putative knowledge of other realities either
reduces to or is inferred from knowledge of mental representations, or
it fails to be knowledge at all. Kant is thus often said to be a *phenomenalist*. Whether this is a just title or not, he certainly does assert that all
knowledge *of reality* is empirical knowledge. Its subject is the range of
spatiotemporal *appearances*. Kant calls these appearances "phenomena," and collectively they constitute "nature." But then he also says that
space and time are "in us" and that "the mind makes nature." Kant tells
us that appearances cannot exist outside our faculty of representations.
Surely they must be mental existences if a mental faculty is the only place
in which they can exist. So, when he is said to be a phenomenalist, Kant
is further understood to think that the idea of objects that *correspond*
to our representations collapses in one way or another into the quite different and ontologically more parsimonious idea that our representations necessarily conform to or exemplify patterns that are expressed by
the laws of nature scientists discover. The necessity of these patterns,

along with spatiotemporal characterization of appearances, is ascribed to our cognitive constitution and not to any extra-mental source.

This kind of idealist reading of Kant need not neglect his commitment to things-in-themselves, although whole schools of Kant scholars think of this as an extraneous element in his theory, to which he is wedded for its envisioned advantages in connection with moral and religious thought. Kant's commitment to things-in-themselves is understandably challenged by those who have adopted an idealist reading, because Kant says that we never get to know anything about things-in-themselves and do not apprehend them. It looks as if, for Kant, things-in-themselves are *real* things entirely independent of us and our minds. They are also, in Wittgenstein's figure, wheels that do not turn with the rest of the machine. Positing them adds nothing to help us in our epistemological situation, so we might as well not posit them. Whether we reject this posit or endorse it, if we are thinking along broadly Cartesian lines, we will contrast, on the one hand, the appearances that reduce to complexes of mental representations and, on the other hand, these unknowable things-in-themselves, which, if they exist, certainly do not reduce to mental representations. So the prevailing conception of Kant's stand as a whole is that he is an idealist concerning appearances and the natural world, and that he also asserts the existence of a nonmental realm of things-in-themselves of which we can know nothing. Some think this nonidealist commitment is superfluous, and others think it an insignificant exception to his idealist doctrine because we are permanently ignorant about all reality save mental reality.

I have set out to show that Kant's transcendental idealism is not properly a form of idealism at all. What is it about positions such as Berkeley's and Descartes's that leads Kant to describe them as "dogmatic idealism" and "problematic idealism" respectively? Plainly, the point is that such views find that we are acquainted with a certain realm of mental realities (ideas) that seem to represent the elements of a further nonmental realm of outer physical objects, but the dogmatic idealist says that there is not and cannot be any such nonmental reality, and the problematic idealist says that we cannot be sure that there is any such nonmental reality. These are both forms of idealism in that they agree that what does surely exist is the range of mental realities, the "ideas," in Berkeley's sense, with which we are acquainted.

Since Kant does not share this opinion, he is not, properly, an idealist at all, and his adoption of the title "transcendental idealism" for his overall view was, as he says himself, regrettable. Kant does not overrule the opinion of "the vulgar" to the effect that the senses acquaint us with material objects outside us. Thus, he does not reduce our conception of such objects to concatenations of mental things, or suppose that our evidence for the existence of material objects is the occurrence of mental representations. Therefore, Kant is not a phenomenalist, as ordinarily understood. Much of Kant's usage of "idealism" plainly expresses exactly the sense of the term that I have just explained. I mean that, for Kant, an idealist is someone who says that outer things are really just ideas or that, in any case, all that we can know for sure is ideas. This is what Kant means by the term when he explains his own "empirical *realism*" and contrasts it with the "empirical idealism" of thinkers like Berkeley. He says that empirical idealists are "transcendental realists." By this he means that idealists hold that empirical objects of perception are mental realities, that is, just "ideas" in the sense of Descartes, Locke, and Berkeley. Thus empirical idealists hold that perceptual experience involves an illusion of outer nonmental reality (that's the empirical idealism), but idealists also think of these inner things, these ideas, as themselves *absolute realities,* that is, they think of their own ideas as if these, at least, are things-in-themselves (that's the transcendental realism). Kant's contrasting view is empirical realism and transcendental idealism. Empirical realism is the doctrine that objects of perception are real, that they are *not* just ideas, and that they *are* immediately apprehended nonmental realities and not the illusion of such outer objects. But for Kant, the mental particulars that we apprehend by virtue of our inner receptivity (which is not, of course, perception) are also appearances and not absolute realities. This is his transcendental idealism that contrasts with transcendental realism. It is not a philosophy that urges, as true idealism does, that everything is, after all, just a domain of ideas. Outer things, on Kant's theory, are not just ideas. Of course, the inner mental reality we apprehend might be called a domain of ideas,[3] but not, according to Kant, a domain of reality considered as it is in itself.

The point is that philosophers, according to Kant, have suffered from the illusion that inner things, unlike outer, are not only mental but also absolute and not subjective realities. Transcendental idealism rejects this conclusion and puts forward a parallelism of inner and outer objects.[4]

> I understand by the transcendental idealism of all appearances the doctrine according to which they are collectively considered to be representations, and not to be things-in-themselves; and that space and time are, thus, only sensible forms of our intuition, and are not determinations that are themselves given, and are not conditions of objects as things-in-themselves.[5]

Outer objects and inner mental things are both subjective appearances, but only inner appearances are ideas, that is, mental realities. The title "transcendental idealism" is misleading because it suggests that Kant claims that the domain of objects is just a domain of ideas, that is, of mental representations, while he really claims that the domain of objects is just a domain of appearances. Kant's repudiation of solipsism follows from the fact that, for him, outer appearances are not mental realities at all, and they are immediately apprehended. They are essentially spatiotemporal, enduring, nonmental, physical, and public things. Inner realities are essentially temporal, transient, and private. The doctrine of the Refutation of Idealism includes the assertion that we could not be conscious of transient inner realities (which are not objects) if we were not conscious, in the first instance, of enduring objects in space. The same doctrine is presented in both the first- and the second-edition versions of the Paralogisms. Further, the establishment of this conception of objects of experience is one of the essential objectives of the Transcendental Deduction of the Categories.

In the first sentence of the Refutation of Idealism inserted into the discussion of the Postulates in the second edition of the *Critique,* Kant introduces a parenthetical qualification concerning the idealism he is about to refute. He begins: "Idealism (I mean material idealism). . . ."[6] No doubt he does this because he is mindful of the danger that he will be taken to refute even his own transcendental idealism. But the explanation of material idealism reveals that by this qualified term Kant means what ordinary readers call simply "idealism." "Formal idealism" is Kant's contrast for the "material idealism" he refutes. The contrast emphasizes that, in so far as empirical objects have a matter (which is manifested in the sensations they engender) and are not merely formal objects (like mathematical objects), no idealistic account of them is correct.[7] That is, objects that are not merely formal are realities that exist outside the mind.

There is an easily followed metaphorical line of thinking (which will be discussed presently) that makes Kant's term *transcendental idealism* intelligible and that conforms in a natural way to what he says about idealism properly so called. But this understanding does not salvage any idealist thesis as something that Kant affirms.

Before presenting the metaphorical line of thinking that makes Kant's use of the phrase "transcendental idealism" graspable, it is important to confine this exposition to *Kant's* thinking. Unlike Kant himself, the German philosophers following him do present views, sometimes under the title "transcendental idealism," that are truly idealist philosophies. That is, they are views that consider some range of things to which we are inclined to ascribe a nonmental reality that corresponds to our ideas or representations, but "correct" this inclination and confine the things in question to the mental reality of ideas or representations themselves. An example of commentary that misunderstands Kant and leads straight to the development of a truly idealist theory is the following statement by F. H. Jacobi in 1787, the year in which the second edition of the *Critique* was published. Jacobi criticizes Kant for asserting that it is empirical objects that affect us by making impressions on the senses:

> for according to the Kantian doctrine, the empirical object, which is always only appearance, is not present outside us and, indeed, is never something other than a representation. Concerning the transcendental object, according to this doctrine, we know nothing whatsoever; and it is also never the thing-in-itself of which we speak when objects come into consideration, for the concept of the thing-in-itself is at best a problematic concept.[8]

The theories of the German idealists following Kant do have the feature that any theory properly called an "idealism" ought to have. These philosophers rejected the thing-in-itself, which they took to be a conspicuous commitment that gets in the way of a thoroughgoing idealist interpretation of Kant.[9] An idealist is, I repeat, a philosopher who finds that reality is, after all, just a question of ideas and other mental things, and not of a nonmental realm that we apprehend and represent. The philosophers who came after Kant understood his transcendental idealism to be a true idealism, and they found their way to their "absolute idealism" and "transcendental idealism" starting from what they took to be his similar commitments. The things that Kant says prominently and repeatedly about space and time and appearances, namely, that the former are the locus of everything we apprehend and are also "in us" and that the latter are constituted of representations and cannot "exist outside our faculty of representations" make it easy to understand how his principal German successors could have taken his transcendental idealism to be an idealist philosophy like their own. But they are nonetheless mistaken. Thus the German idealists are among those who, in an essentially Cartesian spirit, equate Kant's subjectivism with idealism and imagine that he ascribes a mental status to objects in so far as he says that they are, as appearances, irreducibly subjective.

CHAPTER 4

Are Things-in-Themselves Noumena?

The side of Kant's thought that presents his conception of things-in-themselves can be regarded as quite like an idealism, and it is because he perceives a striking analogy with true idealism in the context of things-in-themselves that Kant himself uses the term "transcendental idealism." Those who impute to Kant an idealist account of empirical objects, however, misunderstand the analogy that he sees. Kant says that we have *ideas* of things-in-themselves and, along with these ideas, we have the illusion of metaphysical knowledge of things considered as they are in themselves. This presents a pattern that is something *like* that of idealism, since we do not get any further than our ideas of things-in-themselves *and* we suffer from the illusion that we do get further. The fallacious doctrines explored in the Transcendental Dialectic are expressions of the illusions to which we are susceptible in thinking that we can go beyond ideas and reach knowledge of things-in-themselves. Kant's identification of an illusion of knowledge of things-in-themselves is analogous to the traditional idealist contention that claims to know mind-independent empirical objects are engendered by the illusion that we apprehend outer things directly. To put the point bluntly, the contrast between the phenomena we know and the things-in-themselves that we never do get to know looks like a version of the problem of the external world. If we substitute Kant's term *noumena* for things-in-themselves and note that the very existence of noumena is "problematic" according to Kant, his view appears to be indistinguishable from traditional idealism. This, of course, is just how Jacobi understands Kant in the passage quoted in chapter 3.

Even in this context, however, where Kant is talking about our ideas of nonempirical reality, he does not actually assert any idealist conclusion, which he would do only if he contended that there are no things-in-themselves but only ideas that seem to be ideas of such things, or if he argued that we cannot know for sure whether there are any things-in-themselves in addition to our ideas of such things. These views would amount to a dogmatic or a problematic idealism concerning things-in-themselves. Jacobi seems to adopt the latter position, but Kant himself propounds neither. It is in the context of these understandings that German idealism turns away from Kant's commitment to things-in-themselves.

Although Kant thinks that philosophers suffer from the illusion that they can make defensible judgments that characterize things-in-themselves, the very existence of things-in-themselves is no illusion according to him. On the contrary, he says there are certainly such things, and that the existence of appearances entails the existence of things-in-themselves, although we can attain knowledge only of the appearances.

Part of the general difficulty in understanding Kant springs from his seeming to adopt a double standard for existence or reality. It seems as though, when we are interested in the existence of some thing O, Kant obliges us to conduct two investigations: one into the possibility that O is empirically real and the other into the possibility that O is transcendentally real. This stance with two kinds of reality is a suspicious tenet when it enables Kant to emphasize one reality at the expense of the other as context requires. Thus, when he is a sturdy and hard-headed empiricist, he downgrades anything but empirical existence as mere *Hirngespinst* (fantasy); however, when moral and religious concerns are threatened, he is liable to warn us about exaggerating the reality of appearances. For example,

> Here I want to make the observation that, since the universal interconnectedness of all appearances, in a context of Nature, is an exceptionless law, this circumstance will necessarily destroy all freedom if one insists stubbornly on the reality of appearances. (A537, B565)

Passages in this vein give the impression that if only we could know things-in-themselves, we would regard appearances as a mental froth and not as a domain of real objects. I think that Kant can be absolved of any charge of sharp practice with his two realities, but in any case he is plainly not an idealist when it comes to things-in-themselves. We get no knowledge of them at all, but Kant is certainly committed to their existence. In addition to being the necessary foundation for our conceptions of ourselves as subjects and moral agents, things-in-themselves are the realities that originally affect us and engender representations in us, and they are the things that *appear,* as Kant says himself.

Among his devices for speaking of realities that are not empirical objects, not phenomena, and not mere appearances, Kant also uses the term *noumena.* He tells us that the concept of noumena is a "regulative" concept, that it is "problematic," and a "limiting" concept.[1] All of these characterizations contribute to the unmistakable impression that Kant draws back from an unqualified assertion that there are any noumena. If we were to identify things-in-themselves with noumena, we would have to say that Kant is equally indefinite or tentative in his commitment to the existence of things-in-themselves.[2] His stand on such realities would then be much like that of the problematic idealists relative to the existence of nonmental objects of perception. It is because Jacobi makes just this faulty identification of noumena with things-in-themselves that he calls things-in-themselves "problematic." He has simply transferred to things-in-themselves the term that Kant explicitly does ascribe to noumena. I think that in the history of Kant interpretation, those who have wanted to downgrade the thing-in-itself or eliminate it from his theory have taken encouragement from the patent weakness of his commitment to noumena.

We will have to return to this question, but I will say here that the facts about his text that we have summarized merely serve to underscore the need to distinguish between Kant's concept of things-in-themselves and his concept of noumena. It is not hard to find the right distinction. According to Kant's definition, noumena, if there be a range of objects truly characterizable as such, are things apprehended by a nonreceptive or nonsensible intuition.

> In order that a noumenon signify a true object, distinguishable from all phenomena, it is not enough that my thoughts about it be free of all conditions of sensible intuition. I must in addition have reason to posit another form of intuition than this sensible one, by means of which such an object could be given. Otherwise my thought of a noumenon is quite empty although without contradiction.[3]

The concept of noumena includes the idea of the means of apprehension of the things that would exemplify it. It would be contradictory to affirm the existence of noumena that could not be apprehended by subjects no matter what their cognitive constitution. The concept of things-in-themselves does not include any conditions about the mode of apprehension of such things. Thus, there is nothing contradictory in the idea of things-in-themselves that could not be apprehended by any subject. It is precisely for this reason that skepticism concerning the existence of noumena is not skepticism concerning the existence of things-in-themselves.

It is certainly Kant's view that God does not have to be affected by the realities that God knows. Kant frequently appeals to the idea of divine thought in order to make prominent the contrasting dependence of human subjects on receptivity to outer stimulation from things. Of course, this is only an informal appeal and a conjecture about contrasting cognitive capacities since, though Kant professes his *faith,* he does not claim to *know* that God exists, much less to know the character of God's mental activities and knowledge.[4] Within the speculatively developed contrast, however, it does seem to be clear that God's knowledge of reality would skip what for us are appearances. It does not follow that things-in-themselves are certainly noumena because they are apprehended by the nonsensible intuition of God. That would be the case only if, first, God exists and, second, God's knowledge of things-in-themselves is grounded in some kind of intuition other than sensible intuition. But for Kant these assertions are theoretically just as problematic as the assertion of the existence of noumena.

In any event, Kant sometimes gives his readers the impression that sensible appearances do not have an absolute place in his ontology. This can very plausibly be read as a good reason for thinking that Kant's is an idealist view about appearances and a realist view about things-in-themselves. Another intelligence might not have to countenance appearances at all, as God's intelligence would not. In apparent confirmation of this line of interpretation, Kant does seem to say that empirical objects are only congeries of representations, which are mental things. He appears to be saying that unknowable things-in-themselves are extramental realities concerning which we cannot get any further than ideas, while empirical appearances, and the space and time in which they exist, are, in the last analysis, only representations in our minds.

It seems probable that many readers and commentators ground their ascription of a true idealism to Kant on these broad considerations. Wrongly identifying the concept of the thing-in-itself with the concept of noumenon, such readers naturally see Kant's explicitly problematic

stance concerning noumena as a wavering in his commitment to any realities beyond phenomena, which they (also wrongly) take to be confined
to mental things. The two errors amount to the assignment of a problematic idealism to Kant. But how can this possibly be right? Kant's
"transcendental idealism," whatever it is, goes with an equally clearly
affirmed "empirical realism." We know that space and time are transcendentally ideal, even if we are not sure what it means to say this much
about space and time. Space and time are also and just as securely
"empirically real." When we remind ourselves of this dual formulation
from the Transcendental Aesthetic, we will surely have to say that empirical objects are empirically real too. It is things considered as they are in
themselves that are transcendentally real, and of course they are *not*
empirically real. If we say, "Maybe there are no noumena," and understand that to mean "Maybe there are no things-in-themselves!" we are
saying that perhaps the range of mental phenomena *is reality*. This opinion cannot be ascribed to Kant, because it is precisely the error that he
says the empirical idealists make. They are empirical idealists because
they suppose that there are no (or may be no) nonmental realities of the
sort we seem to apprehend. We have only mental representations and
thus, loosely, only "ideas" of these supposed empirical things. Empirical idealists are also, Kant says, "transcendental realists" because they
think the mental reality that they take to be given is reality *simpliciter*.
The correct view, for Kant, combines empirical realism and transcendental idealism: on the one hand, the seeming nonmental objects of perception are indeed nonmental realities in space and time with which perception acquaints us and of which we have scientific knowledge; on the
other, our ideas of things as they are in themselves are merely ideas, and
we have no knowledge at all of such things. The transcendental ideality
of space and time themselves is not, for Kant, the view that these are
mental entities, but rather the view that they are not entities at all.

There really are noumena only if reality can be apprehended by an
intuition that is nonsensible. An intellectual intuition, for example,
would not have to be affected by apprehended objects, so one may suppose apprehension would occur without any intervening sensible representation. But even if there are no noumena at all, the reality of things-
in-themselves cannot be supposed to be threatened.

CHAPTER 5

The Concept of Representation

If we are to sustain a wholly nonidealist account of Kant's philosophy, we cannot concentrate on Kant's own expressions of opposition to idealism. There are plenty of passages that suggest, imply, or assert outright the rejection of idealism, but idealist readings have generally been adopted by philosophers with full knowledge of those passages. We must be able to adjust our thinking to the texts that most plainly seem to demand an idealist reading. In this chapter, I shall discuss passages where Kant identifies appearances as representations and therefore, it is natural to presume, as mental things. In the next chapter, I will consider passages where he asserts the "ideality" of space and announces the view that space is "in us." In both cases, I will show that the idealistic interpretation is natural only when the passages are read in an environment of Cartesian assumptions. My objective will be to explain how the appearance of idealism falls away when we identify that environment and guard against letting it force an idealist understanding on Kant's words.

In the opening definitions of *intuition, representation,* and *appearance* that Kant presents immediately after the introduction to the *Critique,* he makes it clear that a representation is, *per se,* a mental item. Perhaps a representation is something on the order of a mental picture. A great many passages that seem to espouse idealism come straight out of this conception of representations. For example, in the setting of the subjective deduction, Kant characterizes the combinatory operations of the "three-fold synthesis" as mental activities operating on given representations, and he describes representations as "modifications of the mind."[1] Then he goes on to use the same characterization for appearances:

> Whatever the source from which our representations arise, whether they are brought about through the influence of external things or through inner causes, and whether they are engendered as *a priori* or as empirical appearances, as modifications of the mind they belong to inner sense. (A99)

But appearances are the constituents of nature. They are the only subject matter for science and the only objects we ever get to know in experience. Empirical realities *are* appearances for Kant. If all appearances are modifications of the mind, then empirical objects must be modifications of the mind too. If that is Kant's thesis, he is, of course, an idealist by any standard.

In the exposition of the "synthesis of reproduction in imagination"[2] Kant reaffirms this seemingly idealistic doctrine. Once we understand that appearances are not things-in-themselves, we get our bearings concerning the foundation of the necessary unity of appearances by recognizing that appearances are only "a play of representations" that, in the end, come down to "determinations of inner sense" (A101).

Here Kant has not qualified his claim by restricting it to "inner appearances." It is *all* appearances that are said to be determinations of inner sense. And of course, "inner sense" is that form of receptivity "by means of which we intuit the mind and its states" (A22). Once again, no adventurous interpretation is needed to read this as a straightforward idealism.

These passages from the first edition of the *Critique* are among those that do not appear in the second edition. It is very likely that Kant replaced them, at least in part, because they suggest an idealistic interpretation that he wanted to block. It is not satisfactory, however, to rely on the fact that these idealistic-sounding passages were dropped by Kant, for this leaves open the possibility that they do, in fact, assert an idealistic view that Kant later abandoned. According to Kant's expressed characterization, the changes introduced here and elsewhere in the second edition do not amount to a renunciation of doctrines he had incorrectly espoused. In fact, in discussing the alterations of the text for the second edition, Kant says that he did not find it necessary to change his views at all, but only their exposition, and he accepts blame for misinterpretations by able readers. The second edition, Kant says, attempts to improve on the first where difficulties, darkness, and opportunities for misunderstanding existed, while "in the assertions themselves, and in the arguments for them, . . . I have found nothing to change" (xxxvii). He goes on to say that no substantive changes were needed because he contemplated his views for so long before publishing them at all, and because they fit together in a systematic whole in which any incompatible elements would have stood out from the beginning. Whether or not this explanation can be accepted at face value, it does seem very reasonable to believe that Kant does not think he is renouncing any major view adopted in the first edition. He certainly would be doing that if he had adopted an idealist conception of objects of experience in the first edition of the *Critique* and were dropping it in favor of a realist conception in the second.[3]

It follows that readers who find a doctrine like that of Berkeley in the first edition are misinterpreting what Kant is trying to say. If we hope to sustain this outlook in our own assessment, we still face the job of explaining how these passages can be interpreted so as not to engender the appearance of idealism that Kant himself claims is based on a misunderstanding.

In any case, the culminating drift of these cited passages also appears in the *Prolegomena*—for example, in this statement from §49, where Kant has purportedly just set aside "material idealism":

> The question whether bodies (as appearances of outer sense) exist *outside my thoughts* as bodies in nature can be answered without the least scruple in the negative . . . (Akad., IV, 337)

Kant goes on to assert a parallel relationship between my existence, that is, the existence of my soul in time, and my being the object of my own representations. Whatever we may derive from the parallelism, it seems indisputable that what cannot exist outside my thoughts can only exist *at all* if it exists *in* my thoughts. What does this unqualified negative answer mean if it does not espouse a form of idealism concerning bodies?

Kant brings the term *object* into the context of these themes himself in the following passage from the Transcendental Deduction in the first edition:

> And here it is necessary to clarify for ourselves what is meant by the expression "an object of representations." We have said above that appearances are nothing but sensible representations which, in themselves, by virtue of this status, must not be considered as objects (outside our power of representation). What, then, can be understood when one speaks of an object corresponding to our knowledge and therefore also distinct from it? It is easy to appreciate that this object must be thought of only as something in general = X, since we have nothing outside our knowledge which we could set against it as corresponding to it. (A104)

In the second edition and later writings, Kant never states that he has dropped this line of thinking or even altered it. He gives little or no indication that he is aware of any tension between this view and the realistic conceptions of outer public objects that I have emphasized and that I claim to be his real doctrines. Although the second edition is less emphatic in passages that seem to assert a form of idealism, it contains many passages with this general drift, and it seems indisputable that Kant thinks that the views he espouses in the cited passages are not idealistic, in spite of the ease with which they can be so interpreted.

For a long time, I believed that this passage and others like it did endorse the familiar idealist picture. I thought they must be regarded as lapses into the very conception against which Kant was generally trying to argue. Even if they were idealist assertions, which on the surface seemed to me indisputable, I thought it feasible to suppose that they were merely evidence of the great power of the Cartesian picture from which Kant was struggling, not entirely successfully, to free himself. But I no longer think this is the case. In spite of the ease with which these lines of thought can be assimilated to an idealist phenomenalism, Kant does not so intend them at all.

Kant means, at A104, that we apprehend no object to set against an empirical representation; we have no access to an object distinct from the object that is present to us by virtue of being empirically represented. Empirical representation *constitutes* our access to objects. He means that we cannot, for example, compare our representations with the objects they represent. To think otherwise, to think that we do have a nonrepresentational knowledge of the objects "corresponding" to our representations, and that our ordinary use of "object" is grounded on some contact with things other than the contact that representing them constitutes, would be to suppose that we could compare the object and the representation, perhaps finding the latter satisfactory or a gross distortion. Of course, we cannot do that. Having the representations we do have is what apprehending objects *is* for us. To find our representation of an object faulty is to compare it with another representation that has replaced the representation deemed defective.

There is a background tension in much philosophical thinking about representations that impinges on the issues at stake here. The tension is not confined to Kant's conception of the role of representation in perception. Let's suppose that everyone agrees that a representation is a mental reality. It is also tempting, as I have already suggested, to think of a representation as something like a mental picture. We are able to be in touch with the world around us because we can form mental pictures of parts of it and things in it. If something like an inner picture helps us to apprehend the world, it must be because, in some sense, we can "see" the inner picture. If it seems ill-advised to speak of seeing inner things, we can come up with other ways to express the required apprehension that allows us to benefit from the inner representations in our minds. In this spirit, sense-data theorists speak of *having* rather than *seeing* visual sense data. On no theory will it make sense to think that we can compare the representation and the thing represented by attending now to the one, now to the other. If we could make such a comparison, the whole theory would be vitiated, since we would have some other way of getting at things in the world, some way in addition to having inner representations of them. If this were the case, representation would be expendable in understanding our apprehension of reality. So if we take a mental representation to be a picture-like mental thing, we have to understand that we cannot test these pictures for reliability by comparing them with what they picture. In Cartesian terms, we cannot assess the degree of resemblance between our ideas and the outer objects that we think of as both causes of our ideas and as represented or pictured by those ideas.

I have already tried to indicate the way in which Kant's account diverges from this Cartesian understanding. Having representations *is* our way of apprehending perceivable objects, including outer objects in space. In order to follow Kant properly here, since we are using the term *representations* to refer to inner mental items of some kind, we have to say that we are conscious, in the first place, not of *them,* but of the outer things that our faculty of representation makes it possible for us to apprehend. We experience objects *in representing them* as we do, and we apprehend objects in no other way. That is the force of saying that we cannot get beyond appearances, which are things *as they are subjectively represented* by us. To speak of our sensible representations is not to deny that we apprehend the outer things, albeit subjectively.

This is correct and a step in the right direction. By itself, it is still far short of providing a nonidealist reading of the cited passages. The trouble is that in those passages, Kant says that appearances, which are supposed to be the things we do apprehend, are themselves only representations and, thus, modifications of the mind. This is not just an assumption on the part of careless readers with a Cartesian bias. Kant *states* this identity of representations with (outer) appearances. So Kant does seem to be saying, along with Descartes and the British empirical idealists, that it is the mental picture that we experience, and only with this understanding is it meaningful for him in the *Prolegomena* to deny "without the least scruple" (*ohne alle Bedenken*) that bodies exist outside thought.

We should not be pessimistic about the possibility of finding a coherent view here, partly because it is so very plain, in the text itself, that Kant expects these doctrines to be accepted without an attendant idealism. For instance, this very line from §49 of the *Prolegomena* is part of a discussion the explicit point of which is the repudiation of "Cartesian idealism." The parallelism of inner and outer sense that I have alluded to in previous chapters is alleged to afford a proof that we apprehend "something real outside us," and Kant finds that this easily rebuts "material idealism." What is needed is a reading of Kant's words—his rejection of idealism cheerfully combined with the denial that bodies can exist "outside of my thoughts"—that does not even suggest that bodies are mental things. What is needed is a way of understanding Kant's identification of appearances with sensible representations that does not make mental things of outer appearances.

Cartesian thinking prepares us to identify our inner mental representations as the real objects of our perceptual consciousness. Kant's thinking does not. Kant speaks of the subjective conditions of our human receptivity, but he does not accept the Cartesian explication of these conditions at all. Cartesians suppose that things outside the mind are inaccessible while things in the mind are matters for which the subject is the only observer, although for many philosophers this confinement of the subject carries with it an incorrigible authority within this limited sphere. In the Cartesian view, we do not apprehend outer nonmental things *at all,* although Descartes and most Cartesians think that such things exist, and many philosophers in the broad Cartesian tradition think that our ideas are the basis of some knowledge of, or intelligible hypotheses concerning, *material* reality. But Kant does not adopt this conception of the human subjectivity.

Kantian subjectivity is not a matter of ontology or of subject matter. If a subject S apprehends an object O, and S gets to know something about O, we can ask, Are S's experience and knowledge of O subjective or objective? For Kant, of course, the answer is always the former. We do not experience things as they are. All our knowledge is knowledge of appearances, that is, of things as they appear. When asked within the setting of Cartesian thinking, "Subjective or objective?" is an ontological question. Cartesian subjectivity brings with it a pervasive contrast of private mental objects and public spatial objects. Subjective experience and knowledge are of private mental things. We do not have experience and firsthand knowledge of outer things. Of course, the very idea that S apprehends O at all involves the operation of S's cognitive faculties, and to Kant that means that representations come to exist in S's mind. The general atmosphere of idealism is encouraged because it is so easy to substitute these representations for the object apprehended. This substitution seems to be authorized in the quoted passages. But if it is accepted, the whole framework of Kantian thinking about subjectivity is abandoned. Upon the substitution of a representation in the role of object, it will not be possible to ask whether S's experience and knowledge of this representation O are subjective or objective. The idea of subjectivity will be cashed, as it is for Descartes, in terms of a special range of inner, mental, and private objects. Kant is never tempted by this, and he assumes that his readers know better than to interpret his statements in such a way.

Kant presumes that his endorsement of the parallelism of inner and outer sense will, by itself, put an end to the thought that he may be a "material idealist." Outer sense is receptivity to things in space, just as inner sense is receptivity to things in the mind. We do not encounter outer realities indirectly through inner mental things. No idealism about bodies can be constructed on a foundation that includes an irreducible outer sense.[4]

It is not wholly unreasonable for Kant to expect that his readers will not interpret away his conception of subjectivity and replace it with the Cartesian conception that he expressly rejects. To say, as Kant does, that our experience of outer objects is inevitably subjective is very different from saying, in the manner of the Cartesians, that we do not really experience outer objects at all. Kant allows himself rather loose ways of speaking because he is confident that his frequent assertion that the existence of "outer" objects is established by our immediate experience of them will definitively exclude any such idealism. The history of Kant interpretation shows that Kant's confidence in this regard is misplaced.

Examples can help to set us in the right direction. We used the example of color in order to give credibility to the very idea of subjective features that are not mental. In addition to being sensuous, our perceptual experience is perspectival, and the example of perspective also sheds light on Kant's thought about outer reality. What we actually apprehend of something depends on our particular perspective on that thing. A bridge is visible from my window, but in my view of the bridge, part of it is obscured by an intervening building. Being partly obscured by a building is not an intrinsic feature of the bridge I perceive. It is not true of the bridge, apart from the conditions of my experience, that it is partially obscured by something. This is a subjective feature. All visual experience is irrevocably constrained by such perspectival features. We understand this as a kind of subjectivity without difficulty, but it does not carry with it the implication that what I experience is somehow a mental thing. It is the bridge that I see, the outer public bridge. But within my experience, we can describe the bridge as partially obscured by a building. The terminology of representations is natural here. *In my representation,* the bridge is partly obscured. I cannot get beyond my representation. I cannot move to a nonperspectival and thus *objective* representation of the bridge. Furthermore, to be sure, my representations do not exist *outside my thoughts.* Even when we use the concept of representation in just this way in getting at the perspectival subjectivity of my experience, we are not moving toward the ascription of a mental status to the object I can see. Kant thinks his readers will understand that his talk of representation in connection with sense experience follows this pattern.

In favor of the illustration, I would point out that it fits Kant's global claim that what is radical in his philosophy makes it a Copernican revolution. To be sure, the sun circles the Earth *in our experience,* but Copernicus appreciates that this is only a matter of subjective although inevitable appearance. When we are enlightened on this point by Copernicus, we still identify the sun that rises in the east and sets in the west in our experience with the massive and distant heavenly body around which the Earth is in fact in orbit. We have no use for a mental object here. Given our conditions for observation, the one and only outer sun must appear to us to go around the Earth when it is, in actuality, circled by the revolving Earth from which we make our observations. Copernican subjectivism does not substitute inner for outer objects on the pattern of Cartesian subjectivism.

I do not present the perspectival subjective character of experience as a sufficient guide to Kant's thinking. For one thing, the subjectivity illustrated by a bridge partially obscured in my experience is *personal.* Kant is interested in subjective features of experience that are common to all subjects who share our human forms of receptivity. More important, in the illustration, we can understand the subjective element in my experience by contrasting it with a characterization of the object that is not subjective in the relevant respect. A neighbor's window may give an unobstructed view of the bridge. If an observer could travel to the right places, the Earth would appear to circle the sun as it actually does.

When it comes to the subjectivity that interests Kant, we are not able to contrast the subjectively qualified experience and its object with the relevantly nonqualified experience and object. The spatiality of our outer receptivity is itself a subjective feature. Obviously this subjectivity will not be overcome by moving to another place of observation. Kant says that when reality is apprehended by a mind that is not restricted, as ours is—for example, when apprehended by God—the objects that are *spatial things to us* are not spatial things at all. God does not enjoy a better perspective from which to observe things, or even the best conceivable perspective. In Kant's speculative characterization of infinite intellect, God needs no perspective in order to apprehend all reality.

In its own way, the contrast between human receptive spatial apprehension and divine intellectual nonspatial apprehension of reality is like the contrast between a bridge partially obstructed in my experience and unobstructed in the experience of another perceiver. The important difference in the two contrasts is that we cannot really imagine this divine apprehension, and thus we cannot allow for the subjective spatiality of our experience and understand what a nonspatial apprehension of things would be like. The valuable feature of the analogy with personal perspectival subjectivity is that it is graspable without encouraging the mentalization of the object. It is this feature that we must carry over to the more complex case of the inescapable subjectivity of human experience *per se*. Kant holds that human experience of nonmental reality is necessarily spatial because spatiality is the form of human receptivity to things outside our minds. But the recognition that spatiality is subjective should not incline us to go on to assert the mental status of the object apprehended, even though we are not in a position to illustrate what things are like when they are not marked by this subjectivity. That is, when we have agreed that the objects we experience are subjective appearances and not things-in-themselves, we need not advance to a mental conception of appearances. Note that if, *per impossibile,* we could know what God's experience of things is like, that would not move us to reconstrue our experience of outer things as experience of mental things. So the mere fact that we cannot even imagine objects unqualified by our shared human subjectivity does not in itself encourage a mentalizing move.

I have not adequately addressed the fact that Kant himself seems to *insist* that we mentalize appearances in the very passages I have cited. Therefore, it sounds as if I am presenting a conception of subjectivity that Kant might have espoused but did not. Let us, then, examine the passages in which Kant seems to state flatly that the immediate objects of our experience are objects in our minds.

What nonidealistic interpretation is feasible when Kant explicitly says that bodies cannot exist "outside my thoughts"? For one thing, "outside" may not be the most helpful translation here, since it is so emphatically locative in force. Kant seems to be contrasting existence outside the mind with some kind of inner mental existence for appearances. "Apart from" is at least as good a rendering of *außer* here, and I have used "outside" (as other translators do) only so as to be sure that I do not remove any of the implication of idealism by merely translating Kant in a way that supports a nonidealist construction. Even if we accept "outside," we are still free to take Kant to be saying that except for their conformity to our cognitive apparatus, things would not be spatial. Bodies are spatial. So there would not be any bodies outside the context of our mental life. In terms of our limited analogy, we could also say that bridges are obscured by buildings only in our subjective experience. Outside the context of our experience, or "our thoughts," or "my thoughts," bridges are not obscured by anything. So partially obscured bridges *do not exist* outside our thoughts. That does not mean that when a bridge is partially obscured, and thus when a partially obscured bridge does exist, it is a mental bridge. Bridges are of steel and stone, and the partially obscured ones are no less massive and tangible. It is precisely because they are *out there* that they can be obscured by other things out there. So it is with bodies in the passage quoted from the *Prolegomena* §49.

I want to call special attention to the bearing of Cartesianism on this proposed understanding. The line "Bodies cannot exist outside my thoughts"—the line that seems to mentalize bodies, appears in the *Prolegomena* in a passage where Kant believes that he has just definitively rejected "Cartesian idealism" and "material idealism." A few lines earlier, he has disposed of skepticism about the external world, asserting that

> By means of outer experience, I am conscious of the reality of bodies as outer appearances in space just as, via inner experience, I am conscious of the existence of my mind [*Seele*] in time . . .

Because he has just said that idealism is wrong as plainly as he can, Kant assumes that we are not going to be shopping among idealist theories to interpret the very next few sentences he writes. Having just set aside idealism, and having said that the reality of nonmental spatial objects is definitively established by our experience, as is the reality of our minds, he thinks that we will automatically interpret his "Bodies do not exist

outside my thoughts" to mean that no entities will fit the spatial characterization that bodies do fit except as apprehended by minds like ours.
As should be evident by now, this assertion cannot be construed to mean
that the things that seem to exist in space outside us really exist only in
our minds. The fact is that a great many readers, and I venture to include
my present readers as I include my past self, are so steeped in the Cartesian outlook that Kant erred in supposing that no one would find an idealist theme in the very paragraph in which he had just rejected idealism.
It turns out not only that we are willing to do that, but also that we find
it very hard to keep any non-Cartesian understanding of his words in
focus.

This is not a question of inattention. Readers of the *Critique* today still
think that they see idealism "on every side," just as, in Kant's opinion,
the Garve-Feder review did. One misinterpretation supports another. So
readers are likely to think that there is quite a lot of inconsistency in
Kant's thinking, and that he is always juggling inadequately reconciled
idealist and nonidealist themes, both of which appeal to him. Readers
ascribe to him tireless efforts to accommodate incompatible views. The
big reason for this is that most thinkers suppose that Cartesianism is at
least partly right, although they recognize plenty of defects in this or that
philosopher's version of the general Cartesian outlook. In any given passage of the *Critique,* whatever looks like an inadequately acknowledged
idealism will seem to be merely more of what was "found" in ever so
many other passages. But we are systematically wrong here. Kant is a
truly anti-idealist thinker. His major failing is not inconsistency. It is his
underestimation of the tenacity of Cartesian assumptions among his
readers.

In order to see if this position can bear weight, let us return to A104.
Außer figures twice in this passage, too,[5] and as I have said, opportunities for misinterpretation accumulate around this word. Once again,
"apart from" makes a less misleading translation than "outside" at both
occurrences of *außer.* But we cannot simply choose a translation to suit
one interpretation rather than another. In the first-edition discussion of
the fourth Paralogism, where he presents another rejection of idealism,
Kant himself addresses the meaning of the phrase *außer uns,* in which
there is, he says, "an unavoidable ambiguity," and he makes just the distinction on which I will rely in explaining A104.[6] The ambiguity is that
außer uns can mean outside of our minds in space or independent of our
existence and hence of the conditions of our sensibility altogether.
Neither meaning occasions an idealistic thesis for Kant. Of course,

things-in-themselves exist apart from us and wholly unconditioned by us and our faculties, and things-in-themselves are not located in space outside us. Equally clearly, objects of outer sense, that is, nonmental objects, exist outside us in space. The latter, spatial objects, would not have the character that they do, including their spatiality, were it not for subjective conditions for possible experience that are irreducible for receptivity like ours. Things as they are in themselves obviously do not exist in our minds, but we do not apprehend things as they are in themselves at all. Outer appearances also do not exist in our minds, but they would not have the character that they do *apart from* the context of our subjective apprehension of them. Their spatiality itself is subjective, but they exist, of course, as things outside the mind in space.

Nothing depends on a single word here as long as we bear in mind what the power of representation is according to Kant. It includes an inner sense by which we are able to intuit "the mind or its inner state," but it also includes the capacity "to represent to ourselves objects as outside of us and as collectively in space" (A22, B37). We have no license to read the A104 remark about sensible representations in the middle of the Transcendental Deduction as if it expresses a renunciation of the commitment to an outer sense that, unlike inner sense, apprehends nonmental things. Clearly, the definitional characterization of inner sense in terms of intuition of the mind and mental states would be pointless if outer sense fitted the same definition. Because he assumes that this is obvious to his readers, Kant is willing to adduce his conception of outer sense as a sufficient answer to the ascription of idealism to him.[7]

The cited passage at A104 takes our representation of outer objects to be an apprehension of nonmental things outside us, and Kant does not intend to deny this when he notes that appearances do not exist "outside" or "apart from" our power of representation. He means to emphasize the subjectivity of empirical objects and, consequently, the impossibility of forming any conception that sets them apart from the knowledge yielded by our sensible representations. That is why he says that we have no access to objects as entities *corresponding to our empirical knowledge of them* that would enable us to contrast how things appear and how they are. With this renunciation of a corresponding entity, Kant excludes access to things as they are in themselves. He does not and could not intelligibly exclude access to things in public space.

We have still to deal with Kant's use of the word *representation*. In the cited passages, Kant says that the outer appearance, which is the object of our perceptual experience, is itself "a representation," and as we said at the beginning of this discussion, a representation is a mental reality. Since he certainly does not mean to say that the outer things we experience are mental things, Kant is not using "representation" to cover only mental existences here. Given the explanation I have just developed of Kant's expectations concerning his stand on idealism, I do not find this slackness in his usage a matter of much gravity. At the same time, it is worth our while to understand his usage as well as we can.

When Kant says that an appearance is only is *a representation* of which we are conscious in empirical experience, he does so to emphasize the subjective character of the object *as experienced*, not to ascribe an inner, mental existence to that object. The idea of an object in general = X, introduced at A104, expresses the thought that everything that we can say and know about an object of perception is contained in our sensible representations of it, and there is no characterization at all left over for any concept of an object considered without reference to our powers of representation.

There is a helpful analogy between this discussion of objects versus representations of objects and Leibniz's discussion of Locke's dismissive treatment of the concept of substance when construed as merely "something I know not what." Leibniz points out that our inability to characterize any substance *per se*, that is, in addition to enumerating the "attributes or predicates" of that substance, is hardly surprising. Given our contrast between substance and attribute, our ability to ascribe attributes to their bearers constitutes our knowledge of the substance. A philosopher merely contradicts the terms of the substance-attribute contrast in asking what we know of a substance apart from its attributes. Of course, we know nothing of a substance in addition to knowing what its attributes are, but for Leibniz this does not undermine the existence of substances, as it does for Locke. Even in the use of the phrase "subject in general" (*sujet en général,* where *sujet* stands for the substance and not for the subject of experience), Leibniz's repudiation of Locke's view is suggestive of Kant on the theme of the object as "something in general" (*etwas überhaupt*) in addition to our representations of it. Leibniz says:

> In distinguishing two things in a substance, the attributes or predicates and the common subject of these predicates, it is not remarkable that one cannot conceive of anything in particular in the subject. That necessarily follows since one has already separated all of the attributes whence one might conceive any specific feature. Thus, to require something more in this *pure subject in general* is to require the impossible and to go against one's own

supposition in abstracting and conceiving separately the subject and its qualities or accidents.[8]

The passage continues to develop the thesis that the existence of objects is not refuted by calling attention to the fact that, apart from the attributes we can know, we have only something "in general." Extending the terminology of the topic to include our conception of "pure being in general" and thence to the question of the existence of "objects," Leibniz says,

> The true mark of a clear and distinct notion of an object is the means that one has of knowing many truths about it by means of *a priori* proofs.[9]

I do not assert that this discussion is a model for Kant, although that certainly seems to be possible. Whether that is the case or not, it is the *a priori* truths about objects that we are able to establish by means of our *a priori* concepts of objects, that is, the Categories, that ground Kant's assertion of the existence of objects as distinct from our mental representations in which everything we know about the objects is expressed. Our *a priori* judgments about objects are given footing by the Categories. In these judgments, we recognize our transient representations as representations of objects. As far as consciousness is concerned, we start from consciousness of objects, and our consciousness of transient representations is derivative or mediated.[10]

Those who entertain an idealist understanding of Kant will suppose that Kant's assertion that the object corresponding to our perceptual experience is only "something in general = X" amounts to a denial that there is any extra-mental enduring entity that *has* the perceivable features we make out when we see and touch things. But this is not what he means here at all. On the contrary, he is committed to the idea that there is an enduring spatial object that has now this perceivable feature and now that, while itself remaining the same. That we are perceptually aware of such enduring objects is the fundamental claim of the Transcendental Deduction of the Categories. But Kant considers even spatial character and endurance (temporality) as subjective (not mentalistic) features of the object of perception.

There is a sense in which we always want to be able to contrast representation and the thing represented. Only if we accept a radical reduction can we drop the idea of the thing represented as something other than and distinct from the representation. Kant does not adopt any such reduction. But when he is mindful of the irreducible subjectivity of our knowledge, he sometimes uses the concept of representation to capture that subjectivity itself. In such contexts, Kant allows the contrast between representation and represented to lapse.

Kant's readers, imbued with the Cartesian pattern of thinking, are always ready for a mental identification of objects of empirical consciousness. Since they are ready for a conceptual collapse, they expect Kant to collapse representation and represented into the inner mental item. A collapse in the other direction, *assimilation of the representation into the outer thing*, is not a move for which they are prepared by traditional Cartesian assumptions. But Kant is often willing to identify the representation with the nonmental object and to speak as though representations can be things in space that contrast with nonmental things-in-themselves, which are not conceived of in terms of our subjective faculties.

As I have said, this is not Kant's only use of "representation." It diverges, for example, from his own, perhaps more natural, usage:

> One can add to this the observation that the representation of something permanent in existence is not the same as a permanent representation; for this [that is, the former], like all of our representations and even those of matter, can be highly changeable and transient, and a representation itself stands in relation to something permanent, which thus has to be an outer thing distinct from all my representations. (Bxli)[11]

Here, in the preface to the second edition, Kant expressly asserts that no representation can be an enduring thing, and it is clear that he means to confine representations to *transient mental realities*. It is the subjectively characterized outer object that, in contrast to any necessarily transient representation, has a material constitution and endures. Since Kant also calls nonmental appearances "nothing but sensible representations" at A104, we have to deal with a usage that is inconsistent on the surface. The terminology is inconsistent, but the doctrine is not.

Things-in-themselves, after all, are neither temporal nor spatial, so at Bxli, Kant is not saying that things-in-themselves provide the needed permanence. Only outer appearances, that is, nonmental spatial objects, can possibly be intended. How can we understand Kant's willingness to identify outer things (outer appearances) as sensible representations in some contexts? My reasoned suspicion is that Kant's understanding of space itself leads him to this usage. The subjective character ascribed to space and time make it legitimate to speak of anything spatial as a representation, without entailing that spatial things are mental realities after all.

No doubt because he appreciates the naturalness of thinking of representations as inner mental items as opposed to outer spatial objects
represented, Kant is generally unwilling to ascribe permanence to any
representation. Nonetheless, we can understand how the concept of representation can gravitate toward the inclusion of outer things when we
reflect on our own usage. We could say, by way of expressing Kant's view,

> Things outside the mind are not spatial things, considered as they are in them-
> selves, but they are necessarily spatial *in our representation of them.*

We could restate the same sentiment by saying,

> Though things outside the mind are not spatial in themselves, *we represent
> them as* spatial objects.

And finally, we might move smoothly into Kant's troubling usage by
means of one further restatement meant to convey the very same point:

> Things outside the mind are not in themselves spatial, but *our representations*
> of them are spatial realities.

I have constructed this sequence of ways of speaking about the outer in
terms of representation in order to provide an understanding of how Kant
might have fallen into a pattern of words that generates serious misunderstanding by seeming to call objects of outer sense "representations"
and thus seeming to locate them in the mind. Reflection on the sequence
of formulations makes it seem natural enough for Kant to call nonmental realities "representations" when we remind ourselves that Kant also
calls these outer enduring spatial things "appearances." When appearances are called representations, they *represent* the mind-independent
reality of which they are mind-dependent but not mental appearances.
Thus, in the last of the three formulations, "our representations of them
[outer realities] are spatial realities" does not mean that something mental is spatial. It is precisely things that aren't mental that are spatial.

When a reader has already decided that Kant thinks that all immediate objects of conscious apprehension are mental things, the usage by
which spatial things can be called "representations" will appear to be a
decisive illustration and confirmation of Kant's idealism. If we have not
decided the issue in advance, this usage by no means forces us to such
an interpretation. On the contrary, unless we agree to obliterate Kant's
fundamental contrast between inner and outer sense, we must try to
understand Kant's claim that enduring things in space are representa-

tions without supposing that he takes such things to be mental. This is not really hard to do.

The same assimilation of the concept of representation to that of the outer subjectively apprehended reality is also illustrated in the passage quoted in chapter 4 in which Kant warns of the danger to the concept of freedom that is engendered by insistence on the reality of appearances. "Absolute reality" always refers to things-in-themselves. In the context of that passage, this is abundantly clear when Kant explains the correct view, which does not assign absolute reality to appearances:

> When, on the contrary, appearances are not taken for more than in fact they are, that is, when they are not taken to be things-in-themselves but merely representations, which are interconnected under empirical laws, there must still be grounds for them that are not appearances. (A537, B565)

Here, it is clear that enduring spatial objects, and not mental entities, are the items being called "merely representations." These entities are empirical objects, and these are the things that are connected by empirical laws. They merit the designation "representations" when Kant is speaking in this way just because they are not erroneously taken to be things-in-themselves. These outer empirical objects are subjectively represented in our apprehension of them. This by itself, and not an envisioned inner and transient character, motivates Kant's calling them "representations."

There is a dialectical subtlety here that I think is worth pursuing to the level of a microanalysis. I can imagine critics unimpressed with the claim that Kant sometimes allows the term *representation* to cover outer empirical objects by virtue of their irreducible subjectivity. Such critics might draw attention to passages like Bxli, the very passage to which I have appealed, because such passages demonstrate that Kant does plainly distinguish between outer things that endure and mental representations that do not. The clarity of these passages, it may be urged, cannot reasonably be presented as illustrating Kant's *occasional* respect for the difference between representations and outer things. On the contrary, these passages should lead us to say that Kant does not include outer things under the term *representation*. Thus, it might be argued, my contention that his usage of "representation" varies should be rejected, and with it my understanding of A104 and A537, B565, and other passages. The subtlety that I see here consists in the fact that a critic who wants to reject my interpretation of Kant's usage of "representation" in these passages in order to insist on an idealist interpretation of Kant's identification of appearances as mere mental representations cannot conveniently rest his understanding on passages like Bxli. In this passage and others where Kant discusses the permanence of objects of perception, he is expressing with maximal force his commitment to the existence of immediately apprehended nonmental spatial objects, and thus he is rejecting idealism very plainly. Furthermore, in this particular passage, he is using the issue of the permanence of outer objects of consciousness to express his repudiation of the Cartesian viewpoint as a conceptually feasible starting point for philosophical reflection. Kant calls the solipsistic Cartesian starting point, that is, the perspective from which the subject's mind and its contents are known with security while the existence of any reality external to the mind is still unproved, "a scandal to philosophy and to common human reason" (Bxxxix). The point is that Kant does not adopt any such egocentrism because the external world is immediately accessible to our outer receptivity. Our understanding of experience cannot dispense with a permanent outer thing that is not an intuition and that cannot be identified with my impermanent representations of it. Having asserted this, Kant envisions an objection that involves precisely the issue we are investigating:

> Against this proof, one will be likely to say that I am only immediately conscious of what is in me, that is, of my *representation* of outer things and that, consequently, it remains undecided whether something corresponding to that [representation] exists outside me or not. (Bxxxix–xl, emphasis Kant's.)

In response to this envisioned objection, Kant presses his claim that consciousness of my own mind and its contents is dependent upon consciousness of outer realities. He is careful to insist that outer sense is *experience* of things outside me and not the creation (*Erdichtung*) of objects or mere imagination of outer things, which would leave outer existence unproved. And at the very end of the footnote, Kant sums up, again in terms of the contrast of outer objects and mental representations:

> [The required permanent in perception] . . . must be an external thing distinct from all my representations, a thing the existence of which is wrapped up with the determination of my own existence, and together with it makes up a single experience, an experience that would not unfold inwardly were it not (in part) at the same time outer. (Bxli)

Mindful of the need for a permanent outer, we find Kant asserting here that the object of perception is, indeed, "an external thing" and "distinct from all my representations." At A104, he has said that, just because there is no accessible thing distinct from our representations, the object is merely something in general = X. What a very different thesis seems to be presented at Bxli, on the surface anyway. If readers find Kant's standard use of "representation" at Bxli, they will be unable to use it to ground ascription of idealism to Kant, since Kant flatly rejects idealism in this passage and asserts the immediate apprehension of non-mental outer things. Further, they will have to deal with the explicit contradiction of the first-edition claim that there cannot be any object distinct from my representations. The contradiction is inescapable if we think that "representation" refers to the same things in both passages. In other words, a critic adverting to Bxli in opposition to my claim that Kant sometimes uses "representation" to include nonmental things will actually wind up with the understanding that I confessed to holding for many years. An interpretation of "representation" confined to the sense of Bxli will require recognition of Kant's express rejection of idealism in that passage and his acceptance of idealism at A104.

The passages can be reconciled, but only if one accepts the thought that Kant's use of "representation"—and of "object," for that matter—shifts from one context to another. When he is concerned to reinforce the exclusion of things-in-themselves as objects of consciousness, outer things, which are surely appearances, are also likely to fall within the denotation of "representation." When he is recording the permanence of outer things and the necessity of our immediate consciousness (not mere imagination) of them, he confines "representation" to the inner transient item and is happy to call a spatial appearance an "object," not "an object = X."

When "representation" is confined to inner mental items, a spatial object of perceptual representation will not be merely something = X, because it will be *describable*—for one thing, describable as occupying a certain spatial location, and furthermore as having such and such perceivable features that may change while the object endures. From this vantage point, it is easy to see that an object is intelligibly called merely "something = X" only when all of the descriptions of it have been assimilated to the concept of representation. And to point this out is just to recognize that whenever Kant presents his doctrine of the indescribable object = X, the reality that is describable is being called a "representation." To sum up, when the object can only be called "X," the *representation* becomes the bearer of all characterizations, including spatiality and permanence. Contrariwise, if "representation" is confined to transient mental things, then the contrasting outer objects of perception can be articulately described and are not just "something = X." This is obvious in that, on this use of "representation," the representation is transient and the object is not.

It is worth adding that whether Kant is thinking of the empirical objects as an indescribable something = X or as the describable enduring object that fits the empirical descriptions we make when we are not suffering from any perceptual aberration, the object is not a thing considered as it is in itself. When we consider separately all the empirical properties of something, what is left is still the thing that has those properties. An entity that is correctly said to endure, to occupy space, to be colored, hard, warm, and so forth, does not become a thing-in-itself simply as a result of our deciding to consider the object and its attributes separately. A thing-in-itself could not possibly have *these* attributes.

When Kant says at A104, "We have stated above that appearances are only sensible representations," he does not mean to assert that appearances are all mental realities, for that would mean that all appearances are inner appearances, which would contradict the fundamental conception of inner and outer sense that Kant never compromises. So outer objects of perception are included here among "sensible representations." And why not? Their spatiality marks outer things as subjective, and since they are not things-in-themselves, they are representations. Of course, the contrast of representation and represented has not been utterly obliterated. Creatures with receptivity like ours represent nonmental things as spatial things. So objects in space are representations, but they are not, for that reason, mental things; if they were, they would not be in space at all. They are nonmental realities that we represent spatially but that are not spatial *in themselves*. In Kant's thinking, we have, of course, no conception of what they are in themselves. That we have any conception of nonmental things rests, in the first instance, on our representing them as spatial occupants.

In sum, it seems to me that, after wandering for some years with the idealists in thinking about A104 and similar passages, I now understand it correctly. It is not an assertion of a phenomenalist or idealist account of outer reality. Only when it is interpreted nonidealistically is it compatible with Kant's explicit account of outer sense, with his frequently repeated contention that outer objects are immediately apprehended, with his general claim in the Transcendental Deduction that experience must be of objects, with his claim that only consciousness of outer things makes the representation of the self possible, with his assertion that we all perceive things in one space, with his striking lack of interest in the problem of solipsistic privacy, and with his refutation of idealism, presented explicitly as such. I used to feel a certain uneasiness about A104 and like passages when I saw them as idealistic in tendency. Now it seems to me that those who ascribe an idealism to Kant ought to feel an uneasiness in relying on an idealistic interpretation of such passages. Their interpretation is by no means inescapable, and it engenders massive contradictions when confronted with the major themes of the *Critique*. It is not feasible to think that Kant simply failed to notice what would be glaring contradictions if the idealist interpretation were correct. How could Kant conceivably have thought that the second edition restates the doctrines of the first without major alteration if the second edition says that we apprehend nonmental outer realities directly and the first edition says that we apprehend only mental representations?

Because Kant vindicates the public character of outer objects of perception, it is easy for him to allow for the contrast between subjective and objective that can be made *within* the domain of empirical description. His contrast between judgments of perception and judgments of experience in the *Prolegomena* is devoted to just that issue. A judgment of perception is not intended as valid for every subject, but only for the subject who makes the judgment. This is equivalent, in Kant's exposition, to saying that judgments of perception do not get as far as characterization of the extra-mental. But "when we have reason to take a judgment to be universally valid," Kant says,

> we must also consider it to be objective, that is, we must suppose that it expresses the condition of the object and not just the relation of a subject to his perception, since there would be no reason why the judgments of others would have to agree with mine were it not the unity of the object to which they all refer. They all agree with the object and, thus, they must agree with each other. (*Prolegomena*, §18)

The same message lies behind the quoted passage at A104. Kant is saying that we have no way of comparing objects as they become known to us in experience with those objects considered apart from the conditions of our cognition. Experience can be merely "subjective," in the sense that we can make judgments that do not presume to characterize any objective *public* reality. Only interpersonal validity marks objective judgments, and even these judgments are also subjective, in the sense that they do not characterize anything outside the context of our cognitive powers. In Kant's terminology, both kinds of judgment concern *at most* appearances. In the absence of interpersonal validity, it would not be inappropriate to say, speaking in Kant's terms, that the judgment of an hallucinating subject concerns *the illusion of an appearance.* Indeed, judgments of perception will include the judgments of subjects who suffer perceptual aberrations.

From the perspective of traditional Cartesian philosophy of mind, and for much of the epistemological tradition that rests on it, the merely private subjectively valid judgment is epistemologically primary. From such judgments we *may* be able to advance to judgments about a public reality under the terms of some definitional reduction of objects to private sense data, or within some system of hypotheses that posit outer things in order to account for the occurrence of inner private experiences. There is an expression of this ordering of things in the *Prolegomena*, when Kant advises us that all of our judgments are initially judgments of perception and only subsequently extended so as to have objective reference and to make a claim of timelessness and interpersonal validity:

> At first all of our judgments are merely judgments of perception and they are valid only for us, that is, for our subject, and only later do we give them a new reference, namely to an object, and intend that the judgment shall be permanently valid for us and just as valid for everyone . . . (Ibid.)

This sentiment is not to be found in the *Critique*. It has idealistic implications that are not eliminated by adopting the perspective that we have developed in this chapter. In addition to the temporal priority of judgments of perception, Kant explains that these judgments do not involve "the pure concept of the understanding." This seems to claim, without any foundation in Kant's fully developed theory of judgment, that we are capable of a level of judgment and conscious experience that does not presuppose extra-mental objects and that does not rely on any of the unifying conceptual resources of the Categories. Judgments of perception

> express only the relation of two sensations to the same subject, namely, myself, and also only in my present state of perception. They are not supposed to hold of the object. (*Prolegomena*, §19)

It is possible that these statements can also be understood in a way that does not suggest idealism. I have no proposal for so construing them, and it is also possible, in my view, that they represent an inattentive adoption of conceptions that make no sense outside the idealist tradition that Kant rejects. In any event, the dominant thesis about objects developed in the *Critique* is diametrically opposed to the temporal transition from judgments of perception to judgments of experience that

Kant proposes here. Such a scheme brings with it the hopeless quagmires of solipsism and would casually revoke the intricacies of the theory of the Categories in so far as that theory advances the view that judgments and conscious experience are only possible *at all* because we experience and judge of objects. The very idea that the Categories are at the heart of judgments *per se* and are, at the same time, concepts of an object in general is negligently brushed aside by the thought that we "first" make judgments that are not about objects at all and then extend these, so to speak, reissuing them as objective claims. The primacy of objects for experience excludes the suggested temporal organization of judgments and indicates the opposite ordering. Since objects are required for the possibility of experience, we can say that only perceivers can hallucinate, only a subject who can really experience an object can seem to experience one.[12] A judgment of perception would then be better characterized as a fallback position to be adopted because of the failure of the presumptive objectivity of judgments of experience. Even the passage at A104 that identifies appearances and representations is not part of any proposal to delete the objectivity of the judgments about appearances that we first make.

Finally, by way of confirmation of the understandings that I have developed in this chapter, let us review Kant's discussion of mind-body interaction in the first-edition exposition of the Paralogisms. In considering the prospects for and limitations on "pure psychology," Kant says that he is able to resolve some of the grand problems have been perennially intractable to philosophers. The possibility of mind-body interaction, the coming to exist of minds in a natural physical world, and the nature of death that ends this interaction are intractable and perplexing because philosophers are captives of an illusion within the grip of which

> things that exist only in thought are reified and taken for objects *of just the same nature* outside the thinking subject. Thus extension, which is nothing other than appearance, is held to be a subsisting property of external things even in the absence of our sensibility, and motion is assumed to be the effect of those things, which is thus something that really occurs apart from our senses. (A384–385, emphasis added.)

It is possible to read this as if it expresses a thesis very like that of Berkeley. Kant seems to resolve the problem of interaction by mentalizing objects so that there really is no real interaction to be accounted for. Doesn't he say that the fundamental mistake is to take things with which we are acquainted, things that exist "only in thought," to be outer nonmental things that are independent of our sensory experience? I hope, however, that it is now understood that we need not embrace this idealistic interpretation and need not face the resulting chaotic inconsistencies in our overall picture of Kant's thought.

The essential point comes to the surface if we ask just what the illusion is by which so many philosophers are led astray. They reify something. They ascribe outer existence to something that is only found in the thinking subject. But what is that something? Is it the spatial object of experience that they wrongly suppose to be something that exists outside the mind? The clue here is the phrase "of just the same nature" (*in ebenderselben Qualität*). In a sense, the answer to my question about the illusion is, Yes, it is the object of experience of which Kant speaks and of which he asserts that nothing *of the same nature* exists apart from the thinking subject. If there weren't any minds, there would not be any spatial objects. So spatial objects do not exist apart from the mind. But this thesis does not conflict with the nonmental character of the things that are spatial objects when experienced by subjects with minds like ours. Given that there are subjects such as ourselves apprehending reality as we do, there are extended things *outside us in space.* The spatial things that do exist are not inner, or mental, or private things, even though there would be no spatial things if there were no minds. Furthermore, Kant does not deny that the thing that appears to us *as a spatial object* is a reality that exists apart from our minds and exists whether or not anyone perceives it. Putting his view with all due precision, it is only the extendedness of the extended thing that will never be manifested outside of human cognition. Extendedness is "*ebenderselben Qualität*" with which the object cannot exist apart from the forms of our receptivity. The nonmental realities that we are able to apprehend by ordering them in space will not cease to be nonmental realities outside the context of human faculties. They will cease to be spatial things.

The Paralogisms are the primary locus of the explicit argument *against* Cartesian idealism in which Kant urges that the existence of things outside the mind is *proved* by outer experience. I want to spell out the naturalness with which this contention can be upheld along with the idealistic-sounding passages that we have investigated once one grasps the intended force of Kant's remarks about what is dependent for its existence on thought and on the thinking subject. Outer sense proves the existence of nonmental realities in that it affords us apprehension of them. Space is a mere form. To apprehend spatial objects, we have to be affected. When it is just our own minds and their states that affect us, we get only temporal representations. Only when nonmental realities affect our sensibility do we generate spatial representations. These outer representations *are* outer appearances.[13] They are nonmental things in the form in which we are able to apprehend such things. Therefore, Kant is entitled to say that outer sense proves the existence of extra-mental reality and refutes idealism. On that usage, the sensible representations that Kant identifies as appearances are not merely mental things. To say that they would not exist without the mind is not to say that the thing that we apprehend *as a spatial thing* would not exist *at all* in the absence of our minds and their powers. It would not exist as an object *of just the same nature.*

In elaborating an understanding of the passages that lend themselves to an idealist reading, I have argued that there is a sense in which our sensible representations can be said not to exist at all outside our mental life, and that this is compatible with a sense in which outer objects of perception are *per se* nonmental things that do not depend for their existence on our experience of them. As a final matter for this discussion, we should decide just what we take the nonmental reality of outer things to be. Kant's claim is that we apprehend nonmental things by spatializing them. This can be taken to be the thesis that things-in-themselves affect us and, as a consequence of the receptive component of our cognitive constitution, things-in-themselves appear to us as objects in space. The spatiality of these appearances is subjective; hence, they can be said to be merely representations. This is Kant's concept of spatial intuition. Spatial appearances, though subjective, are not mental things. Kant's discussions are burdened by ambiguity because he sometimes confines the term "representation" to objects of inner intuition, namely, mental picture-like entities. The contrast between inner (mental) and outer (spatial) realities is always a contrast within the domain of subjective appearances. It must not be confused with the contrast between things as they appear and things as they are in themselves.

Kant holds that outer appearances—that is, objects in space—are enduring entities. They endure, for example, through temporal intervals between episodes of perception by one or another perceiver. A thing-in-itself cannot be said to endure. Endurance is no more properly ascribed to things-in-themselves than is extension. A certain conditional form of expression and allusion to *possible experience* is inescapable in any Kantian spelling out of this endurance of extended things. That an extended object exists unperceived is going to involve the thought that episodic spatial representations are possible experiences *of such objects.*

Given that I experience an enduring object, were I observing it at another time I would have relevantly similar experiences, and were another subject suitably positioned, that subject would have experiences like mine. The domain consisting of experiences that actually occur and those that do not actually occur but would in the right circumstances is the realm of possible experience.

Such conditionals are conspicuous in various versions of idealism. In the setting of these theories, categorical assertions about enduring non-mental objects are sometimes reduced to, or defined in terms of, conditional assertions about experiences. It is understandable that readers think they hear the familiar rhythm of phenomenalist reduction in Kant's text, although he has no reductionist program in mind at all. There are two contrasting ways in which a philosopher may connect the truth of counterfactual conditionals about possible experience with the assertion of the existence of enduring public objects. The reductive thesis of the phenomenalist is a sophisticated use of counterfactuals in comparison with the ordinary and relatively naive thought that the existence of enduring public objects explains why the counterfactuals are true. That there is really a warm stone *there* explains not only why I have my present sense experience but also why I would experience the same sensations of warmth and color at other times were I to be appropriately positioned and sensorially competent. That there is a *public* warm stone there explains why others would have like experiences were they appropriately positioned and competent. This relatively naive view posits public enduring objects to explain the existence of and the patterns among private transient experiences. The sophistication of phenomenalism finds such posits both expendable and more or less unintelligible. We don't know what we are talking about when we are tempted to posit enduring public things, because our imagination goes no further than the sort of things with which we are directly familiar, and these are all private and transient. So the reduction explains talk about enduring objects as being no more than talk about patterns in our experience of private transient objects. Both of these philosophical stances are idealistic, within the frame of Kant's thinking. Both take it that we apprehend directly only transient private realities. The two philosophical attitudes toward counterfactual assertions about private experiences correspond to Kant's contrast between dogmatic and problematic idealism. The naive empiricist is willing to posit enduring objects to account for private mental data, but he cannot test his hypotheses, so his view does not get beyond problematic idealism. The phenomenalist deletes the idea that there is anything to be apprehended other than private mental items, so he is a dogmatist as exemplified by Berkeley.[14] Since Kant rejects both forms of idealism, there ought to be a way of understanding his thought concerning counterfactual assertions about experiences that differs from both of the well-known philosophical lines of thought that we have sketched. And in fact there is.

We find the right understanding of Kant without difficulty as long as we do not impose on him the thesis that both idealist theories share, namely, the contention that the objects of immediate experience are private mental things. The general thesis of the Transcendental Deduction is that we could not have experience at all, including experience of ourselves and our transient mental states, if we did not experience objects, that is, entities that conform to the Categories. "Just what do the Categories call for?" we must ask. Of course, the answer is complicated, but the relevant characterization, and the short characterization to which Kant very often adverts, is that they must be enduring objects collectively constituting a unique, causally interconnected objective reality. Kant does not deny that we have transient private experiences of objects. But he does not authorize us to restate that truism by saying that the things we experience in those transient episodes are transient mental realities. We could say that the point of the Transcendental Deduction is to exclude just that understanding of the objects of experience. Collectively, the Categories are concepts of an "object" in the sense in which an object is something that endures between transient experiences of it. If we did not experience enduring, causally connected objects immediately, we would not have experience at all and could not even be conscious. Some of the details of Kant's reasoning in support of this position will be discussed in chapter 12. The global contours of the position exclude both of the idealist styles of thought that readers mistakenly ascribe to Kant.

To think otherwise is not merely a question of finding inconsistencies in Kant. There is no point at all in Kant's elaboration of the Categories as concepts of an object and as conditions for the possibility of experience, including self-consciousness, if at the end of it all he means that transient private mental things are the things of which we are directly aware in experience. In the same way, there would be no point in his repeated and emphatic contrast of inner and outer intuition if he were going to accept the idealist view that we apprehend only inner mental things directly. So in spite of the great tradition of idealistic interpretation of the *Critique of Pure Reason,* I think such an interpretation deserves to be called preposterous, once we see that it is not obligatory.

At this juncture, support for any nonidealistic interpretation of Kant's philosophy demands an assessment of the ontological bearings of the contrast between appearances and things-in-themselves. In spite of Kant's seeming willingness to develop this dichotomy in terms of contrasting realities, it is not fundamentally an ontological contrast at all. That Kant sometimes downplays the ontological standing of the contrast has always been appreciated. It is quite clear in Kant's moral philosophy that the empirical self and the self as it is in itself must be, in some fundamental sense, the same entity, although we can only *think*, and cannot *know*, the self as it is in itself. The same presupposition of identity is expressed in a theoretical context in the second-edition version of the Transcendental Deduction of the Categories, at §24, where Kant investigates the seeming paradox of the self affecting itself and, therein, being simultaneously active and passive.[15]

Following the findings of Gerold Prauss, I will say that the concept of the "thing-in-itself" and of contrasting appearances is never presented as an ontological distinction by Kant. Kant usually includes some version of the longer epithet "things *considered as they are* in themselves," versus "things *considered as they appear to us,* "and when he does not, this idea is implied, or the short "thing-in-itself" terminology is intended as an abbreviation.[16] How very unlikely it would be to think in ontological terms, and to suppose that we might doubt or deny existence in the referent of one but not the other contrasting term, if we expressed the two as "things considered as they appear to us" and "things considered as they are in themselves." Two ways of considering the things that exist are not two ontological commitments. Given the full designations, a philosopher could not deny the existence of things considered as they are in themselves, or regard their existence as problematic, without extending the same denial or doubt to appearances.

For application to Kant's account of perceptual experience, we should also stress his thesis that things-in-themselves are presupposed by empirical appearances in that they constitute the reality *that appears.* With this understanding, the counterfactual elaboration of the claim that an outer nonmental appearance endures between my perceptions of it will be intelligible and will not be a brute and intellectually impenetrable hypothesis. We cannot express this explanation by saying that the counterfactual is true because the thing-in-itself endures unperceived, any more than we can say that the perception of an extended thing at a certain point in space is possible because there is a thing-in-itself at that point in space. This is prohibited by the circumstance that spatial and temporal characterization fit appearances because they are the forms of our receptivity. We are not left utterly speechless, even though we cannot describe things-in-themselves at all. The point is that transience is the mark of mental status, and the manner of existence of nonmental reality is what we represent as spatial existence or extension. It is the nonmental thing-in-itself that can appear to us at various times, although the temporality of appearance as well as all the other features of the appearance are subjective.

CHAPTER 6

"Space Is *in Us*"

The discussion of the fourth Paralogism (first edition) contains another line of thought in which Kant's explanation of his rejection of idealism reinforces the reader's conviction that he is most certainly an idealist.

Things go badly following this strange comment on what counts as idealism:

> . . . we must not take an idealist to be one who denies the existence of outer objects of the senses but, instead, one who does not admit that that existence is known through immediate perception. (A368–369)

Kant then distinguishes between the correct "transcendental idealism" and the defective "empirical idealism," emphasizing the idea that all objects are *appearances* according to the former and things as they are in themselves according to the latter. For one thing, this makes it hard to resist the idea that transcendental idealism is a form of idealism. As transcendental idealists, we can say that since outer objects, as mere appearances, are simply representations, our apprehension of them includes direct contact and there is no room for doubt about these spatial things called "outer objects." We don't actually go beyond the contents of our own conscious experiences in affirming their existence, even though they are spatial, because, after all, "space is in us"(A370). So it is no surprise to find Kant apparently endorsing the Cartesian perspective as the first step of the Paralogism that asserts the "ideality" of outer existences.

> Thus Descartes was right to limit perceptual knowledge, in the strictest sense, to the proposition: I exist as a thinking being. Thus it is clear that the outer

does not exist in me, I cannot encounter it in my consciousness or in perception, which is actually only a modification of my consciousness. (A368)

Then it seems to readers as if Kant accepts this limitation and secures the existence of what are vulgarly called "outer things" at the considerable cost of finding them in his own conscious mind as purely mental realities.

To many readers of Kant, the supposed rejection of idealism achieved in this fashion looks like a bad joke. Kant seems to state that even if you flatly deny the existence of outer objects of the senses (and he surely implies that you accept only inner mental objects), you are not, for that reason, an idealist. It is tempting to try to insert an "only" ("we must not take to be an idealist *only* one who denies the existence of outer objects of the senses") so that Kant could at least be understood to say that although the denial of the existence of outer things is idealism, that is not the *only* form of idealism. One is *also* an idealist if one depends on causal reasoning for inevitably inadequate evidence of the existence of things outside the mind. But Kant includes no hint of such an "only." If we take him at his word, it promptly comes to seem that he means just what he says. The transcendental idealist asserts direct acquaintance with outer objects, but in order to do so, he also brings the outer object, the spatial domain, and space itself into the mind. If this were Kant's idea of a rejection of idealism, then I for one would say that he is a thoroughgoing idealist who is merely playing with words.

But this is not so. On the contrary, it is we are who are imposing meanings on Kant's words that he does not intend at all. It is helpful to notice that before any of this discussion, Kant has given titles to the view he will reject and the view he will sustain. The former is "idealism," and it asserts uncertainty about all objects of outer sense, which Kant rephrases as "the ideality of all outer appearances." The latter, which allows for possible certainty about outer objects, is called "dualism." If we understand Kant's ensuing discussion as a process that secures certainty about "outer objects" by making them inner objects, his stance will hardly fit the title "dualism."

The issue of space and spatial reality is so close to the heart of idealism that it deserves a separate treatment. I say that Kant's claim here is a way of expressing his view that space is subjective and that things wouldn't be spatial at all were it not for our cognitive constitution. I will argue, as I have previously, that subjectivity is wrongly equated with mental status here even though "in us" is so naturally taken to be short for "in our minds." I want to draw attention to the features of Kant's view that seem to put the subjectivity of space into conflict with the public and interpersonal accessibility of the spatial. Kant plainly believes that, in itself, an irreducible subjectivity need not engender conflict with the uniqueness of space and the public accessibility of spatial occupants. Nonetheless, when Kant says that space is, after all, *in us,* and that space would be *nothing* without us and our cognitive faculties, we are inclined to think of these statements as an assertion of an idealistic conception of spatial things and of space itself. Thus understood, a space that is in us will have to be a *mental space,* and one mental space will exist in one mind. But we have also to say that dualism would be definitively excluded by such an understanding.

Kant's view of space strikes us as idealistic only because we are tacitly or explicitly setting aside his commitment to the publicness and uniqueness of space. We do this partly because we do not have anything to put under the heading of a subjective but public space. Furthermore, the traditional idealistic conception of a private mental space is very familiar, and it inevitably operates as we try to give significance to Kant's assertion of the existence of space "in us." We assimilate Kantian subjective space to a private "one man, one space" account, even though that requires substituting "in me" where Kant says "in us," and even though it cancels the uniqueness of space at a stroke.

But do we have alternatives here? Much depends on whether or not we should ascribe to Kant a conception of space as a single entity, that is, as a container-like individual. Several Kantian views suggest a container-space. The curious problem of incongruent counterparts preoccupied Kant for decades and was a significant determinant of his thinking about space. Kant proposes to solve the problem by understanding, for instance, that a left-hand glove and a right-hand glove necessarily take up different regions of space itself.[1] This solution seems to rely on thinking of space as a container somewhat like the absolute space of Newton. The idea of a *pure* space in which we are able to construct the *a priori* objects of geometry also seems to envision something like an empty container-space in which mathematical objects are the constructed pure representations, that is, as though constructed of regions of empty (pure) space.[2] Similarly, Kant's exposition of the necessity of space that draws on the idea that, though we can imagine space empty, we cannot "think space away," as we can think away empirical objects (A24, B38–39), lends itself to a conception of a container that inevitably remains when emptied of all contents.

These themes, together with Kant's theory of the concatenation of objects of experience via the synthesizing powers of the understanding, give us reason to think that Kant endorses some version of the idealist picture of private mental space. To say that space is subjective means that it is a feature of our cognitive constitution that we produce spatial representations when we are appropriately affected by reality. Space is generated by us and is not a feature of the affecting items. If space is also an individual object that we produce, then Kant is saying that human mental faculties create this container-like individual. Whether this is a good account or not, it seems that one cannot avoid thinking that Kant has in mind private spaces, if space is both subjective and a container-like individual. Construed as such an individual, space itself is not *out there*. This seems especially clear if space is generated as *pure space*, without benefit of any stimulation from extra-mental reality. We can understand the theory according to which my mind makes an inner private container and arranges empirical representations in it. But we cannot envision human beings collectively making a subjective public object. We cannot imagine arranging our private mental representations in an outer public entity that people have somehow managed to create jointly.

In sum, if space is subjective and is an object-like particular, then it will have to be private. The doctrine of the uniqueness of space will collapse, and with it the pretension to advance a nonidealistic outlook. The only way of avoiding this unfortunate result for the interpretation of the *Critique* is to deny that space is an object-like particular and a kind of container. Fortunately, we no sooner put the issue in these terms than we find powerful evidence that, for Kant, space is not really an object-like particular, nor any kind of container.

In the Aesthetic, Kant offers three conceptions of space and time, as though they exhaust the plausible possibilities for deciding just what these fundamental elements of our world are:

> Now just what are space and time? Are they actual entities? Are they merely determinations, or even relations of things, but such that they would apply to things-in-themselves even if such things were not intuited? Or are they such that they attach only to the form of intuition and thus to the subjective constitution of our mind, without which these predicates would not be ascribable to any objects at all? (A23, B37–38)

Kant explicitly sets aside the first hypothesis, that is, the Newtonian doctrine that absolute space and time are "real entities" that exist independently of any spatial or temporal occupants,[3] and he also sets aside the second option, that is, the Leibnizian doctrine that space and time are not anything at all *per se* but are only systems of essential relations between simultaneous and successive existents. The third option, which is endorsed by Kant, rejects the claim that space and time are entities in themselves, but it does not substitute the claim that they are subjective or phenomenal *entities*. To this extent, the third option is compatible with Leibniz's rejection of a thing-like status for space and time. Indeed, the asserted "empirical reality" of space and time at the end of the Aesthetic does not identify these "forms" as phenomenal objects. On the contrary, the above-quoted *Erläuterung* expressly denies that the reality of space and time can be thought of as the reality of objects of any kind.[4]

A recurrent theme of the *Critique* is that space and time are not themselves perceivable, which is precisely what phenomenal objects are. So in this passage at least, a thing-like character for space does not emerge at all. For the work as a whole, Kant never identifies space and time with phenomenal objects and always denies that they are things-in-themselves. There are no other conceptions of thing-like existents in Kant's conceptual arsenal to which space and time might be assimilated.

Of course, another passage very close to the one quoted and also retained in all editions of the *Critique* is the standard source of the supposition that Kant *does* think of space as an individual. I refer to the third point in the metaphysical exposition of the concept of space, which is the fourth point in the somewhat differently organized A edition. Kant says that space is not a general concept but a pure intuition. It is easy to construe this as asserting that space is an individual.

Even if the final meaning of this passage is uncertain, it is clear enough that the objective is the assertion of the uniqueness of space. One main point, if not *the* main point, is to eliminate the idea that each subject's outer intuitions are located in a private space that is not spatially related to the private spaces and outer intuitions of other subjects. If we use this passage to anchor a thing-like interpretation of Kant's concept of space, we will guarantee that it leads to a conclusion opposite to the one intended by Kant. A thing-like subjective space will be, as we have already said, a private space, but Kant's objective in affirming the uniqueness of space is to secure the publicness and hence the unity of the system of spatial occupants and of physical science.

On the other hand, we can accommodate the features of space that Kant adduces in this passage without interpreting Kant's space as a thing-like container at all. The first point under this item of the metaphysical deduction is that "we represent to ourselves only one space." I think it will be conceded that Kant does not mean, "We represent to ourselves one space *each*." The unifying power of the concept of space would be squandered at once by such an interpretation. Kant's assertion of uniqueness requires only that spatial predicates be employed in such a way that all things that exist in space are somewhere with respect to each other. This requirement does not entail that space is thing-like, while it does exclude private spaces.

The second point is that *spaces* have to be considered to be parts of and not instances of space. The part-whole relationship strongly suggests a structured entity or thing. Kant says nothing to inhibit us from adopting this suggestion. But once again, it is not a requirement of the point that he wants to make. That point is captured just as well by the idea that all locations and regions are somewhere with respect to one another; and that there is always a single region containing any two regions, whether they are partially, wholly, or not at all overlapping. Kant also says that space is essentially a unity (*"wesentlich einig"*) of which spaces are limitations. Here, too, the unity of the system of assigning spatial locations satisfies the claimed unity without presupposing a thing-like space. This leads to Kant's final point here, which purports to justify the idea that space is a *pure* and not an empirical intuition. This distinction does not impinge on the thing-like character of space at all. The supposition that the system of spatial predicates is imposed by the subject will make the unity of the system *a priori* with or without a thing-like interpretation of space.

The crucial point is that we can successfully suppose, within the framework of Kant's text, that the system of spatiality is a subjective imposition making possible the representation of the nonmental while retaining the idea that the resulting space and spatial occupants are publicly accessible. The uniqueness of space and its *a priori* standing leave open the possibility that all human perceivers apply the same devices for representation to *public* unarticulated elements of outer intuition so that the articulated product becomes the public spatial world.

Space is a shared system of representation, that is, its use is characteristic of all who have a cognitive constitution like ours. Kant says that ours is a constitution that organizes but does not create a sensory input (sensation). The things that affect us are not private things, and neither are the articulated appearances that result from their spatial and temporal organization. Objects of inner sense *per se* are private, but this is because the inner sense only enables us to represent our own minds. In inner sense, I represent my mind and its states, not your mind and not the states of your mind.[5] So privacy results not from the subjective imposition of the forms of intuition but only from the intrinsic privacy (mental character) of the affecting reality, namely, my own mind. When I am not representing myself to myself but instead representing the world outside of me (nonmental reality), the affecting reality is not private, and neither are the causally connected appearances that figure in our knowledge of nature.

At the very end of the third item in the metaphysical exposition of the concept of space, Kant appends an appeal to geometry as further evidence of the *a priori* status of space *per se*. We have *a priori* knowledge of facts such as that the lengths of two sides of a triangle taken together are always longer than the third. That this cannot be understood to be empirical knowledge shows that space is not just an empirical object that we apprehend. I mention this only to draw from it a further support for finding in Kant a non-thing-like concept of space. It is easy to sympathize with Kant's idea that the triangles of which we speak in geometry are somehow accessible to our thought and are not the empirical boundaries of perceived physical objects such as geometrical diagrams. But if we do think in terms of pure objects created for the sake of mathematical reasoning by the combinatory power of the subject, these pure objects will not be located anywhere with respect to empirical spatial occupants.[6] They will not be public objects, and it will not be possible to say that I apprehend the same one that you apprehend. They will not be private objects either. We are tempted to interpret Kant as asserting that we are able to apprehend geometrical truths because we can intuit the relevant features of geometrical figures in private *a priori* objects that we construct in our minds. But apprehension of private objects would exclude the needed generality of geometrical truth. If the objects of which mathematical theorems speak were private, Kant would have to worry lest the sum of the two sides of a triangle *of mine* turn out to be shorter than the third, even though this is never true of *his* triangles. These reflections have to be understood to indicate the limitations that must inevitably confront the concept of individuals that are not public individuals. Along with the fact that I could not discover that I apprehend the same pure triangle that you apprehend, I could not discover that I no longer apprehend the triangle I apprehended yesterday. Re-identification and the distinction between numerical and qualitative identity belong only to the unique public space. Pure geometrical objects are not locatable in that space, and this just goes to show that our conception of them is only metaphorically a conception of objects.

These points are not asserted on grounds like those Wittgenstein sometimes suggests: the absence of public "outer criteria" demolishes the distinction between what seems to be so to me and what is so. For Kant, rather, reidentification cannot have footing in the private realm because there is no conceptual foundation for endurance in that realm. Candidates for reidentification simply cannot arise given the essential transience of objects of inner sense. The spatiality that makes room for endurance cannot be mental, and mental status is the essence of privacy.

We find confirmation of this outlook on mathematical objects in the B-version of the Transcendental Deduction. Kant emphasizes that synthetic *a priori* knowledge is confined to knowledge of possible objects, or to objects of possible experience. Here he states this qualification as the contention that "pure" knowledge in mathematics would not be knowledge at all if empirical objects of experience did not actually exist. Given that there are objects, synthetic *a priori* truths express knowledge of "an object in general." In the absence of actual objects, there would be no such truths to be expressed. Knowledge depends upon the provision of intuitive materials to be shaped into determinate objects by the active mental powers we possess. Of course, I do not deny that Kant envisions the application of *a priori* concepts to either empirical or pure intuition. It is tempting to suppose that he means that objects outside the mind are required for the former application but not for the latter. Then we would take him to posit objects internal to the mind as the subject matter of mathematics. This, however, is not his meaning. According to Kant, we can indeed possess knowledge of objects in mathematics by virtue of pure intuition alone:

> Through determination of the former [pure intuition] we are able to possess *a priori* knowledge of objects in mathematics, however, only with respect to their form as appearances. Whether things can really be given that require to be intuited in this form is not decided by such *a priori* knowledge. (B147)

In other words, this "*Erkenntnisse a priori von Gegenstände*" cannot provide its own object and does not amount to knowledge except in so far as it is presupposed that there are things that fit the forms of pure sensible intuition and thus can be presented to us. Thus,

> In consequence, all mathematical concepts do not yield knowledge in themselves except in so far as one presupposes that there are things that only admit of being presented to us as conforming to that form of pure intuition. (Ibid.)

Even this passage can be understood to mean only that mathematics involves intuition, that is, *pure intuition,* and not understood to appeal to the existence of empirical objects as a condition for mathematical knowledge. But this possibility is expressly ruled out in the next sentence:

> Things in space and time are only given, however, in so far as they are perceptions, that is, representations accompanied by sensation, and thereby only through empirical representation. Therefore, the pure concepts of understanding, even when they are applied *a priori* as in mathematics, can become knowledge only when such intuitions and, by their mediation, also the pure concepts of the understanding are applied to empirical intuitions.

Mathematical knowledge is not subsumed under empirical knowledge here. But Kant is saying that mathematical knowledge would not be knowledge if it were not for the availability of the empirical world in which perceivable objects exemplify mathematical concepts. In keeping with this subtle stance, mathematical propositions are not empirical, for no appeal is made to the character of perceived objects in establishing a mathematical theorem. But mathematics qualifies as a domain of knowledge in light of the existence of a reality in which these formal relations are realized, and thus only by virtue of the existence of an empirical domain. The reason for this is that knowledge has to be knowledge of *something,* and there is no reality to be known save empirical reality, in Kant's view of things. Geometry is true of all possible nonmental realms, but were there no such realm at all, geometry would not be true of anything and, to that extent, would not be true *simpliciter.*

This doctrine emphasizes the primacy of empirical ontology. Although Kant speaks of pure space and time as providing *a priori* objects for mathematics, the understanding explained here considerably deflates the ontological standing of pure objects. If there were no empirical objects filling space and time of which mathematics could be knowledge *in general,* there would be no mathematics.

In spite of Kant's willingness to speak of space as *a pure intuition,* he does not intend it to be taken as a subject matter in itself, complete with its own inner objects. Mathematics is knowledge of possible empirical objects. If some of those possible objects are also actual, mathematics is true of those objects. But taken for itself, it is only knowledge of the form of appearances and not of any objects at all.

If we express our understanding of Kant in terms of the three options he examines in the Aesthetic, we should say that he rejects both Newton's absolute space and Leibniz's relational theory because they both fail to appreciate the subjective character of space. Newton's absolute space is transcendentally real according to Kant, and as such it falls beyond the scope of empirical knowledge into a region about which we can make no claims. This much is rather Leibnizian, for Leibniz raises verificationist objections to Newton that amount to the view that Newton's absolute space and time have no empirical significance.[7] We then come to the second option:

> Are they in fact mere determinations or even relations of things, but such as they would apply to things-in-themselves even if such things were not intuited . . . ?

This alludes to Leibniz's view. Kant sets aside Leibniz's opinion, not because it proposes that space is merely a system of relations of things, but because it is a system of relations that is said to apply to things-in-themselves. Even though Leibniz's theory is reductive from an ontological point of view, it shares the perspective of transcendental realism, and that is why Kant rejects it.[8]

The third option announces the subjectivity of space and adopts the stance that Kant calls "transcendental idealism" and "empirical realism." But to say that much still leaves undetermined just what it is that is subjective and transcendentally ideal. Is it Newton's container-space that is properly regarded as subjective, or is it the Leibnizian relational conception that survives in corrected form in the Kantian theory? Judging from this text, the case for the latter is overwhelming. The vocabulary of the third option is taken over from and relies on the second. In fact, the third option is formulated as a clause in the sentence that presents the Leibnizian relational account.

> Or are they such that they apply only to the form of intuition and thus to the subjective constitution of our mind, . . . ?

Kant means to answer in the affirmative. "They" are subjective and without our minds would not characterize any objects. But what are "they"? What is the antecedent of "they" here? The same question arises for the German text.[9] Plainly, it is to the spatial and temporal "determinations" and "even relations" of the second option to which Kant alludes. The rhetorical point of the sentence is the contrast of the Leibnizian view, according to which these determinations attach to things even if they are not intuited, with the third option being introduced, according to which "they" are confined to the subjective context of intuition. Thus in this passage, Kant, like Leibniz, reduces space to "Bestimmungen oder auch Verhältnisse der Dinge" and differs from Leibniz only on the issue of the subjective origin of these "determinations or relations."

Kant thinks that the subjective status of space, and not its character as container, suffices for the solution to the problem of incongruent counterparts. In other words, the spatial determinations conferred on representations that make up a left-hand glove differ from those conferred on representations that make up a right-hand glove. The shortfall of Leibniz's relational theory, as Kant understands it, is that the relations are just those that stand, in the example, between the elements constituting the gloves or, generally, between space-filling objects. Intrinsically, there are no differences in spatial relations between parts of a left-hand and a right-hand glove. The Leibnizian theory provides nothing more than intrinsic relations of the parts. In consequence, were one glove the only spatial thing to exist, it would not be a right-hand glove or a left-hand glove. Kant thinks this is unacceptable, and his theory does provide something more. The difference between the gloves is marked in the spatial system of things that subjects like us impose in the process of apprehending nonmental reality. Kant can reasonably suppose that whatever explanation of the difference between incongruent counterparts an absolute container-space would provide will also be provided by a *subjective* relational theory.[10]

Therefore, all of the sources of support for an individual container-like interpretation of Kant's conception of space do not really require such an interpretation. Kant's thinking can be understood to be quite Leibnizian, with the proviso that the system of relations that is space is subjectively imposed. This is not to say that Kant's conception of intuition and of perception of spatiotemporal things is close to that of Leibniz. The Leibnizian "intellectualization" that regards perception as merely a confused form of intellectual cognition is definitively rejected by Kant.

All of this discussion of space has the local objective of providing an interpretation of the assertion "Space is in us" as it functions in connection with the fourth Paralogism. Now we can restate Kant's claims on behalf of transcendental idealism so that his rejection of idealism *simpliciter* is not a bad joke, while his claim to present a dualist philosophy is vindicated and his praise for Descartes can be understood. Let us begin with the last item. Descartes is right because he understands that outer objects cannot simply be found in the mind by some kind of introspective procedure, and because he recognizes that the argument for their existence as the cause of inner ideas cannot successfully repel skeptical challenges. So Kant's praise for Descartes is aimed at his correctly posing the problem of the external world for all who think that it is known on the basis of inference from some mental item that is immediately accessible. But this also means that Kant is not planning to offer a justification of the kind that he has just praised Descartes for ruling out. He is not going to say that we can apprehend outer objects, because these are, properly understood, inner things, and he is not going to say that we can successfully argue that inner things must be known only as the effects of outer causes.

When Kant points out that inner and outer objects are only appearances, he is stressing the parallelism of the two forms of receptivity and is not assimilating outer sense to inner. His claim is that we have just the same title to certainty about things directly apprehended by outer sense as we do about mental things (like thoughts) apprehended by inner sense. The Kantian point here is captured by emphasizing that inner objects *too* are only appearances. We do not get to absolute reality in inner sense any more than in outer sense. We get to a representation of reality (reality as represented), and as everyone agrees, we are entitled to certainty about the existence of that inner reality because we encounter it directly in inner experience. Kant's claim is that the same holds for outer objects. Outer objects, that is, things in space, are also merely representations (reality as represented), and we are entitled to the same security about the object of outer sense as appearance as we are about the object of inner sense. We directly apprehend both kinds of appearance. There is no reason to think that we have to move to an internal surrogate for the object of outer sense in order to attain this certainty. Certainty attaches to it as the immediate object of our conscious experience. This becomes clear in the fuller discussion in this very context. Kant says that, for all we know, an outer thing, "in the transcendental sense," may cause perceptual episodes in us:

> . . . this [transcendental object], however, is not the object that we understand via representations of matter and corporeal things, for these are only appearances, that is, kinds of representation that always occur in us, and the reality of which rests on immediate consciousness, just as the reality of my own thoughts does. The transcendental object is just as unknown in respect to inner as to outer intuition. (A372–373)

In other words, through all of his discussion of outer objects as mere appearances and representations, Kant never means to erode the outerness of objects of outer sense. The sense in which we know them with certainty is limited. We do not know them as they are themselves but only as appearances, as things as we represent them. But in that respect they are known to us immediately, just as inner things are known to us. In both cases, we directly apprehend the subjectively conditioned reality. In both cases, the form of intuition—time in the case of inner things, space in the case of outer—comes from us. And that is what Kant means when he says that both time and space are in us (A373). In neither case do the forms constitute the reality apprehended, a mental reality in the case of inner sense and a nonmental reality in the case of outer sense. Only thus does it make sense to speak of dualism. Kant has distinguished his view from that of Descartes, who cannot be certain about outer objects, and from that of philosophers like Berkeley, who simply deny that there are any nonmental things. Mental things are mental and spatial things are not mental, and we know them both in immediate experiences of them.

CHAPTER 7

Outer Causes of Perception

Kant rejects the familiar idea that nonmental objects in space cause our perceptual experiences. Stating this rejection in the context of the fourth Paralogism discussed in chapter 6, Kant uses the very terminology to describe the allegedly defective idealism of Descartes that he used earlier to express his own doctrine of the subjectivity of perception. Once again, he gives the impression that his own theory of perception is not different from that of the idealists he claims to refute. Cartesian idealists who posit external objects as causes of inner perceptual experiences recognize that doubts can always be raised about the justification of such posits. In the context of the discussion of the Paralogism, Kant says,

> In consequence, the relation of perception to its outer cause remains permanently doubtful; whether this [cause] can be taken to be inner or outer, and thus whether all so-called outer perceptions are not a mere play of our inner sense [*ein bloßes Spiel unseres inneren Sinnes*], or whether they stand in relation to real outer objects as their causes. (A368)

Because outer causes are mere hypotheses, our putative experience of outer things may be a "mere play of our inner sense." So the causal theory generates a form of problematic idealism that Kant opposes. But in the Analytic, in the discussion of the synthesis of reproduction in imagination, Kant has said,

> when we are mindful of the fact that appearances are not things in themselves, we quickly appreciate that they are the mere play of our representations [*das*

bloße Spiel unserer Vorstellungen], which eventuate in determinations of inner sense. (A101)

Does Kant not embrace here the very conception of perceptual experience for which he condemns those who posit outer causes of the *play* of our inner representations? Kant thinks that Cartesian idealists wrongly contrast the insecure hypothesis of outer objects (as causes) with the secure knowledge we possess of inner representations, which is a matter of immediate apprehension and not of explanatory hypotheses. He insists that we have secure knowledge of *outer* objects and need no inference or hypothesis. His strategy is to replace the shaky inference with immediate apprehension of outer things so that a parallel knowledge of inner and outer objects can be sustained. But it seems that this security is achieved only by dropping the idea that outer things are truly external to the mind. Outer reality is only a question of the existence of outer *representations* that are *nothing apart from us and our minds.* This internalization of the outer, along with the passage at A101 that proposes the same internalization, seems to be a Berkeleyan subjective idealism.

The investigation conducted in previous chapters of Kant's use of the term *representation* and of the concept of representing objects is immediately pertinent here. As we have seen, Kant sometimes collapses the distinction between object and representation into the outer, subjectively apprehended reality. When he does so, the term *representation* comes to mark the subjectivity and not the mental status of the item it refers to. Though we are prepared to allow for this potentially confusing usage, the present context focusing on the causes of representations will still prompt idealistic interpretations of Kant. Even as I now reread this discussion at A367 to A381, the possibility that transcendental idealism is not really different from ordinary dogmatic idealism looms as a powerful and unwanted thought. Kant's own contention that he is *rejecting* idealism here by identifying outer realities with representations in our minds seems unwarranted and sophistical. If the principal resource for confidence in the existence of things in space consists in altering our conception of the gap between representation and represented, Kant's own view seems to collapse into the idealism he purports to escape. The object is still outer (spatial), but the outer itself is now inner.

Is the only leverage that Kant envisions for avoiding Cartesian idealism this move that drops the claim about external causes and thus makes the so-called *object of perception* a kind of internal object? It is not. A much more robust anti-idealist argument emerges in this very discussion, right after the distinction between two senses for *außer* at A373—a distinction that could itself fit in with a weak and disappointing, or even sophistical, anti-idealism. I will quote this passage in full.

> Space and time are representations *a priori* that reside in us as forms of our sensible intuition, before any real object of the senses has been determined through sensation for representation under these sensible relations.[1] However, this matter, this real thing, this something that has to be intuited in space, necessarily presupposes perception, and it cannot be created or produced by any imaginative power independently of this perception, which alone indicates the reality of something in space. Thus sensation is that thing that marks a reality in space and time, according as the one or the other kind of sensible intuition is involved. Once sensation is given, if it is applied to an object in general, without specifying that object,[2] it is called perception. Once sensation is given, as a consequence of the variety in it, all sorts of objects can be invented that have no empirical position in space and time outside the imagination. This is entirely certain: whether one takes into consideration the sensations of pleasure and pain, or the external sensations such as color, warmth, and so forth, it is perception through which the matter must first be given in order that we be able to think objects of sensible intuition. Thus, if we confine ourselves here to outer intuition, this perception represents something real in space. For, in the first place, perception is the representation of a reality just as space itself is the representation of the mere possibility of simultaneous existence.[3] In the second place, this reality is represented as present to outer sense, that is, as in space. In the third place, space itself is nothing other than mere representation, and thus, only that which is represented in space can be validly said to be real in it, and conversely, what is given in it, that is, what is represented in space through perception, is really present in it; since if it were not really present in space, that is, immediately given through empirical intuition, it also could not be imagined, since one cannot just think up the real in intuition *a priori*.

Three points are adduced here on behalf of the claim that what is perceived in space really exists in space: (1) The difference between space itself and the perceived content of space is just the difference between the possibility and the real existence of external things; (2) In the mode of representation that constitutes perception, outer objects are simply apprehended *as existing in space*. This form of receptivity does not require inference any more that the apprehension of inner, temporally organized items requires inference; (3) Since space is, in the absence of spatial things, "merely representation" and not any represented thing, it is only objects in space that can be said to be real outer existences. These assertions are intended to rule out the possibility that the things we perceive in space do not exist in space. They rule out the possibility that perceptions are all just concoctions, or illusions—that is, that they are just mental realities to which nothing external to the mind corresponds. This is ruled out not by an argument supporting the correspondence (like the causal argument) but by understanding perceptual experience so that there is no question of a "corresponding" object. Objects are perceived in space. That is how outer things are present to us. A seemingly real thing in space would not actually be a real (although inner) object if it were just dreamed up or imagined. We would still have a certain mental content that we might wrongly take to indicate the presence of a reality in space, but there would not be *anything there*. Whatever Kant means by describing perception as "a mere play of representations," he intends that the description be compatible with these summarized understandings of the contrast between apprehension of real objects in space and mere thought or imagining of such objects.

One of the important features of the discussion here is that Kant asserts the priority of perception over illusion and imagination. Of course, he does not rebut the possibility of illusions or dreamed realities. He does refuse the title "perception" to these cases, without trying to establish an absolute test for distinguishing revealed realities and illusions. After all, the fact is that we have no absolutely secure test, as philosophers have stressed since the advent of the skeptical method. The point is that we can only hallucinate and dream and cook up imagined realities if we have first perceived actual realities.

This is not a new principle or an ad hoc device to reach the security about outer realities that is Kant's objective in the fourth Paralogism. It is, rather, a reassertion of the theme that Kant has endorsed throughout the *Critique* to the effect that our sensibility is receptive. We provide the form of outer intuition, but the matter has to come from a source outside us. Once perception as apprehension of outer realities is achieved, the diverse sensuous materials with which we become familiar can figure in dreams, hallucinations, and imaginative concoctions of all sorts. All of these things rely for their occurrence on the reality of outer objects of perception.[4]

In the case where I do hallucinate, Kant's view is that there is a representation present similar to the representation that would exist in me were my experience perception and not hallucination. Idealism gets a secure footing by means of very little development from this kind of concession that the inner realities of hallucination and perception are similar—similar enough to make it conceivable that I might be mistaking what is really hallucination for perception on any given occasion. In a sense, Kant does not reject this degree of similarity. Indeed, he could not reject it, since there are plenty of cases where hallucinations deceive subjects into the belief that they are perceiving something. Global considerations and not case-by-case analysis block the possibility that "perceptions" do not reach as far as a truly outer reality. These global considerations include the point just made: only perceivers can possibly hallucinate or imagine perceived reality. We have no power to generate the matter of outer representation *a priori*. Without any matter we have neither perception nor hallucination, and with matter we have perception and the possibility of hallucination. It is the reality of perception that gives us the ability to imagine things and to suffer from perceptual aberrations.

Although Kant will presumably describe an hallucination in terms of a mental representation, he is not saying that when we perceive, we are correctly inferring the existence of an object corresponding to an apprehended inner representation, while when we hallucinate, we are *incorrectly* inferring the same thing. That is the insecure causal argument that Kant rejects. For him, when we perceive, the element of sensation is immediate cognitive contact with the outer object and cannot exist without the outer object. Given perception in which outer realities are apprehended, it is possible to generate mental representations that may result in our mistakenly thinking that we perceive, that is, that we apprehend an outer object directly. The fact that this kind of error is possible does not mean that, in either perception or hallucination, we are inferring the existence of one thing from the given existence of something else. Perception is immediate apprehension of something extra-mental, and a hallucination that deceives us is a situation wherein we mistakenly take ourselves to be apprehending something although we are not apprehending anything. The problem in hallucination is not that the object exists but only in the mind. The problem is that the object does not exist at all. There isn't any such thing. The hallucinating subject is just "seeing things."

This understanding of perceptual aberrations is essential if we are to offer a coherent account of the direct perceptual apprehension of nonmental things in space. It is only such an account that will sustain the proof of the existence of outer things that Kant states again and again in the Paralogisms. To my knowledge, Kant never expresses this idea explicitly, and he may never quite realize that the representation invoked to *explain* a perceptual aberration cannot be presented as an object that is apprehended. He does repeatedly assert that apprehension of outer things is noninferential. Outer sense either reaches objects in space or seems to. If it merely seems to get as far as a spatial object, then it fails to reach any object. It does not sometimes find an inner mental thing that, somehow, seems to be a spatial thing. The subject of an hallucination might remark, when he appreciates that he is not perceiving anything in space, "Something very odd must be going on in my brain." This *conjecture* is reasonable, but it is a conjecture and not a report that relocates what the subject really does apprehend, assigning it to an inner locus. Hallucinated objects are "seen" in outer public space. The location offered by the subject (for example, "hovering in the doorway") is as authoritative as the description (for example, "a horrid severed head"). The recognition that this is a case of hallucination depends on the correctness of the subject's assignment of a location to the putative object. It is an hallucination because there is no such thing hovering in the doorway, not because there is such a thing but it is hovering somewhere else inside the subject.

Such a conception of hallucination is accessible to Kant just because he has accepted a single and a public space. If a spatial object does not exist at the point in public space where it is "seen," then no spatial object is actually apprehended at all, however much we remain inclined to insist, "But I *see* it *right there*." We will explain this residual insistence by saying, "It is just something going on in your nervous system." *This* explanation adduces inner realities but does not present them as either spatial *objects* or as things apprehended by the subject. The explanation does not provide a substitute spatial object of consciousness and does not claim that the subject is *really* conscious of the inner neural goings-on that play an explanatory role. Instead, it explains why the subject is in a position where he may mistakenly think that he apprehends an outer spatial thing. This whole stance is dictated by Kant's assertion of the uniqueness of space. Any move toward making the hallucination a private object is blocked by the consideration that such an object would be a spatial thing but it would not be locatable with respect to other things, like the doorway. By the same token, the conception of private objects, familiar in idealist thinking about hallucination, is dependent upon the deployment of a concept of private spaces, one for each subject.

Although he never explicitly speaks in these terms, Kant's thinking about representations and objects is perfectly suited to the claim that there is a representation, which we do *not* apprehend, that explains our seeming to perceive an outer object. Apart from the context of illusory experiences, Kant is, of course, generally committed to the existence and functioning of unconscious representations throughout his account of the development of consciousness. The overall plan of Kant's account of experience involves the idea that consciousness is of objects and is attained only when elementary representations of which the subject is not conscious are suitably concatenated. Thus the idea that representations can be posited for explanatory purposes and are not always objects of consciousness is at the very heart of Kant's thinking, and no special machinery is needed in order to invoke representation in an explanatory role in the context of hallucination.

This argument will still seem to be in jeopardy because of Kant's compromised conception of the "outer" that appears to figure in the disappointing "sophistical" rejection of idealism noted above. Kant distances himself from the idealist tradition not only in insisting that the possibility of hallucination is conditioned by prior perceptual experience of real things in space but also in his conception of what it is to speak of real things in space. We will not be able to take satisfaction in his refutation of skeptical empirical idealism if the reality in space of which he proves the existence is too far removed from the reality whose existence is doubted by the empirical idealists. To put this another way, the argument for the reality of perceived things in space will sound good to us— assuming that we want to find such an argument—just to the extent that it establishes a certain kind of extra-mental reality. For considerable stretches of the discussion of the fourth Paralogism, Kant seems to agree altogether with the idealist sentiment that we cannot make any secure statements about outer reality because we have only our mental representations at first hand, and through these stretches of discussion, it sounds as if the main burden of anti-idealism is going to be borne by the thesis that we can be secure about the objects of outer sense because *they are not really outer.*

This line of thinking is eliminated, however, if we see alleged internalization as a way of expressing the subjective character of space and not a way of limiting the reach of outer intuition to mental realities. I have developed this at sufficient length already. We can properly invoke this understanding on the strength of Kant's own words in this passage. In particular, it is space that is "in us," and because that is so, we are able to insist with complete confidence that there would be nothing spatial were it not for us and our minds. The particular line that is essential in this context is the third supporting claim in the passage cited. Since space is *"bloße Vorstellung,"* the only thing about which we might even raise the question "Is it real?" is the thing that exists in space, the thing that sensation marks. Kant is insisting on the reality of this thing, which is contrasted with what is "merely representation." Therefore, in the last analysis, he does not compromise the outerness of spatial reality in asserting our security about the existence of such things. The weight of the argument is not carried, when all is said and done, by noting that space is merely representation and not really external to us at all. In so far as this is true, Kant says, space accounts only for the possibility of things existing together and outside one another. We are entitled to go beyond possibility and to assert real existence, not of space itself, but of spatial objects of perception. The subjective representational character of space is *not* what gives us the title. The credentials of perception rest with the sensory component, with *Empfindung* and not merely *Vorstellung,* which has to be taken to be immediate contact with non-mental reality. Then the fact that we could not imagine such a reality, or dream it, if we did not also perceive it guarantees its existence.

Is Kant's assertion that space is merely representation and thus *in us* just a false start and not a working part of Kant's argument here? It appears to be nonfunctional when we realize that Kant is not going to say, in this setting, that spatial realities exist only in that they too are merely representations and therefore nothing outside the mind. But in fact, more or less at the last minute, Kant makes another use of the merely mental status of space. It is precisely because space itself *is* merely a representation that we have to look elsewhere for a foundation for the reality of the things that are in space. That is just what Kant says here: Because space itself is merely representation, "only that which is represented in space can validly be said to be real" (A375). Furthermore, this is by no means just a consideration adopted for this context. It is the standard Kantian view that we have to be affected in order to get as far as knowledge of any reality. Far from saving the reality of the spatial by the disappointing claim that everything spatial is only representation and therefore a mental reality, Kant asserts here that the representational character of space itself forces us to look elsewhere—namely, to the represented—in order to respond to questions about the reality of objects.

In *Reflexionen,* no. 5653, Kant explicitly says that the occurrence of illusionary experiences of outer existence in dreams does not counter his contention that the intuition of outer things only occurs when something that is not in the subject determines the subjective representation. Dreams and illusions do not ground an object because, Kant says, they have to be preceded by perceptions, that is, instances of apprehension of something real. In the same passage, Kant even asserts that "as a matter of fact I cannot think of any space as existing within myself." I am confident that Kant sees no contradiction between this assertion and any of the frequent occurrences of "Space is *in us*" in his writings. By the latter slogan he means to affirm only the subjectivity and not the metaphysical "location" of space and spatial things. Space itself has no location, and spatial things are all located *outside* in space. A bit further on in this same passage, Kant says that what is involved when something not in the subject determines the intuition of an outer spatial object is "none other than the subject's original passivity." *Original passivity* can only mean our capacity to be affected by things-in-themselves and thus to obtain an input available for synthesis by the active powers of the mind. In other words, the outer something, the thing that belongs to the realm of things-in-themselves, affects the subject, and *this* is the ultimate foundation of the outerness that is represented spatially as a domain of permanent perceivable substance.[5]

CHAPTER 8

Kant Not a Foundationalist

Like the idealist, Kant is preoccupied by the mind and by mental representations. His theory of objects assigns a conspicuous role to the creativity he finds in the human cognitive constitution. The fact that we can think a world of objects at all is ascribed to mental combinatory powers that operate on an input of representations. These representations are understood in prominent and relevant passages of the *Critique* to be transient and private mental items. In the absence of mental synthesizing activities, all of the elementary or original intuitive representations are simple and momentary. They exist in radical separation and dispersion that is only overcome by mental activities. Complex representations of enduring objects of perception that are constituents of the natural world are *constructed* by these creative combinatory activities. That these complexes do represent objects is rendered, by Kant, in the idea that the patterns in representations of objects instantiate universal laws. An *a priori* element in the laws of science is grounded on the constitutive activity of the creative synthesis of mental representations. The central doctrine of the possibility of a synthetic *a priori* turns on the subjective origin of space and time and of the Categories. The mind simply finds in nature what it has put there itself. Thus the mind makes nature, at least in the sense that without this constructive activity, conscious experience could not be experience *of objects,* and in consequence we could have no experience at all or be conscious even of ourselves and the contents of our minds. The intellectual level of judgment, and with it, the attainment of propositional attitudes and the deployment of the concepts of truth and falsehood, are all rooted in the mind's combinatory and creative activity and would find no foothold in the realm of unsynthesized original representations without the constitutive activities of the mind.

The reader who has accepted the idea that we must ground our claims about the world on inner objects of consciousness will see in this sketch of the familiar Kantian moves an irrevocable commitment to the idea that all the objects we apprehend are, properly speaking, mental. This understanding, of course, requires an assumption that elementary objects, properly speaking, are precisely those representations that are fodder for our creative powers of synthesis. The original representations are, without any doubt, mental representations, and the activities that operate on them are mental activities with mental input and mental output. When Kant goes on to say that objects created by these mental activities working on this input are only *appearances,* that appearances can exist *only in our faculty of representations,* and that the idea of a *corresponding* object is just the idea of "something in general = X" and has to be cashed in terms of laws to which our representations themselves conform—when Kant says all of these things, the reader will hear the traditional idealist view that he expected from Kant in the first place. In consequence, such a reader will approach my contention that Kant is entirely opposed to idealism with skepticism.

To confront this natural skepticism about the general feasibility of the understanding of Kant that I am presenting here, it is necessary to consider the fact, and the implications of the fact, that Kant is not a foundationalist philosopher. A foundationalist, for our purposes, is a philosopher who thinks that knowledge claims about the world must be defended, if they can be defended at all, by finding a secure base of ultimate evidence. When such a base is available, defensible claims will be those that are appropriately related to the undisputed knowledge the base affords. The relationship between defended claims and the evidence base can be different in different versions of foundationalist thinking. Knowledge claims can be more or less translated into complexes of assertions in the base, as in reductive phenomenalism, or they may be merely hypotheses that are deemed to be sufficiently confirmed because they entail propositions that belong to the base, as in hypothetico-deductively organized radical empiricist accounts of knowledge. On the whole, foundationalism has been pursued by philosophers who have adopted a Cartesian philosophy of mind, because that conception of cognition brings with it the idea that although we are certain only of the existence and character of the mental realities that are *given* in our consciousness, at least we are absolutely certain of something. Since we are alleged to be entirely secure about that inner subject matter, the Cartesian outlook identifies the needed epistemological base of ultimate evidence with the subject's acquaintance with his own inner states, including the immediate inner objects of his perceptual consciousness, his own beliefs, and the other immediately apprehended mental items directly present to his consciousness.

Whatever variety may be found in foundationalism, all versions contrast with nonfoundationalist epistemology, which does not look to a Cartesian base of evidence restricted to the subject's acquaintance with the contents of his consciousness, and does not posit any other base, but instead gives up the very idea of ultimate evidence as unworkable. Leibniz is not a foundationalist, and this is one of the many respects in which Leibniz is followed by Kant. In his discussion of Descartes's philosophy, Leibniz rejects the method of doubt, and he does not express any aspiration to identify some privileged inner subject matter in the Cartesian manner. In particular, Leibniz says of the hyperbolic Cartesian doubt about even the most evident things,

> if this doubt could once be justly raised, it would be straightway insuperable, it would always confront Descartes himself and anyone else, however evident the assertions presented by them.[1]

The Cartesian notion of the conscious subject influences Leibniz's concept of a monad to some extent. The influence never takes the form of a move toward a base of ultimate mental evidence. Philosophers who recognize that Leibniz offers no foundational organization in his system are liable to ask, What considerations does Leibniz suppose will move us to accept his assertions? His numerous articulations of his metaphysical system, of which the best known is the *Monadology*, largely restate his doctrines with insufficient indication of grounds for them. Why does he expect us to agree with his accounts of both phenomenal and metaphysical reality and with his account of the relations between the monadic and phenomenal realms? Prominent modern interpreters have answered on Leibniz's behalf that all of his philosophical views are supposed to follow from a few general logical principles.[2] This seems to me to be, as much as anything else, an expression of the interpreters' conviction that the abandonment of epistemological foundations leaves only logical principles as matters to which appeal might be made, so those *must* be the sole defense of Leibniz's views. If this view were valid, we would have to regard Leibniz's philosophy as if it were intended as somewhat like a series of theorems of logic. Such an understanding is, in my opinion, completely untenable. Leibniz does not read as if he thinks of his philosophical assertions in this way. It is pretty obvious that his wide-ranging metaphysical speculations do not in fact follow from any logical principles, and it is ungenerous to Leibniz to propose that he thought they do.

Instead of this implausible logical foundation, we have to say that Leibniz rests his case on the overall power of his views to account for *everything*. Leibniz's metaphysics is designed to offer an explanatory setting for the system of our ordinary concepts and to make intelligible and expectable the distinctions on which we rely in everyday and scientific experience. The same scheme of things is supposed to bring mathematical knowledge into the sphere of intelligibility and to make natural room for our moral and religious commitments. By no means least important, Leibniz's system is intended to save the insights of other philosophers. Unlike many of his fellow philosophers, Leibniz inclines to think that other philosophers, of all periods and schools, are very often right in their doctrines. He regularly finds in the thought of others an expression of the truths, seen from another perspective, that he is trying to articulate and clarify himself. His theoretical claims are alleged to provide a convincing and stable understanding of all of these matters and the relations between them. This understanding is supposed to replace uncertain and unstable conceptions that confront us as philosophical problems. Far from confining himself to logical premises, Leibniz uses whatever imaginative, metaphorical, and inspirational means come into his mind, and draws freely on many traditions of past thought, in order to develop a philosophical account that is supposed to make good enough sense of all these things to command our acceptance of it.[3] Kant inherits this general stance from Leibniz.

The significance of this inheritance should be understood in the context of Kant's repudiation of traditional metaphysics, which is far removed from Leibnizian ecumenism. The *Critique of Pure Reason* addresses an agenda of theoretical problems that includes the nature of space, time, and matter; the self-conscious mind and its relation to nature; causality and freedom; possibility and necessity; the source of mathematical truth; the relation of general concepts to individuals; and the existence of God. These are the principal subject matters assigned to metaphysics as traditionally conceived. Kant calls his philosophical treatment of this roster of problems "critical philosophy," and this philosophy is

better viewed as Kant's attempt to replace metaphysics than as a metaphysical system in competition with others. In the *Prolegomena to any
Future Metaphysics,* where he offers his most detailed metaphilosophi-
cal reflections, Kant is willing to say,

> This much is certain: whoever has once tasted the critical philosophy will be
> thereafter repelled by all the dogmatic rubbish with which he has previously
> been obliged to be satisfied because his reason demanded something to sus-
> tain it and he could find nothing better.[4]

The implication here is that metaphysical treatments of the grand questions prior to his achievement of a critical philosophy amount to repellent rubbish.

No doubt, Kant lets his rhetoric get somewhat out of hand here. But
there is a clear sense in which he is trying to replace, and trying not to
engage in, the kind of enterprise that in the past has culminated in metaphysical views. Of course, "metaphysics" can be virtually synonymous
with philosophy at its most abstract, general, and theoretical. Thus conceived, Kant's handling of these issues, whatever its originality and dis-
tinctiveness, is itself inevitably metaphysics. But this broad sense of the
term contrasts with the conception of metaphysics that is the subject of
the pessimistic allegory in the preface to the first edition of the *Critique.*
Metaphysics was the "queen of the sciences," but her dogmatic despotism has been undermined by the attacks of nomadic skeptics, her right
to rule by *a priori* dicta has been confronted by the challenge of empiricists, and after failed efforts to restore her dominion, she is now treated
with contempt or humiliating indifference (Aviii–x). The *Critique* is not
another attempt at the restoration of the traditional despotism of metaphysics, for Kant identifies "the kernel and specific character of metaphysics" as

> the concern of reason merely with itself and, in the course of brooding over
> its own concepts, its supposed direct apprehension of objects, without hav-
> ing any need of the mediation of experience and, indeed, without being able
> to attain such apprehension through experience.[5]

This identification becomes a potent challenge to any thinker who proposes metaphysical doctrines in the traditional mode. In so far as an
assertion claims the support of experience, we can understand why it
must be given a hearing. Many empirical assertions are hard or impossible to evaluate, given our resources, but this never amounts to a ground
for dismissal out of hand. Beyond the domain of empirical fact, there is

a realm for nonempirical assertion, namely, the realm of logic and mathematics. Of course, the nature of logical and mathematical truth is not obvious or agreed upon. Even so, it does not seem rash to suppose that there is such a realm where true and false can be distinguished. In any case, it is not logic and mathematics that Kant takes to be an arena for the generation of repellent rubbish, in the production of which schools of thought vie with one another without any cumulative effect or agreed-upon achievement.

What is the source of traditional metaphysical claims if it is not the metaphysician's brooding over his own concepts and promoting the claims that his reflections manage to put him in touch with reality and that this access, in some mysterious way, dispenses with the need for experience? Perhaps we can answer this question in some way that does not force us to follow Kant in the critical philosophy or to drop metaphysics altogether in the manner of the positivists. Kant obliges any metaphysician to attempt such an answer.

Kant asks in the *Critique,* as in the *Prolegomena,* How is metaphysics, thus conceived as knowledge of reality without need of experience, possible? His answer is that it is not possible. The hope for a compelling metaphysical doctrine actually engenders only illusions of knowledge and endless dialectical vacillation between opposed contentions. What is possible, and also actual, is metaphysics as "a natural disposition of human reason." In this sense, metaphysics

> is, in its fundamentals, implanted in us by nature itself, and cannot be looked upon as a product of an arbitrary choice or an accidental extension during the advance of experiences (from which it is entirely distinct).[6]

The critical philosophy cannot alter the fact that no satisfactory metaphysical knowledge of reality will ever be forthcoming. Its task, on the contrary, is to counter the effects of the illusions reason naturally spawns and to recast our ineluctable metaphysical impulses in their proper role as regulative principles that do not contain information about any objects of knowledge at all. Critical philosophy deals with our natural and irrepressible disposition to metaphysics, but not by generating a metaphysical theory. Therefore,

> Metaphysics as a natural disposition of reason is real, but in itself [that is, as doctrine] . . . it is dialectical and illusory. To try to derive fundamental principles from this source and to use them in pursuit of this natural but nonetheless false semblance can never engender science but only vain dialectical

artifice in which one school can surpass another while none can ever acquire justified and lasting approval.[7]

Kant is thus willing to assert that the ultimate sum total of metaphysical knowledge is, and will always be, *none at all!* This outcome will be accepted by the rational critical philosopher "notwithstanding all the prized and revered dreams that are thereby set at nothing" (Axxii). In this intellectual renunciation, Kant is a *modernist,* and his views prefigure analogous renunciations by twentieth-century positivists, by Wittgenstein and followers of Wittgenstein, by the conception of philosophy as therapy, and by attempts at a "postphilosophical" outlook.

Of course, understanding why we can never attain metaphysical knowledge is itself an invaluable addition to human wisdom. Within the critical philosophy, Kant believes that he establishes a body of secure, hitherto misunderstood *a priori* truths. But this yield cannot be considered an attainment of the goals of metaphysics. To say that metaphysics is a disposition of human thought means that we have a permanent aspiration to a kind of knowledge of reality, and that this aspiration will always be disappointed. The defeat cannot be avoided if we deal with the aspiration by trying to satisfy it. That effort has prompted the enterprises that generate the illusions of knowledge Kant exposes in the Transcendental Dialectic. The task of critical philosophy is to explain this in a way that will eliminate our willingness to credit any of the metaphysical theories that are spun out when philosophers yield to the temptations created by our disposition to metaphysics.

Like other revolutionaries, Kant thinks of his critical stance as liberating. For one thing, it relieves us of a burden of conceptually defective expectations. But this is not the whole story. The permanence of the metaphysical aspiration also entails a permanent and real disappointment that criticism does not mitigate. When it comes to the main issues on which we look to metaphysics for instruction—issues such as the existence of God, the freedom of the human will operating in mechanistic *nature,* and the immortality of the soul—it is Kant's judgment that no compelling view can ever be established by rational means.

The point is not that we can never go beyond empirical knowledge and have no resources for establishing *a priori* or necessary truths. Nor is it that our capacity for *a priori* knowledge is confined to formal matters that contain no information about reality. On the contrary, within the *Critique,* Kant identifies logic, mathematics, and natural science as areas of intellectual enterprise in which *a priori* necessary truths are established, and in mathematics and natural science, the *a priori* findings amount to knowledge of objects and not merely to knowledge of barren tautologies. Kant himself claims to establish synthetic *a priori* truths within critical philosophy itself. But in all cases, the *a priori* truths we can know fall short of the pretensions of traditional metaphysics and hold out no hope for the ultimate satisfaction of our metaphysical aspirations.

Physics (or more generally, science) does generate secure *a priori* knowledge of the extra-mental, but the scope of its truths is limited to the world of sense experience. Kant thinks that all empirical physical laws have a core of synthetic *a priori* truth. The empirical law always fleshes out an *a priori* skeleton. The law of gravitation, for example, while itself an empirical generalization, embodies an underlying truth graspable *a priori*. In this case, the underlying truth is that a law covering forces of attraction between massive particles must be an inverse square law.[8] Although there are, in Kant's view, *a priori* generalizations about the universe that belong to physical science, such truths, like empirical truths, have only the domain of experience for subject matter. The *a priori* in physics goes beyond what we in fact experience, but the realm of its application is confined to what it is possible for us to experience—in short, confined to the empirical universe.

An *a priori* core explains how it is that physics can reach true laws at all and why we are not confined to the level of generalizations about observed cases. Therefore, the attainable *a priori* in physical science makes possible the rejection of Humean skepticism about the possibility of certifying strictly universal propositions and necessary truths. But the rescued propositions are not metaphysics, properly so called. They are not attempts to establish truths without reference to the empirical scope and limitations of human experience.

Perhaps this degree of critical limitation has still to be qualified in order to make Kant appear to rescue a part of traditional metaphysics, even though he abandons most of it. The positive doctrines that are asserted as the culmination of the Transcendental Analytic cannot all be brought under the heading "formal or analytic truth," nor are they all truths of mathematics or *a priori* skeletal laws of empirical science. Synthetic *a priori* findings are presented in the *Critique* which are broadly *philosophical* and that cannot be relegated to any other field. It seems that only verbal pedantry can resist the thought that these ideas formulate a Kantian metaphysics. The very concept of a *critical philosophy*, however, stands against the temptation to regard these claims as akin to traditional metaphysics. No synthetic principle that Kant is officially willing to defend in

CHAPTER 9

The "How-Possible" Questions

Since Kant is not a foundationalist, since he does not try to find secure premises for knowledge claims, he is obliged to start from the ordinary and putative scientific knowledge of things that we are confident we have when we are not testing it against a philosophical skepticism. Taking ordinary knowledge at face value, Kant asks how it is possible for us to have this knowledge. This is the order of Kantian transcendental arguments. It is the stance from which Kant formulates the famous "how-possible" questions in the introduction to the *Critique* and elsewhere.

The outlook of the "how-possible" questions contrasts most sharply with that of the foundationalists, who are willing to deny that we do possess knowledge of ordinary things outside us and to deny that we have achieved any scientific penetration of nature. Generally, foundationalists think that we are committed to such a skeptical denial if we cannot exhibit our claims as suitably derived from some fail-safe epistemic base. Skeptics among them think that such derivations are permanently beyond us. In just that spirit, Hume finds it "vain to ask whether there be body"—vain because we can produce no satisfying argument passing from premises about our impressions and ideas to conclusions about bodies, and *for that reason* we cannot know that there are any. Hume contemplates the universal causal laws discovered by Newton that express our deepest and best understanding of the physical world. Although Hume thought well enough of Newton's accomplishment to aspire to be a kind of Newton for the mind and to provide three laws of "gentle attraction" or association in imitation of Newton's three laws of motion, he is not able to construct a satisfactory intellectual picture that really endorses Newton's presumption that he had found out something deep about nature. From Hume's perspective, Newton's laws are actually spurious claims in so far as they purport to express such knowledge. There is a double skepticism here. First, strictly universal assertions inevitably involve a rationally unjustified extrapolation from observed cases. Second, Hume's stance concerning the existence of *body* implies that we do not know that any physical realm exists. To this extent, we cannot establish that there is anything that offers a subject matter about which physical laws might be true or false. This is part of the precarious position that Hume finds himself forced to occupy, a position according to which we do not find rational justification for the central claims we want to make about reality and are forced to fall back on appeal to beliefs implanted in us by that "human nature" of which Hume's great work is *A Treatise*.

Kant's famous awakening by Hume's philosophy does not include a willingness to join Hume in permanently excluding the hope of rational justification. The attainments of the human mind in mathematics and physical science are too conspicuous and too grand to allow them to be set at nothing on the strength of Hume's radical skeptical arguments. According to Hume, no assertion of a law of nature can be more than an expression of a natural human disposition to go beyond what we can really know. For Kant, it is the premises of those skeptical arguments and not the success of Newton in understanding nature that must be called into question. This is expressed in the overall organization Kant proposes for his book, when he promises to investigate the question, How is it possible for us to have synthetic *a priori* knowledge in various domains, and in mathematics and physics in particular? Kant entitles this "the general problem of pure reason" (B19). Whether we do have such knowledge is not a topic for investigation! Unlike Hume, Kant was actually a scientist himself, with a grasp on the meaning and scope of mathematical physics. He does not regard it as feasible to redescribe the fundamental laws of physics, much less all scientific knowledge, as rationally unjustified extrapolations from observation of an outer reality the very existence of which is not wholly secure.

Hume's arguments are of great value to Kant because they do prove that the necessity and strict universality of these examples of human knowledge cannot have empirical origins. Thus, for Kant, Hume's work raises questions that are left for others to answer. "How is such and such knowledge, knowledge that we do possess, possible?" That is Kant's question. The nonfoundationalist order of thought is patent here. The knowledge is given. The philosophical problem is to account for the possibility of this knowledge. More generally, Kant not only accepts Newton's laws and the theorems of mathematics as propositions the truth of which we have come to appreciate *somehow,* he also accepts the ordinary world and our ordinary conceptions on which scientific thinking is erected. He takes as given that we are, each of us, enduring subjects of experience, that we have a corrigible but workable understanding of the world we experience, that the world we experience is one of relatively stable objects in space, and that our own thoughts and experiences are nonspatial realities that exist in time. Kant's system offers a philosophical explanatory account of these ordinary conceptions. He purports to explain how it is possible for us to apprehend enduring objects in space, and how we are able to have a representation of our self as subject and thus be both conscious and self-conscious. The explanations start from the putative facts and not from special skeptical restrictions. Kant does not refuse to make any use of these ordinary conceptions before they have been certified by a process that relates them to a secure base of evidence. Idealist interpretations of Kant are generated only by first projecting something like the foundationalists' skepticism onto his thinking.

In the introduction to the *Critique of Pure Reason,* Kant makes plain his reliance on the fact that we do possess synthetic *a priori* knowledge in mathematics and natural science, as required for the "how-possible" perspective he adopts. There is no comparable text in which Kant expresses his acceptance of our ordinary concepts of ourselves and of objects of perceptual experience, and our ordinary concepts of space and time. Kant does not simply affirm our possession of a reliable concept of outer material things or bodies as objects of perception and then expressly raise the question, How is it possible for us to have this concept of bodies? On the contrary, it is pretty obvious that nothing except our possession of synthetic *a priori* knowledge prompts this familiar Kantian move. Because he restricts the scope of "how-possible" questions to the rather technical context of knowledge of synthetic *a priori* truths, it may seem unconvincing to claim that his procedure constitutes a justification for our everyday conception of bodies and our ordinary assumption that it is outer physical things that we apprehend in sense experience. But upon reflection, I think it will be conceded that this is just what Kant's procedure aims to establish. The Aesthetic makes the public status of objects of outer sense a synthetic *a priori* truth via the uniqueness of space and the contrast with inner sense. The Deduction of the Categories establishes as a synthetic *a priori* truth that the outer realities apprehended are enduring objects. These are the ordinary understandings that human beings share unless they are undermined by the skepticism of a foundationalist philosopher.

In order to bring to light the force of this understanding of Kant, let us contemplate, first, the discussion by means of which he identifies the *form* of sensible intuitions. Following the preface and introduction, this argument appears at the very beginning of the *Critique*—in fact, on the second page of the Transcendental Aesthetic, about forty lines from the beginning of Part One. Having informed us that the object of any empirical intuition will be an "appearance," Kant introduces the distinction between matter and form with the help of a kind of thought experiment in which we start from the representation of "a body" and take away from it in thought everything but the form. Kant stipulates that representations will be "pure in the transcendental sense" if they contain nothing that belongs to sensation. Of course, we are in the process of identifying the pure elements of *intuition,* so contributions of the understanding to our representation of a body—and that means all conceptualization—must also be set aside. So the thought experiment is a twofold process in which, when I first

> separate from the representation of a body what the understanding ascribes to it, such as substance, force, divisibility, and so on, and then in the same way separate away that pertaining to it which belongs to sensation, such as impenetrability, hardness, color, and so forth, there remains something left over to me from this empirical intuition, namely, extension and figure. These belong to pure intuition, and they reside in the mind, without a real object of the senses or sensation, as a pure form of sensibility. (A20–21, B35)

I have given prominence to the fact that this appears just a few lines into the *Critique* in order to make it clear that there has been no deployment of a technical concept of material things to serve us in this thought experiment. Kant is invoking our ordinary, prephilosophical shared notion of "bodies" as objects of perception that we can classify conceptually because we experience their hardness, color, and so forth. In fact, although page 1 is packed with more or less technical definitions of *intuition, sensibility, thought, sensation, empirical,* and *appearance,* no special philosophical guidance at all is offered on the question of what a representation of "a body" might be. There is every reason to think that Kant is just appealing to the fact that ordinary experience, taken at face value, provides everyone with abundant examples of representations of bodies. For one thing, having presented the thought experiment starting from "*der Vorstellung eines Körpers*," Kant repeats the whole procedure in more abstract theoretical terms as a characterization of the overall content of the Transcendental Aesthetic that he is about to develop. In the repetition, he leaves out the appeal to "a body," which has served merely as a handy example from experience of things around us:

> In the Transcendental Aesthetic we will first isolate the [faculty of] sensibility by taking away from it everything that the understanding ascribes to it with the help of its concepts, so that nothing is left except empirical intuition. Second, we will again detach from this everything that belongs to sensation, so that nothing but pure intuitions and the pure form of appearances remains, which is the only thing that can be offered by *a priori* sensibility. (A22, B36)

Ultimately, Kant has to eliminate the example of "a body" in order to state the general point, because he wants it to emerge that time is a pure form parallel to space, and as a pure form, time will not be brought to our attention by taking conceptual and sensual features away from *a body*. Kant does this because he is about to assert a strict separation of inner and outer: "Time cannot be outwardly intuited, any more than space can be intuited as something in us" (A23, B37).

It is within the setting of the common understanding of bodies, and not philosophical theory, that Kant is able to say that the form of our representation that remains when we have eliminated both the conceptual and the sensual is something that is not taken into the mind but is contributed to experience *a priori* by us. The passage implies that it is plausible to ascribe this "form" to the mind because the element that gives the object a real existence, that is, the "matter" that cannot be ascribed to a mental realm, has been removed from consideration in the thought experiment. That implication fits the contrast of outer and inner sense that Kant gives only a few lines further along. It is a defining characteristic of inner sense that by its use the mind is able to intuit itself and its states, while outer sense is analogously defined as representing objects outside us in space.

If Kant is not a Cartesian foundationalist, if he does not try to identify a level of absolute security in the contents of the mind immediately accessible to the subject, it will be natural for him to accept the ordinary conception of inner thought and outer bodies. We have seen that he does accept scientific reality when he asserts that we possess synthetic *a priori* knowledge in natural science. This assertion surely presupposes the concomitant acceptance of the existence of the physical world, a world of bodies. We cannot make sense of an outlook that takes the law of gravitation to be an example of established knowledge and is, at the same time, skeptical or uncommitted about the existence of the massive bodies that provide all of the exemplifications of that law. We should notice that the illustrative concepts belonging to the understanding that Kant mentions include "force" and "divisibility," and these are concepts with the help of which Newtonian laws, and thus synthetic *a priori* truths, are framed. So it would be bizarre if Kant did not think it legitimate to draw attention to our representations of bodies as a source of examples that can be taken at face value. Bodies are "real objects," and they do not "reside in the mind." They are things outside us that engender our sensuous experiences and fit the concepts of our understanding, among which scientific concepts are prominent. There is every reason to think that Kant does assume that a familiarity with bodies can be exploited in introducing his central philosophical ideas. The taking-away procedure that enables Kant to identify *a priori* forms is just a case in point.

In the same spirit, we should now return to the points that Kant makes about the concepts of space and time under the heading "Metaphysical Exposition." At the beginning of the discussion of space, Kant repeats the characterization of inner and outer sense in a way that, again, implies that outer sense does not reveal mental realities, for this is just what distinguishes inner sense from outer. Then Kant raises the question of the character of space and time and offers the three options we have discussed in chapter 6. The job of the Transcendental Aesthetic is to explain the correctness of the third option. This is essentially the thesis of the transcendental ideality and empirical reality of space and time, but in each case Kant prefaces transcendental considerations with a list of "metaphysical points." The contrast between "metaphysical" and "transcendental" expositions is actually added in the second edition of the *Critique,* together with some rearrangement of the points. But the points are the same in both editions, and the contrast parallels the contrast between the Metaphysical Deduction and the Transcendental Deduction of the Categories.

Now the question to which I want to draw attention is this: What is it to which Kant makes appeal in supposing that we will accept the metaphysical points concerning space and time? Here again, I propose that Kant takes for granted our nonphilosophical conceptions derived from everyday experience of spatiotemporal reality, and especially of objects of perception. For the sake of brevity, I will consider only the concept of space. The four metaphysical points are that space is (1) not an empirical concept; (2) an *a priori* and a necessary concept; (3) a singular rather than a discursive concept; and (4) a concept of something infinite. Kant's presentation of these points in the Metaphysical Exposition seems to consist of a series of flat assertions for which a little elaboration but no arguments are given. The text reads as though Kant expects these assertions to be accepted by any intelligence able to apply common sense to ordinary experience and to recognize general truths that can be appreciated through that simple-minded procedure.

Consider the first point: space is not an empirical concept. Kant says that the concept of space is presupposed for, rather than derived from, experience. To see what he has in mind, it is useful to refer to another similar point that he often makes later in the *Critique*. Unlike ordinary empirical objects, space is not itself perceived. So space is not a concept like the concepts *cave* and *closet*. I choose these examples because they are concepts of container-like objects, and space seems to us to be something like a super-container. *Cave* and *closet* are empirical concepts that we possess because we encounter such things as caves and closets in our perceptual experience. Of course, space might be an empirical concept, although not an object of perception, if it figured in hypotheses belonging to an explanatory theory, in the way the concept of a gravitational field figures in theories that explain the perceived motion of objects. The point I want to stress is that Kant takes it for granted that we all know what it is to perceive something like a closet, and we know that we do not perceive space. It is in the arena of ordinary experience that Kant expects us to test the metaphysical points.

Kant's second metaphysical point rules out any theoretical status for the concept of space. Space is necessary for any outer experience at all, while theoretical objects are doubly contingent and never necessary. Theoretical objects are contingent, first, because the facts they are introduced to explain are contingent facts. But they also have a second kind of contingency, because they may always be repudiated in favor of other theoretical commitments that explain the same facts even better. The status of space is nothing like this because there could not be any facts of outer intuition without space.

Therefore, when it comes to the second metaphysical point, Kant supposes that we will accept the assertion because, reflecting on experience at the commonsense level, we will agree that space is not just something that happens to be there as caves and closets do. We can readily imagine a universe with caves and space but no closets but we cannot intelligibly posit an experienced outer world with caves and closets but no space. So space is a necessary condition for outer objects of perceptual experience, while it is not one of them.

We can think space *empty*, but we cannot think it *away*. The inhibition on thinking space away is related to the fact that space is not something we detect by perceiving it or experiencing it. Things that we do detect by perceiving them, things like caves and closets, we can think of as empty (caves empty of bats and stalagmites, and closets empty of clothing and tennis rackets, respectively), and we can also think such things away, that is, think a universe without caves or closets among its constituents. Now thinking space empty is simply thinking away *all* of the constituents of the outer universe. But since there is nothing else that might disappear from the outer beyond the things that appear in it, and since space itself is not one of these things, thinking away space is impossible. Kant asserts the necessity of space because of facts like these.

We can now give a plausible account of the third metaphysical point: that space is not a discursive concept, as the concepts *cave* and *closet* are. No discursive concept could carry the sense of uniqueness that attaches to space. There is just one space in which all outer things are located. The plural, "spaces," indicates only parts of space and not instances of space, while caves and closets are instances and not parts. Once again, it is as proprietors of ordinary experience and not as technical thinkers that we are expected to assess this claim favorably. Of course, our ordinary concept of space carries with it the feature that everything in space is somewhere with respect to everything else. For this reason, I think that philosophers who try to test this point by imagining cases in which we might confront disconnected spaces are going beyond the intention of Kant's assertion. He does not purport to derive uniqueness from some abstract concept of space, for he presents no such concept. It is the space of our ordinary experience of things that he is confident we will agree to describe as essentially one space.[1]

In Kant's discussion of the fourth claim, the infinity of space, the total absence of argument is particularly conspicuous. What discussion there is presupposes that we have already accepted the assertion without *any* argument. Kant proceeds at once to the auxiliary thought that the *a priori* status of the concept of space can be read from its infinity because of considerations that are reminiscent of his derivation of the *a priori* status of strictly universal truths from Hume's proof that they could not be empirically grounded. Here, he seems to have in mind that the infinity of space could not be understood as a shared element in a multiplicity of empirical representations of spatial things, as, for example, yellowness is a shared element in representations of lemons. Thus the infinity of space has to be given intuitively, not abstracted as a concept that fits all of a range of individuals. Kant assumes that we already agree that space cannot be finite, that a line however long could always be extended, a sphere however great could always be expanded, and so on. This idea is a commonsense reflection that motivates the geometrical assertion of infinity.

None of this discussion would make minimal sense if Kant were a foundationalist trying to put all our philosophical beliefs beyond doubt. He assumes that familiarity with the spatial world suffices to enable us to *see* the points about space to which he is merely directing our attention. And once again, we have to be mindful of the standpoint of the "how-possible" questions, which assume and aspire to explain our possession of synthetic *a priori* knowledge. Our everyday conceptions of space, time, and bodies are a required framework against which the law of gravitational attraction, for example, is intelligible. Of course, a philosopher who takes it as given that this law illustrates synthetic *a priori* knowledge that we do have is free to draw on our ordinary conceptions of space and time and bodies. The acceptance of the law of gravitation as embodying synthetic *a priori* knowledge is flatly inconsistent with the foundational attitude toward the external world characteristic of Cartesian and British empiricist thinking. Therefore, Kant is naturally taking the world of ordinary experience for granted in elaborating the metaphysical expositions of space and time.

Kant describes the goals of the Transcendental Aesthetic in terms of the identification of *a priori* forms of intuition:

> By this investigation it will be discovered that there are two pure forms of intuition as principles of knowledge *a priori,* namely, space and time, with the consideration of which we will now occupy ourselves. (A22, B36)

Once we recognize that these discoveries are made possible by attention to and reflection on features of our ordinary experience of objects of perception, we will not be inclined to think that Kant is suggesting that we are confined to the apprehension of our own mental representations. It

CHAPTER 10

The "Clue" for Finding the Categories

Kant's preliminary acceptance of everyday thinking provides the setting for the more elaborate "metaphysical deduction" of the Categories starting from the familiar forms of judgment. Kant does not present foundational arguments for the points he makes in these passages where fundamental philosophical steps are taken, nor does he present these points as if they are in need of foundations, or as if he means to defer provision of a needed justification for them. They can be stated because they just say what everyone knows, or what they will accept as soon as it is articulated for them. In this case, Kant introduces the logical forms of judgment, saying that they have already been identified by logicians, and he relies on these forms for his identification of the Categories. Neither Kant's thinking here nor the thinking of logicians is imagined to proceed by relating claims to an epistemological foundation of privileged propositions. He adverts to judgments on the strength of our shared familiarity with them, since we make judgments all the time. Our appreciation of the forms of judgment depends upon the familiarity of ordinary judgments, much as our appreciation of the forms of intuition depends on our familiarity with bodies and our ordinary perceptual apprehension of bodies. Judgments are presumed to be something accessible at the level of ordinary thinking, and logicians have arrived at the forms of judgment by eliminating all elements of content in a way that is much like Kant's "thinking away" the material aspects of bodies so as to arrive at the spatial form. The appeal to such forms is not an allusion to an epistemological base.

Kant uses the word *clue* (*Leitfaden*) in the title of several preliminary sections of the metaphysical deduction of the Categories. He is engaged in trying to identify the primordial devices of combination by means of which our active mental powers are able to synthesize elementary representations and make of them complex representations of extended and enduring material objects. It is understandable that we need a clue here. Kant does not imagine that we can introspect these first synthesizing steps that ultimately issue in conscious experience. In the nature of the case, we must start from the experience we have. But why should anything in our conscious experience support a conjecture about the battery of primitive combinatory devices that must have operated in engendering that very experience? Kant's conjecture in answer to this question is relatively simple, although the details of the discussion can be questioned at every point.

What is judgment but the combination or bringing into relation of the subject and predicate terms?[1] The terms represent the matter that is combined in the judgment, and the rest is a question of form. We are trying to identify our basic repertoire of mental powers of combination. Kant supposes that our combinatory resources are open to observation, so to speak, at the level of ordinary conscious judgment. He takes it that attention to the forms of judgment affords access to the very same devices for combination that must operate in primitive, preconscious combinatory mental activity.[2] Can we not say that *combination is combination* and therefore plausibly expect (perhaps "hope" is more realistic) that unobservable mental activities follow the pattern of those of which we are conscious? It is in this sense that ordinary judgment provides a clue for the identification of the Categories, and this is the reasoning on which Kant relies in using the table of forms of judgment as a foundation for the table of Categories. Once again in this passage of thought, the starting point of ordinary experience and the "how-possible" outlook are prominent.

I do not suggest that Kant simply assumes the correctness of all sorts of metaphysical doctrines for which we would like to see arguments. He is quite aware that nothing that he says will stand if, after he has presented his account, it appears that no satisfying *theoretical* foundation for our ordinary views has been given. But if, when Kant's philosophy has been erected, a theoretical ground for ordinary views is in place, he takes for granted that we will not complain that he did not derive the metaphysical expositions of space and time from incontestable ultimate evidence and did not provide a phenomenal base of absolutely secure evidence for his assertions about the system of ordinary judgments that lead him to the Categories.

I do not mean to imply that Kant's table of the forms of judgment is correct or truly illuminating. It is often pointed out that any basic classification of forms of judgments will depend on free decisions made by the classifier as to what counts as a "basic" form and on the resulting possibilities of interdefinability of forms of judgment. Kant ignores both of these considerations, and as a result, by present-day standards, his discussion is both naive and unsatisfactory. Kant has to work rather hard to fill out the pattern of four groups of three judgment forms and four groups of three Categories, a pattern that for some unknown reason was enormously attractive to him. His claim to have a definitive and reliable method for generating the exhaustive schedule of Categories—a method he contrasts with Aristotle's haphazard "rhapsodic" procedure—is by no means convincing. It is clear that in spite of his claims about a definitive method, he fiddled with the list of Categories and designed the table of judgments so that it would reach the desired Categories. It is hard to find a satisfying parallelism in the elements of the finished schedule. The two Categories of substance and causality play an enormous role in Kant's system, far greater than that assigned to any of the others. It is hard to see the modal distinctions as combinatory devices at all, but they are said to be such by Kant. Although it is hampered by these difficulties and by his dubious architectonic, Kant's deduction of the Categories is full of remarkable insights.

Notice that Kant's Transcendental Analytic takes as its explanatory burden the need to provide a theoretical account of the possibility of knowledge of objects and also of the possibility of conscious experience itself. Of course, conscious experience is *given,* but for Kant this does not mean that some propositions about conscious experience can function as ultimate evidence for a subject. On the contrary, Kant is interested in consciousness not because, in the manner of Cartesian thinking, consciousness provides unassailable premises, but because he is trying to identify the conditions upon which consciousness itself rests. The original representations that are combined by mental synthesis into objects of consciousness are not themselves objects of consciousness for Kant. We do not consciously apprehend atomic momentary representations and then consciously build up complexes of these. On the contrary, neither the original representations nor the first combinatory workings of the mind are conscious matters, and such things are not *given* at all.

All commentators ought to be agreed on this point. Both the elementary representations and the first syntheses of them are posited and cannot be described or reported by a subject. Both are to be accepted because they enable us to explain how it is that one is able to be conscious of enduring objects and conscious of oneself as an enduring subject.

The assumption that original input consists of simple momentary representations is supported in Kant's thinking by principles that ascribe any complexity in representations of objects to combinatory activity. All complexity that is potentially analyzable presupposes a prior synthesis by our combinatory faculties. Kant insists that nothing is initially "received" in complex form. This thought contains an echo of the *a priori* demand for simples in the opening of Leibniz's *Monadology,* and it is probably also confirmed, in the thinking of both philosophers, by the reflection that familiar everyday experiences, like the unified visual representations in conscious visual experience of objects, must result from the concatenation and integration of myriad more elementary events that take place in the course of the stimulation of the eye, the nervous system, and the brain. Kant takes it for granted that these elementary sensory events, of which we are not conscious, themselves have the status of simple representations. Although it is not without rationale, this demand for absolutely simple representational input is far from being unassailable. For the present discussion, I do not mention this thesis in order to endorse Kant's contention that posited simple representations *must* be the original input of inner and outer receptivity. I merely want to make it entirely clear that this is his view. The broad structure of argument illustrates the fact that Kant is positing simples that *are not given* in the course of his account for the possibility of ordinary perception of objects that is *given.*

In spite of the more or less universal appreciation of the posited character of Kant's original representations and mental activities, much of the willingness to see Kant as an idealist is wrapped up in the inconsistent assumption that Kant's theory of mental construction takes simple original representations as *given* and that he accounts for the existence of complex objects by saying that they are constructs built by mental activity out of the original manifolds of simple elements. This is the procedure of Locke, who, in the elaboration of foundationalist theories of human knowledge, does think that "simple ideas" are given, and that complexes are concatenated in the mind out of these simple ideas. A comparable outlook enables Berkeley to say that we do not really apprehend material substances but only congeries of sensuous properties. Similarly, Locke raises doubts about the idea of substance, proposing that we really experience only batches of sensuous properties that are regularly exemplified together and that we do not apprehend any substantial proprietor of those properties.

These empiricist reconstructions are no part of Kant's project. I do not mean that Kant takes the existence of enduring objects in space to be an incorrigible datum of ordinary experience. In any particular episode of what seems to be experience of an enduring outer reality, we cannot definitively exclude the possibility that we are suffering from some kind of illusion and that there is no such enduring object. When we start out with Kant to seek the conditions for the possibility of experiencing everyday objects, we do not know for sure that we will succeed. With this initial perspective, we may well worry that we will be unable to provide a coherent account that sustains our everyday convictions— an account both of our mental life and of physical reality. Before we have conducted this investigation, we might fear being driven to recognize that our ordinary conceptions of experience and its objects are false. Kant's contentions purport to exclude these possibilities.

How would things be if this most unwelcome conclusion, namely, the falsehood of our everyday convictions about the world, were established? Our everyday belief that our experience is generally of enduring complex objects, together with illusions or hallucinations that pose as such experience, would be shown to be false. Were that the upshot of our investigation, we would have to say that we are conscious of only our own transient mental contents, and we would have to drop the pretense that we know anything about outer enduring things. This outcome is excluded because conscious experience of transient contents is itself only possible for a subject who has real experience of enduring objects outside the mind. This thesis is presented prominently and in various settings in the *Critique*. It is inconsistent not merely with the conclusions but especially with the preliminary outlook of Locke, Berkeley, and Hume.

As we have seen, Kant does not take as his first step in philosophy the setting aside of everyday convictions in favor of a conception of evidential foundations. He does not take the first step of the Cartesian method of doubt. Remember that Descartes counsels us to dump out the whole barrel of apples of everyday belief. For Kant, the everyday world is one from which the philosopher should be driven only by compelling argument. In fact, he cannot vacate the world voluntarily and take up—even temporarily—lonely residence within the confines of his own mind. Kant is not tempted to endorse anything along the lines of the "methodological solipsism" proposed by Hilary Putnam and Jerry Fodor. On the contrary, it is just that alleged alternative to ordinary thinking, the possibility of a solipsistic vantage point, that Kant takes to be incoherent. Generally speaking, the foundationalist starts with the aspiration to explain our wonderful capacity to apprehend the world around us, but when he has finished, his foundationalism has become an idealism that does not offer any such explanation. Idealism ultimately denies that we possess any such grand capacity to know the outer world. We are unable to directly apprehend anything outside our minds. We suffer an illusion of getting at the outer. Kant is particularly sensitive to this inadequately acknowledged feature of the idealistic "reconstructions," which must actually deny that we have any knowledge of outer things to be explained. His distance from the idealists is expressed in his frequent insistence that for him, *Erscheinung* is not *Schein* and perception is not illusion or mere imagination.

An emphatic and ironic paradigm for the sobering shortfall in idealistic epistemology is Descartes's account of vision in his book on optics, where he models sight on blindness. The sighted man gets his knowledge of the world by interpreting the causal consequences of physical processes, just as the blind man interprets the pressures he feels from his stick as he probes with it.[3] Vision extends no further out into space than does blindness. The foundationalist construction proposes that what we really know is only the raw material for the construction of complex objects. The project assumes that we are not simply acquainted with such complex objects. Kant, on the contrary, posits simple raw materials and combinatory activities to account for our experiences of complex outer objects, which are the things with which we are acquainted to begin with.

Kant's thinking consistently takes the conscious experience of objects and conscious judgments as given and as a subject matter the examination of which can ultimately yield the character of the pure forms of intuition (space and time) and the pure forms of understanding (the Categories).

CHAPTER 11

The Parallelism of Inner and Outer Sense

Sensation grounds our ability to give empirical descriptions of the things we perceive. Without sensation, our representations would have no empirical content. The empiricist foundation of Kant's thinking is registered in the doctrine that sensation provides the *matter* for our empirical representations and is our only resource for the representation of existence. We shall see that the absence of an intuition of the subject and of any sensation-based experience of the self is explicable as a consequence of the fact that sensation does not play a part in inner receptivity that is in any way comparable to its role in outer sense. There is, in fact, no *matter* in representations of inner sense to convey the existence of an object of inner perception. Objects figure in representations of inner sense only at second hand. Transient representations of outer sense constitute the only "stuff" to which inner sense is receptive. No transient things are true objects. By "true objects" I mean entities that conform to the subjective norms expressed by the Categories.

Both the parallelism of inner and outer sense and the serious limitations of that parallelism are expressed in this passage from the Transcendental Aesthetic:

> By way of confirmation of this theory of the ideality of the outer as well as the inner sense, and therewith of all objects of the senses as mere appearances, the following remark is especially apt: namely, that everything in our knowledge that belongs to intuition (excluding feelings of pleasure and pain and the will, which do not amount to knowledge) contains nothing but mere

relations, that is, relations of place in an intuition (extension), relations of change of place (motion), and relations as expressed in laws in accordance with which these changes of place are determined (motive forces). What it is that is present in these places, or what takes place in the things themselves beyond change of place, is not given in intuition at all. How things are in themselves is never known through mere relations, so it is easy to appreciate that since nothing is given to us through outer sense but mere representations of relations, this sense can contain only the relation of an object to the subject, and not inner relations that attach to the object in itself. Just the same holds for inner intuition. This is so, not only in that representations of outer sense make up the actual material to which we apply our minds, but also because the time in which we place these representations, which itself precedes consciousness of them in experience and lies, as a formal condition, at the foundation of the way in which we take them into the mind, itself contains relations of succession, of simultaneity, and of that which exists with the sequential (the enduring). Now that which as representation can precede all mental acts of thinking anything whatever is intuition. When it contains nothing but relations, it is the form of intuition. Since this form represents nothing except in so far as something is put into the mind, it can be nothing other than the way in which, through its own activity, the mind affects itself, namely, through the placing in the mind of its own representation. Thus, that which as representation can precede all other mental acts of thinking can be nothing other than an inner sense in respect of its form.[1]

Here is the picture that Kant wants to emerge in this passage. In outer sense, we are affected by realities that exist apart from our minds, and this engenders simple spatial representations that are elementary intuitions of outer sense. These representations are themselves, of course, mental realities, but they are not objects of experience. They are raw materials for mental activities that will eventuate in apprehension of complex enduring objects in space. These objects occupy places and change positions in accordance with laws. Mental activity creates complicated representations that include the representation of endurance, but these complex mental representations are not objects of consciousness and not enduring objects of experience that conform to the Categories.

We must advert to the faculty of understanding as well as that of intuition in speaking of the combinatory activity by means of which complex representations are engendered. Kant alludes to the powers of understanding in the quoted passage when he says, "representations of outer sense make up the actual material to which we apply our minds." We are not conscious of either the original representations of outer sense or of the application of the mind to them, for conscious experience is the ultimate product of this mental activity. A creature in whom the concatenation of representations reaches fruition has experience of objects that are located in and take up space and endure in time. As spatial things, these objects of experience are not mental things. Our apprehension of them, but not their existence, is a product of our own creative activity. (This point will be examined more fully in chapter 14.) Because our characterization of these nonmental independent realities can never be separated from their relation to our forms of receptivity and understanding, all of our descriptions of such objects are irreducibly relational and subjective, and this is what is meant by saying that they are only *appearances*.

In order that the original representations of outer sense be accessible to our combinatory powers, they must themselves be apprehended, and this is the fundamental business of inner sense, at least as far as knowledge is concerned. Inner intuition is not a further source of inputs for knowledge of reality. On the contrary, in so far as inner objects bear on the attainment of knowledge of reality, the representations of outer sense are the only inner items with which the mind is concerned. Inner sense (and I should emphasize again the restriction, *as far as knowledge is concerned*) is a matter of apprehending mental realities that are, in the first instance, none other than the representations of outer things that the stimulation of outer sense engenders. Kant even speaks of the need for "inner perception of the manifold already given in the subject" (B68). Therefore, in so far as there is an empirical manifold of inner sense, it will contain representations *of the representations* that make up the manifold of outer sense, plus whatever additional mental things there are—feelings and volitions, for example—that do not contribute to our knowledge of reality. The mind must affect itself in order that these mental representations belonging to the manifold of outer sense become objects of *sensible intuition*. According to Kant's general doctrine, to which he allows no exceptions, our human receptivity is sensible, and that means that we have to be affected by what we are able to represent, albeit subjectively. The concept of the mind affecting itself, however, is not exemplified by the production of representations *of the mind itself*. That is, when the mind affects itself, the mind does not become the object represented. Henry Allison, speaking of this passage, says, "Quite simply, this means that there are no sensible representations which we can recognize as representations of the soul, mind or self."[2]

We have said nothing so far about the prominence given to "relations" in this passage and to Kant's claim that intuition grounds knowledge of relations only. He uses this motif as a quick way of reaching the desired "ideality" of objects of perception, whatever that means in the present context. Knowledge of relations, Kant says here, contrasts with knowledge of things as they are in themselves. The "relation-representations" (*Verhältnis-vorstellungen*) that come into being in outer intuition do not contain what belongs intrinsically to the object in itself, but only the relation of that object to the subject. This much is the familiar Kantian thesis that we never apprehend the thing considered as it is in itself. This understanding does not imply or support, or suggest in any way, the idea that the object of outer intuition is a mental object. As I have previously said, because outer intuition is not able to free our apprehension from relation to the subject, it is subjective at the core, and thus mind-dependent, but not mental. The passage is confusing, because the relational status of intuition is expressly said to exclude intuitive representations of features of things-in-themselves, whereas, at the beginning of the quoted passage, it seems as if Kant is saying that since outer representations are confined to relations, they do not directly characterize objects of any kind. This would be a disastrous doctrine, but Kant does not assert it.

The emphasis on relations, and especially the contention that the confinement of our knowledge to relations is a consequence of the *forms of our intuition,* namely space and time, sounds a familiar Leibnizian motif: the relational account of space and time. Kant devotes the next section, number III of his summary of the Aesthetic, to repeating his rejection of the ascription of "objective reality" to space and time. Of course, the Kantian alternative is not to ascribe *subjective* reality to space and time but, rather, to insist on their status as subjective forms of intuition. To repeat our earlier finding, Kant accepts Leibniz's relational characterization of space and time, with the understanding that the origin of this system of relations is our cognitive constitution in so far as it is receptive.

Since spatiality expresses the relation of outer nonmental things to our receptive capabilities, and temporality expresses the relation of the mind to its own contents, it makes no more sense to doubt whether outer things are *really there* in space than to doubt that thoughts are really there in time. So Kant points out that his outlook does not lead him to say that "bodies only *seem* to be there outside of me, or that my mind *seems* to be given in my self-consciousness."[3] That discussion culminates in Kant's use of the parallel security of the existence of outer objects in space accessible to outer sense and of mental things to inner sense, in refutation of Berkeley's effort to concede security to inner sense while rejecting outer sense altogether.[4]

Just what does Kant intend to limit to relations when he says that "what belongs to intuition . . . contains nothing but mere relations?" Two very different answers to this question are suggested by the quoted passage at B66–68. At the beginning, Kant says that everything belonging to intuition goes no further than relations, as far as our knowledge of reality is concerned. This seems to embrace both matter and form. Does Kant mean that sensation also is a matter of mere relations? He might mean to include sensation on the grounds that sensuous representation like spatiotemporality cannot eliminate a relationship to the subject. Redness is a property things have *in relation* to creatures equipped with receptive faculties like ours. And this understanding seems to be encouraged when Kant contrasts knowledge of spatial relations of things not with sensible properties of things but with knowledge of things-in-themselves. Later in the passage, however, Kant identifies just "the form of intuition" as a representation that "contains nothing but relations," and this does not take in the *matter* of intuition, which, by implication, is *not* merely a matter of relations. This also makes sense. There is a natural way of thinking in which questions like "What region is occupied by X?" concern relations, while "What color and texture does X have?" does not concern relations but rather features of objects perceived or perceivable.

Kant makes no express mention of sensation here and does not adjust his views to considerations of the empirical sensuous character of objects of experience, because these only emerge in the setting of the functions of consciousness and understanding that have not been broached as yet. Nonetheless, when we try to fit sensible features of things into the assertions he makes here, we encounter a significant difficulty in Kant's thought. Where he is thinking just of outer sense, he explains the relations in question as relations of place and of change of place (motion), and as relations expressed by laws of change of place. Once again, these are all formal and leave the matter—that is, the sensuous element in empirical outer intuition—out of consideration. It may be that Kant intends throughout to assert that the form of intuition consists of relations only and not to include sensation in this characterization, although sensation is something that "belongs to intuition" and Kant says that "everything" belonging to intuition can contain only relations. The impression that he includes sensation as relational, although it may be a misleading impression, is heightened when he does expressly state an exemption for feelings and the will but includes no exemption for sensation.

This is important, because Kant's account of things-in-themselves as opposed to appearances is threatened by his handling of the relational character of intuition. In the very next sentence, after giving the details of spatial relations of extension, motion, and motive force, Kant says that what is present at a place and what is really going on that underlies change of place are not captured in the relations to which he alludes. He makes it clear that these matters that are not relational also go beyond what is merely *appearance,* for the vocabulary of *Dinge selbst, Sache an sich,* and *Objekt an sich,* is immediately deployed. That we do not get to know what is present at a place is supposed to illustrate the fact that we only do get to know appearances. But this way of putting the point involves Kant in a mass of difficulties.

For one thing, a thing as it is in itself cannot be said to be what is non-relational and actually present at a place, even with the proviso that we cannot know anything about it. Things considered as they are in themselves are not spatial realities. It is only empirical things, things considered as they appear to us, that are spatial, since spatiality is simply the way in which empirical things become accessible to our cognitive powers. Furthermore, we certainly do get to know what is present at a place in experience. We do not know only that, whatever it is, it is spatially related in such and such ways to other things, whatever they are. We know that the cold moon is at a place, and that it is spatially related to the hot sun, which is at another place. This is all knowledge of appearance. No doubt Kant feels free to ignore these candidates for what is present at a place because, here in the Transcendental Aesthetic, he is thinking within the abstract limits of pure intuition. Intuition, in the absence of matter provided by sensation, does not provide us with knowledge that the cold moon is what exists at such and such a place. This is achieved only by sophisticated functions of the understanding that enable us to move from the level of transient intuitive representations to representations of enduring perceived objects, of which the moon is one. It remains the case that Kant very misleadingly suggests that knowledge of what is really present at a place would be knowledge of a thing as it is in itself. It is possible that he means that such knowledge of what is present at a place, *if it were wholly intuitive and not partly due to understanding,* would be knowledge of things as they are in themselves. Even with this qualification, Kant should not propose the thing-in-itself as what is present at a place, because, abstracting altogether from the functions of the understanding, sensation, as a component of outer sense, has to be spatial.

Of course, it is correct to say, within the framework of Kant's thinking, that intuition does not give us a conscious starting point by itself. We do not start from any passive experience of "Red, here, now," but this is because there is no consciousness or experience at all apart from the functions of the understanding. Nonetheless, the character of outer intuition that is, for example, the apprehended color of objects when we have attained conscious experience, does not become outer and spatial merely as a consequence of synthesizing activities we perform.

The most important difficulty in the passage under discussion concerns the disparity of inner and outer sense that Kant introduces and then fails to acknowledge adequately. He raises the issue of the disparity in saying that inner sense has elements of the manifold of outer sense for its proper objects. Inner and outer sense are supposed to be parallel faculties for the apprehension of mental and nonmental reality respectively. We have seen how Kant's attention to the relational character of the form of intuition gives rise to unanswered questions about the element of sensation that is so prominent a part of empirical outer sense. When he turns to inner sense in this passage, he assures us that things stand just as they do with outer sense. But since he also says that the representations of outer sense are the only relevant objects of inner sense, the parallelism is immediately jeopardized, if not utterly wrecked. Kant makes it look as though he is demonstrating a parallelism when he adverts in detail to the elements of relations that are prominent in temporal characterization.[5] If form were to exhaust everything belonging to intuition, as Kant misleadingly suggests in the context of outer sense, then there would be a parallelism here, even though inner sense is a question of further relations that come into play when representations of outer sense become material for inner representation. Because Kant has not dealt with the issue of sensation in connection with outer sense, he can present a parallel treatment of inner sense in terms of form and mere relations. But the striking difference between inner and outer sense merely goes undiscussed.

It is easy to understand what the element of sensation is in the context of outer sense, while it is impossible to imagine what sensation could possibly be in the setting of inner sense. Kant says that the mind must affect itself in order that its representations be material for inner intuition. He also speaks of inner *perception* of the elements of the manifold of outer sense. However, if such talk were to be meaningful, if it could be taken literally, there would have to be another range of sensations generated when the mind affects itself. There is not. Kant gives no indication that he expects sensations beyond those connected with outer sensibility, that is, with the senses. These sensations are obviously not qualified to serve as the matter of inner intuition, if only because they are already identified as the matter of outer intuition. Kant does not envision any other sensuous component. The representations of outer sense, with their sensuous character, are the items that are manipulated by combinatory powers of the understanding to issue in apprehension of enduring objects. The sensations that are part and parcel of outer intuition appear, when conscious experience is attained, as the sensible features of perceived objects. No other range of sensation is given footing in Kant's conception of our receptivity. How can we understand inner sense on the model of outer sense when sensation, an indispensable side of outer sense and an integral part of Kant's general characterization of intuition, is no part of inner sense?

The contrast of appearance and things as they are in themselves threatens to unravel because of this difficulty. If the contrast were maintained, we would perceive our own outer representations not as *those representations are considered as they are in themselves* but only as they appear to inner sense. The absence of a component of sensation in inner sense leaves us unable to understand this distinction.[6] Of course, this double subjectivity in inner sense is completely undesirable from the viewpoint of epistemology and phenomenology. But it seems that there certainly would be such a layer of "appearance of representations" if inner sense were really parallel to outer sense. Kant imagines that our outer representations are merely placed in time when they are apprehended as mental states. He does not also envision an appearance of those representations that contrasts with how they actually are. If he did, a second layer of appearance would be engendered. We would not be able to say that the mind combines outer representations and ultimately reaches the level of apprehension of enduring objects, for the mind would not have access to outer representations any more than it has access to things as they are in themselves. Inner sense would provide us with *representations* of outer representations, and only these would be available for mental concatenation.

It is fortunate that Kant does not flesh out the parallelism of inner and outer sense that he advertises. Such a parallelism corresponds to nothing in our epistemological circumstances. What Kant's omission shows is that his assertion of the parallelism of inner and outer sense is driven entirely by theoretical demands of his systematic thought. When he distinguishes form and sensation in connection with outer sense, he is trying to incorporate obvious features of our world and our epistemological outlook in his theoretical system. When he asserts the parallelism of inner and outer sense, he is trying to force features of his theoretical system into our thinking about perception and knowledge. Here the mind may not quite dictate to nature, but Kant tries to do so himself.

I want to emphasize that the failure of parallelism of inner and outer sense is natural. This is not something that we ought to try to overcome. When Kant overemphasizes the parallelism, he is letting his impulse toward theoretical symmetry override his sense of how things are. It is very easy for us to think of our mental states, including feelings and intentions as well as perceptual experiences and memories, as objects of a kind of inner apprehension. But we cannot think of this apprehension of the inner as anything like perception of an inner realm (in spite of the fact that Kant sometimes speaks in exactly these terms), because the concept of perception is tied up with that of organs and media of perception and with the role of sensation. This machinery of perception necessarily brings with it the contrast between appearance and reality. Inner sense provides a setting where there is no such machinery. We have no idea how we might try to replicate the contrast between appearance and reality in thinking and speaking about perception of our own mental representations. We cannot successfully model our contact with mental things on the idea of objects of perception.

As we shall see in chapter 12, crucial parts of Kant's overall account of possible experience actually rely upon the nonparallelism of inner and outer sense. Kant properly registers this when he restricts the matter of experience in general to sensations of outer sense, which enter into the sphere of mental activity only because inner sense takes the representations of outer sense for its objects.

How can we understand Kant's views about space and time at all once we appreciate that the asserted parallelism of the two forms of receptivity fails in such a fundamental way? If there is no sensation in the generation of representations of inner sense, then these cannot be related to real existence in anything like the way in which representations of outer sense can. Kant is entirely clear that sensation is the vehicle through which our representations are connected with the *existence* of objects. At the same time, spatial representation provides the key to endurance, in that space is the locus of unperceived reality. This is the essential wedge between representation and object on which Kant relies in asserting the permanence of the objects of transient outer representations. But we have to understand this fundamental doctrine as the thesis that unperceived endurance of the outer object is necessarily presupposed by conscious experience and not that endurance is *given in any experience* that is merely inner or merely outer. The combination of spatiality and sensation is necessary for the very idea of endurance of the nonmental object of perception. But no spatial representation is *per se* an enduring entity. In Kant's thinking, the reality of the spatiotemporal outer object of perception (and no mere spatial representation) is required to account for the reality, and therefore the possibility, of conscious *transient* perceptual experience. In contrast, inner sense gives no setting of intelligibility to the continued existence of the inner item before the onset or after the cessation of the representation, nor to the existence of an inner object where such an object would be an enduring entity bearing transient features.

The difficulty in Kant's doctrine that I want to bring into focus is visible in the famous "threefold synthesis" of the first edition. Of course, the details proposed here of the combinatory work of the mind are totally speculative, and it is passages like this that make Strawson's characterization of transcendental psychology as a "fictional" discipline plausible. Kant's pattern of thought has to be understood as governed by the assumption that something like this *must be what happens,* otherwise how on earth could we get from the transience of all our mental representations to the representation of an enduring world? Since we are working with a wholly transient input, the imagination gets the job of making the step to the representation of endurance. The imagination can engender a representation of a mental state that is not present (but, in fact, past) and thus make past representations accessible for combination with other mental contents past and present. It is commonly thought that the story of mental creativity told in the threefold synthesis is far too committed to an assembly-line conception of the manufacture of experience and its objects out of mental raw materials. It is also common and understandable to think that this inevitably idealistic picture of things is deleted in the second edition because it conflicts with the anti-idealist elements Kant came to emphasize later. As I have already said, I think the transition between the editions is not a change of doctrine but merely of exposition, as Kant himself asserts. Therefore, I do not think the threefold synthesis presents a construction of enduring objects out of transient raw materials.

This first-edition discussion is an adventurous and purely speculative theory, but it is confined to accounting for the construction of representations of the outer and does not purport to explain why we should be confident that there is an enduring reality that representations of endurance would appropriately represent. Once again, we have to see this passage in the spirit of the "how-possible?" project. The synthesis does not have to explain the existence of enduring things and our experience of an enduring world. That enduring world is what is given. Of course, if we were working in the skeptical tradition of the Cartesians and the British empiricists, we would not think that experience of enduring reality is given. The things actually present to the mind are all, as Hume expresses it, "perishing existences." Accepting any such conception of our starting point, we would have to be concerned that our everyday representation of an enduring outer world might turn out to be spurious. So readers who place the threefold synthesis within the skeptical tradition mistakenly suppose that Kant is presenting the *source* of our confidence that there is an outer world that we are representing. And, of course, the threefold synthesis would be, within the assumptions of that perspective, an idealistic reduction of endurance. If it were intended to show that we are right to believe that there is an outer world, this invocation of the imaginative synthesis would have to be offered as a phenomenalist reduction. But since it is only a speculative account of the existence of our *representation* of the enduring world, it contributes nothing to confidence in the correctness of that representation, which is presupposed in ordinary and in scientific thinking and defended against philosophical skepticism by Kant. Kant's argument expounding the conditions for the existence of an objective time order in experience is an example of the repudiation of philosophical skepticism and the vindication of the ordinary assumption that we perceive an enduring world. There is no room for a reductive argument here. The ordinary view of things is not derived from anything, but it is defended against idealist threats.

There is a subtlety in Kant's thinking, but his conceptions are not really hard to grasp once we dispose of the wrong assumptions. I say that for Kant, the experience of enduring objects is *given,* but this is not to say that ordinary experience is itself a fail-safe foundation for science or philosophical reconstruction. The idea of endurance does have to be defended, and it is not defended merely by saying that it is what we experience at first hand, although it is true that we do experience enduring objects at first hand. Ordinary experience, is, *prima facie,* experience of enduring things outside of our bodies. This *prima facie* character of experience has to be defended by Kant against potential skeptical arguments. The defense is the claim that if it were not correct, we could not have a concept of the self, we could not have conscious experience even of inner reality, and we could not have an objective time order in experience. This

being entirely decisive in favor of the soundness of the *prima facie* interpretation of experience, we are not faced with the questions

> Are we right to generate a representation of enduring things? Might there
> actually be none? Might *esse* be *percipi?*

We are only faced with the question, How is it possible for us to arrive
at the representation of enduring things given what Kant takes to be
compelling grounds for the view that (theoretically speaking) we have
to start from simple transient representations?

Now let us go back to the question, How can we understand Kant's
conceptions of space and time in light of the great failure of parallelism
that stems from the absence of sensation in inner receptivity? We have
to say that even the separation of receptivity into distinct outer and inner
modes is itself part of the construction of an answer to the question, How
is experience possible? The possibility of experience is the great unifying motif of the *Critique of Pure Reason.* The investigation of that possibility, the real existence of experience being given, captures the essence
of the *critical* stance in philosophy. Just as the *Groundwork* as a whole
explores the possibility of duty, that is, of action that is required although
it does not answer to any inclination in the agent, and just as the "metaphysics of morals" is engendered entirely by the idea that the reality of
duty is given, so in the *Critique,* the whole metaphysics of experience is
engendered by the idea that we really do have experience. I mean that
the theories of space and time, and of the Categories, and the resulting
accounts of synthetic *a priori* truth in mathematics and natural science,
follow only if experience of an enduring world is given. It is conceivable
that philosophers should reject this perspective and decide that what
seems to be such experience is no such thing. This is parallel to the
thought of a thoroughgoing moral skepticism, that is, the view that there
is no duty and that all action springs from inclination. Such a skeptical
perspective, if feasible, would cancel the conclusions Kant presents in the
Groundwork and in the *Critique,* respectively. But for Kant, these potential starting points are not options that we are free to adopt. The arguments concerning the subject of experience, the time order of experience,
and the dependence of inner experience (consciousness) on the existence
of permanent objects of perception are meant to exclude the skeptical
outlook definitively and to certify the *prima facie* natural and everyday
understanding of our access to the enduring world. In the *Groundwork,*
there are parallel efforts to exclude the moral skepticism that would vitiate all of Kant's contentions. At the outset, Kant appeals to our natural

conviction that action from duty is possible even if difficult and even if duty is never exemplified, which is all that he really needs. Toward the end, in a spirit much like that of the *Critique,* he presents the view that we are unable to think of our actions as simply caused. The adoption of the view that everything we do and think is caused is self-defeating, since we cannot intelligibly affirm that that hypothesis itself is both correct and something we are merely caused to endorse. As Stuart Hampshire once put this Kantian point, to regard our opinions as caused is to renounce them.

The important point here is that the separation of space and time as distinct forms of receptivity to nonmental and mental reality respectively is itself justified by the role it plays in the explication of the possibility of experience. Kant thinks the separation is easily agreed to, and this assumption is prominent in the metaphysical expositions of space and time. But the Kantian doctrine is not presented as simply part and parcel of ordinary experience. It may be that the difficulties that are generated by the fact that sensation attaches only to outer sense are so great that Kant's radical separation of the objects of spatial and temporal receptivity cannot itself succeed. In ordinary experience, we do not entertain the idea that temporality applies, in the first instance, only to mental things. We take for granted not only that the objects of outer sense exist outside our minds but also that they endure in the intervals in which they are not perceived.

Kant does not doubt that we are right to think of our experience in this way. I am persuaded that this defense of the ordinary is a profound achievement in Kant. At the same time, I merely describe and do not endorse the detailed machinery that Kant thinks must operate to achieve this ordinary conscious experience of things: the theory of simple representations, the separate modes of receptivity to the spatial and the temporal, the theoretical identification of our powers of synthesis through the forms of judgment, and the transcendental function of imagination that is needed to bridge the gaps that Kant's theory itself creates. I think Strawson is wrong to turn his back completely on Kant's speculative transcendental psychology. Surely the result is a *Hamlet* without the Prince. But I also agree with Strawson in finding enormous merit in Kant's global convictions and little or none in his detailed conjectures about our mental activities.

In sum, Kant proposes theoretical reconstruction aiming to show how ordinary experience, as ordinarily understood, is possible. He never denies that everyday conceptions of the objects of perception are correct. On the contrary, the theory of the Categories has as its objective to account for the correctness of our ordinary conception of experience as of *enduring,* and hence temporal, objects in space. The separation of inner and outer intuition and the contention that the outer is essentially spatial and the inner essentially temporal belong, together with the resulting difficulty concerning the confinement of sensation to the outer, to Kant's theoretical construction of the possibility of experience and not to the ordinary and scientific understanding of the world that his theoretical work vindicates.

CHAPTER 12

The Subject of Experience

The inner sense by means of which the mind [*Gemüt*] itself or its inner state is intuited provides no intuition of the soul [*Seele*] itself as an object. (A22, B37)

Foundationalist epistemologists require and commonly simply presuppose the existence of the enduring subject surveying the self-contained contents of its own private consciousness. Although this conscious subject is the "I" whose existence Descartes proves with the *cogito* argument, a difficulty with it is pretty conspicuous. Even in the *Meditations*, the assertion of the nature of the subject as an enduring *res cogitans* has a theoretical flavor that contrasts with the character of transient mental representations that, according to the method of doubt, exhaust the truly given. In the second *Meditation*, having established definitively by the *cogito* not only that "I exist" but also that the immediate contents of my mind are as they seem to be as long as they are merely contemplated *as contents of my mind,* Descartes has to reflect on just what this "I" is. He has to eliminate the natural thought that would lead him to identify the "*I*" as a person with parents, with a life history, and most important, with a body. The *res cogitans* is a fallback theoretical identification for Descartes, after this naturalistic candidate is eliminated on the understandable ground that it is part of the domain of the perception-grounded realm of things that he has resolved to set aside as dubious. At this point, at the very moment of birth of the egocentric perspective in epistemology, it emerges that the contents of the mind are indeed given, while the subject, the *"I"* that thinks, is elusive, featureless, surely required, but not really given at all.

Just as Kant is not generally skeptical about strictly universal and necessary laws that scientists purport to know, but instead investigates the conditions for the possibility of this scientific knowledge, so, too, he is not tempted to raise doubts about the general conception of the unified and enduring self that we all employ. Instead, he proposes a philosophical explanation focused on the conditions for the possibility of a representation of the subject under the circumstance that no self is simply given as an object of consciousness. Of course, every conception of a synthesis of representations that makes conceptual room for objective judgments and for articulate experience absolutely requires that the materials available for potential combination be accessible to one and the same agent, namely, the agent that is doing the combining. There could not be any cognitive combination of two representations unless both were present to the same mind. Kant registers this inescapable demand for a subject in his principle of original apperception. He calls this mental unity both "original" and "transcendental."[1] It is original because it is presupposed for any mental activity at all, and it is transcendental because it is itself *a priori* and it is a condition and source of synthetic *a priori* knowledge of objects yielded by the theory of the Categories. The fact that there is an original unity itself is just the fact that all of a subject's mental representations and thoughts are connected in that they are *his* mental representations and *his* thoughts. We cannot make any sense at all of active mental faculties without this unity, which expresses the access of the subject to the raw materials for its own thought and experience. Kant does not present this consideration as a synthetic *a priori* principle, because he recognizes it as an analytic truth from which no existential claim can be deduced. Given our possession of a manifold of inner representations spread out in time, the endurance of the subject follows. Kant appreciates that this conceptual requirement of a subject is not accompanied by an intuition of the self as an enduring proprietor of temporally diverse representations. Just because we have no intuition of a "constant or enduring self,"[2] the unity of consciousness cannot be understood as grounded in the relation between all of the contents of consciousness of one subject and that subject itself. The second term for such a relationship is simply missing as far as intuition is concerned.

The special problem of the self as an enduring object is rooted in the ultimate asymmetry of space and time when these are taken as the two forms of our immediate cognitive relation to reality, as Kant proposes.

As I have shown, the asymmetry that inevitably puts the subject (as an object) at a greater cognitive distance than any spatial object consists in the fact that there is no element in inner intuition parallel to sensation in outer sense. For the most part, Kant's stress on the symmetry of inner and outer is understandable as a central element of his repudiation of idealism. He insists on an indispensable receptivity in opposition to the Leibnizian contention that all cognition is *thought*, of which the perceptual component is *confused* thought, and as against the British idealists, it is by virtue of outer receptivity that cognition gets all the way to reality or existence outside the mind. But this commendable motivation leaves unaddressed the fundamental structural differences between inner and outer sense identified in the previous chapter.

The "objects" represented by inner sense are the contents of consciousness and not the subject of consciousness. Kant means to include our feelings, intentions, memories, and perceptual experiences among the states of mind that he thinks of as inner objects of experience. As I have said, the use of "objects" here is very permissive. No items apprehended only by inner sense are true objects, that is, realities conforming to the Categories. A sensuous aspect enters inner sense only through the outer perceptual experiences that are themselves apprehensions of outer nonmental things. A perceptual experience involves sensation in that it is cognition of the sensuous character of an outer thing. However, a perceptual experience, as something of which a subject may be conscious, has no sensuous character itself, any more than thoughts, intentions, and hopes are sensuous entities. In so far as it is right to say that I am aware of a perceptual experience of something yellow in addition to being aware of something yellow (and it is not obvious that it is right to say this at all),[3] the experience is not a yellow inner object, and as an object of consciousness it has no sensuous features at all.

The absence of sensations belonging to inner sense directly generates the special problem of apprehending the subject itself. Although Kant says that the self affects itself, this cannot duplicate the pattern of affectings by outer objects that ground the possibility of our coming to appreciate the features of the outer things. Like the perceived substance that exists outside the mind, features of outer things are also out there even though they are subjective. Only a surface can be yellow, and there are no inner things with surfaces. Thus sensation is the element in outer sense that stands for the *existence* of the apprehended reality in our representation. Sensation contributes the only real news from the outer nonmental realm that affects us. Kant never suggests any parallel element carrying the weight of the existence of the mind, nor any parallel source of real news when he considers the mind as affecting itself. From this perspective, it is no surprise at all that we cannot have intuitions of the self.

Both inner and outer sense figure in our overall empirical consciousness, according to Kant. This seems appropriate enough when we are considering, as examples of inner receptivity, our self-conscious apprehension of our experience of outer things. Here the empirical character of our experience involves the spatiotemporality of perceived objects and the temporality of our perceptual experiences themselves. However, even in the context of consciousness of perceptual experiences of the outer, inner sense is not itself a locus of any kind of *perception,* as this concept is generally understood. For empiricist epistemologists, for example, sense perception is the foundation for knowledge. Thus understood, perception is limited to vision, touch, hearing, and the other sense modalities, perhaps including proprioception in which sensation does play a part. In Kant's theoretical reconstruction of experience, all of this receptivity is assigned to the faculties that comprise outer sense. Neither our perceptual experiences nor our thoughts, nor any other strictly inner "objects" of consciousness, are perceived. Our access to the mind and its states is not perceptual access, and to that extent, *the mind falls outside the empirical.* This is what lies at the foundation of the fact that inner sense does not offer examples of sensation, and it is also at the foundation of the special problems of our knowledge of our selves as subjects of experience.

We have seen that Kant writes as though the analogy of inner and outer sense is much closer than it can possibly be. In particular, following the pattern that has its intelligibility in the perceived world of spatiotemporal entities, Kant says that inner intuition is the faculty by which the subject construed as an absolute reality (thing-in-itself) affects itself, yielding materials that are synthesized as an *appearance* of the self. In the setting of the Transcendental Deduction, he expresses these ideas drawing attention only to the superficially paradoxical ascription of simultaneous active and passive roles to the subject (B152–156). The problem of the nonperceptual character of the inner materials that have to serve as input for the construction of appearances of the subject is not mentioned, although it affects Kant's discussion throughout.

The absence of anything to play the role of sensation in inner intuition undercuts the very idea of an appearance of the subject. When it comes to nonmental things represented spatially in outer sense, the subjective appearances in question are enduring objects that are immediately apprehended in transient episodes of perception. The appearance *is* the enduring outer object. When the level of enduring objects and consciousness is reached, the component of sensation can be cast as the sensuous character of the perceived object: the redness of a rose, the warmth of a stone. Kant does make room for a kind of consciousness of, or acquaintance with, these mental representations *of outer things*. That is, in addition to enduring outer objects, we can be conscious of our own transient perceptual representations. When apprehension of perceptual representations occurs, it exemplifies inner intuition, since perceptual experiences have a place in the temporal stream of mental realities and have no spatial position with respect to each other as outer objects always do. Objects represented in perceptual experience are spatially related to one another, but our representations of spatial objects are only "received" by inner sense and are not spatially related either to outer objects or to each other. Furthermore, characterization of these inner mental states as perceptual experiences is conceptually dependent on prior acquaintance with outer objects, as I have stressed in explaining Kant's assertion of the dependence of hallucination and imagination of outer things on prior perception.

Sensation grounds our ability to give empirical descriptions of the things we perceive. Empirical descriptions are not restricted to perceivable features of objects. The sensuous finds a place within the nonempirical categorial framework for characterizing an object in general. In this rich conceptual environment, descriptive discourse that goes beyond the sensible surface of things gains a foothold. Thus concepts like *momentum* and *gravitational attraction* can figure in empirical descriptions although they are not immediately perceivable features of things. The robust empiricist element of Kant's thinking is registered in the doctrine that sensations provide the *matter* for our empirical representations, and in the consequent thesis that sensation carries the burden of representing nonmental existence. The absence of an experience of an enduring self is thus explicable as a consequence of the fact that we do not have sensations of inner sense; there is therefore no matter, in Kant's sense, from which empirical description might be concatenated. Thus cognition of the self as an inner object must be mediated by cognition of outer things. The world for us is an outer world, and we get to a definite conception of ourself as the subject of experience only by locating ourself temporally in the system of temporal characterization that applies to public outer things.

When we contemplate Kant's treatment of our representation of the subject as itself an enduring entity, that is, when we are mindful of his account of the subject as an object for its own thought, we find conceptions very different from those that he proposes in his account of outer objects. Kant does not make these differences clear enough. There is something that falls under the heading of "empirical self-consciousness," according to Kant. This involves acquaintance with mental realities that are to be regarded as appearances. The constraint is dictated by the general principle that no receptivity is access to things as they are in themselves. So Kant warns against the error of the idealists who think of inner sense as such access. He insists on a strict parallelism so that both inner and outer sense yield knowledge of appearances only. The doctrine of the subject as an appearance, however, does not offer an example of an object of consciousness that, as in consciousness of outer objects, results from synthesis of intuited materials by means of our formal categorial resources.

Of course, it is part of Kant's overall understanding that we have to make room for the application of our combinatory powers to the manifold of inner sense as well as to that of outer sense. But whatever Kant means by empirical consciousness of the self, he does not mean that synthesis of inner intuition yields a representation of the subject as an enduring entity. The central argument of the Transcendental Analytic, the argument for the necessity of outer objects of experience—that is, the argument that makes apprehension of outer realities a condition for conscious experience in general—would be set at nothing if Kant were to suppose that the enduring self is something we simply experience as an inner object, as we experience outer things. The culminating argument presents our immediate apprehension of enduring spatial realities as a condition for the possibility of representation of an enduring self. Such reasoning would make no sense at all were the self simply given. But Kant never so regards the self, and instead emphasizes the absence of any intuited self as an object of consciousness. His defense of the reality of enduring outer things brilliantly exploits the fact that the self is not and could not be simply intuited or perceived.

Why does it seem right to say that synthesis of inner intuitive materials cannot achieve experience of an enduring self, while synthesis of outer intuitive representations can achieve experience of enduring objects in space? Kant's thinking about this central question is guided by what might be called *phenomenological* considerations he inherits from and shares with the British empiricists. It is guided also by constraints of the technical conceptual apparatus he has already put in place. The technical constraints and the phenomenological considerations are mutually supporting. In citing phenomenological considerations, I am alluding to the fact that, from a preanalytic viewpoint, within experience itself we do not encounter the self or subject at all, or at any rate, not in a manner comparable to that in which we experience perceivable objects.

We do not have an "idea" of the subject, as Berkeley puts this point. Berkeley's use of "idea" is not Kant's. Berkeley means that we do not have any item of immediate perceptual apprehension that naturally presents itself as perception of the self. Kant agrees with this much, although his terminology is not Berkeley's. Of course, Berkeley deletes the very concept of a substantial owner of sensuous qualities in the case of things we do experience, like cherries. His repudiation of the concept of substances as objects of perception entails his reduction of the concept of such outer things to the joint manifestation of what we vulgarly take to be their sensuous features. Perhaps wisely, Berkeley does not simply eliminate the substantial subject of experience because there are no perceptual ideas to which the subject might be reduced in the way in which perceived objects are reduced to clusters of ideas. Instead, he introduces the ad hoc "notion" of a "spirit" or subject-owner of experiences to make up for the missing idea of the subject. This move is not just an intrusion of ontological largesse in a system otherwise noteworthy for its parsimony. The point is that Berkeley thinks that an empirical object like a cherry can be explained reductively as an exemplification of a characteristic set of features that are naively understood to be the features of *something*. Of course, for Kant, the rejection of any such reduction is conveyed by the traditional concept of substance as the needed owner of perceivable attributes, and then by the Category of substance, which expresses permanence through alterations.[4] The absence of ideas of the self means for Berkeley that we have nothing to which we might reduce the concept of the subject of experience, though this circumstance does not lessen the felt need for an owner of experiences. In this respect, the notion of a spirit, which amounts to a posited subject, is an *a priori* commitment of Berkeley's philosophy akin to Kant's *a priori* unity of apperception.

The same phenomenological point is expressed in Hume's celebrated observation that when he consults inner experience, it does not acquaint him with himself but only with "another perception."[5] Hume does press on to a reductive elimination of the substantial subject of experience parallel to Berkeley's elimination of substantial outer objects. Since there are no perceptions of features of the self to which the concept of a substantial self might be reduced, Hume is obliged to constitute the subject out of the same transient materials that go into the idealistic construction of outer objects of perception in his own as in Berkeley's thought. The resulting outlook, rehabilitated in the later philosophy as *neutral monism,* involves the conspicuously inadequate "bundle" theory of personal identity. The fact that the subject must be bundled from the same elements that figure in the "constitution" of outer objects reflects, in Hume's thought, the absence of any sensations peculiar to inner sense or introspective apprehension. An inner object-like subject would be found only by *looking within,* and only if there were characteristic intuitions of such a subject.

Kant's treatment of the unity of the self, and of the subject of experience as an enduring object, develop out of his acceptance, adopted from and shared with Berkeley and Hume, of the fact that we have no experience of a "*stehendes oder bleibendes Selbst*" (constant or abiding self). Kant's contention that we do have an "empirical self-consciousness" may seem to contradict this claim and to reveal an outlook opposed to Berkeley and Hume on this point. We might be tempted to think that, according to Kant, the shortfall is not in consciousness of the subject *per se.* We attain empirical self-consciousness and lack only a transcendent apprehension of the self as a thing-in-itself. In this respect, we would then suppose, Kant's treatment of inner sense is just like his treatment of outer sense. In both cases, intuitions yield only a subjective appearance and not a thing-in-itself. The defect in this line of thought is twofold. First, as I have already emphasized, inner sense does not offer any sensuous *matter* parallel to the sensations generated in the perception of spatial objects. We do not apprehend an enduring self. If we did, that self, as a temporal existent, would be an appearance. Therefore, to say that we do not apprehend the subject as an object is not to make the standard Kantian comment that we do not get as far as the thing-in-itself, in this case, that we do not reach the self considered as it is in itself. That is not the point in saying that we do not know an enduring self. An enduring self, if we did apprehend such a thing, would be a subjective appearance by virtue of its temporality. Second, the representation of the subject as an *enduring* entity cannot be accounted for on a foundation confined to the unrelieved transience of the inner. Nothing enduring could possibly be concatenated of elements accessible to inner sense alone, because transience, which excludes endurance, is essential to the inner. It is objects of inner sense, the inner items that Hume calls "perishing" existences, for which it is natural to assert that their very being is identical with our consciousness of them. Only space can provide conceptual room for the endurance of objects through intervals between periods of observation. There is a deep and intimate connection between the idea that mental realities are locatable in time but not in space and the idea that their *esse* is *percipi*. Time alone does not offer any scope to the existence of the unperceived mental reality, just as space alone offers no scope to endurance of nonmental reality.

Now, without losing sight of these phenomenological themes, let us turn to a more theoretical perspective on the subject. We know that a subject of experience is an irreducible conceptual demand. But inner sense cannot generate consciousness of an enduring subject, because time is the form of inner sense. For example, I contemplate the inner perceptual experience I have when I observe the bridge that is visible from my window. Then I close my eyes. Common sense does not require me to think that the bridge ceases to exist, or that its being is threatened in any way by the cessation of my experience. But everyone certainly understands that my visual experience itself does cease to exist. There is no significance to attach to the idea that the item I think of as an inner experience might continue to exist unobserved. Even this way of speaking is not satisfactory, since it is misleading and not at all natural to say that a visual experience is itself *observed* before it ceases to exist. These considerations confirm the idea that access to mental states is not a matter of inner perception. If receptivity to the mental were a kind of apprehension of true objects, inner intuition would be like perception and the concept of observation would naturally have footing. In any case, a visual experience ceases to exist when I cease to be conscious of the visible outer object. The inner item is a consciousness of the bridge, and its continued existence would be a contradictory reality: the continued existence of consciousness of mine of which I am not conscious. When we restrict our consideration to the inner range of apprehension of "the mind and its states," that is, to the domain of things to which inner sense affords access, we understand that an essential transience extends to all of them. There is no question of potential endurance to raise here, and no conceptual machinery with the help of which we could try to raise it. Small wonder, then, that we do not apprehend an abiding self and that Hume found none when he looked within.

It is worth noting that, having reminded ourselves of the essential transience of the inner and mental, we are in a position to understand the absence of any analog of sensation in inner sense. The function of sensation is wrapped up with the fact that outer sense apprehends a reality that is not mental. The existence of the object of outer sense is conveyed by the element of sensation, and it is because of this element that "*esse* is *percipi*" does not apply. When we contemplate consciousness of our own perceptual experience, or of our own bodily feelings, it is entirely natural to think that the existence of the mental "object" coincides temporally with our consciousness of it. Space, in Kant's doctrine, is the device that we employ to be able to entertain the thought of the continued unperceived existence of the objects of outer sense. In so far as we empiricists very well understand Hume's characterization of the contents of the mind as "perishing" existences, we also understand that we can make no use of any comparable device for inner sense in the role Kant assigns to sensation.

While Kant makes no comment at all on this issue, he ought to say that the essential transience of so-called objects of inner intuition exempts these objects from conformity with the Categories. One might object that, within the setting of transcendental logic, Kant is not contemplating the empirical content of experience at all. In consequence, the doctrine of the Categories is not dependent upon the fact that outer sense, in its empirical manifestation, always involves sensation as the mark of the existence of the nonmental reality intuited. For the purposes of transcendental logic, what Kant thinks of as "pure intuition" involves no sensation, whether or not we consider pure spatial or pure temporal intuition. Since the Categories are "deduced" without reference to sensation at all (that is, since it is shown that the Categories must apply in any cognition of reality that is based on intuition or receptivity), we might be tempted to conclude that the absence of sensation in inner sense is not a ground for claiming that things accessible to inner sense are not subject to the Categories. After all, in the abstract atmosphere of the deduction of the Categories, pure outer intuition does not involve sensation either. This would be a mistake.

It is quite correct to say that, prior to the schematism and the doctrines that expound the *a priori* principles such as the Analogies, the Categories *per se* are merely so many abstract concepts derived from the patterns of combination allegedly visible in our ordinary forms of judgment. The contention that they must be deployed in any experience founded on receptivity has no definite meaning until we see what that amounts to in our experience. Titles such as "substance" and "causality" are given to the abstract Categories prospectively, and they do not actually deserve any such titles until we see the arguments of the Analytic of Principles, which flesh out the abstract *a priori* concepts of an intuited object in general. When the Categories are given the definite significance that they have for us (the relevant case is the Analogies) and it is possible to assert, for example, that all changes in objects of experience are alterations and none involve creation or annihilation, we are certainly entitled to note that things accessible to inner sense alone cannot be included under such a conception of objects of experience since they will not satisfy this categorial condition.

I am not asserting that Kant appreciates this line of thinking, but I do assert that he is irrevocably constrained by it. It seems to me to be a virtue of his thinking that it leads to the downgrading of the standing of purely mental realities without anything like a behavioristic or materialistic reconstruction of the mental. In this sense, I believe Kant is broadly Wittgensteinian in his perspective on the mind and the world. Concerning the range of objects for which the Categories hold, no mere cessation of existence is possible. All changes in the world of empirical objects, as Kant expresses this point, are *alterations*.[6] So we never accept as an explanation for the fate of any space-occupying object that it simply ceased to exist. That assertion, preposterous for outer objects, is unproblematically applicable to inner mental items. When they no longer exist, it is not pertinent to try discover what has become of them, as we do when we look for the fragments of something smashed or the ashes of something burned. Mental things cease to exist without alteration. So we have to interpret the idea that Categories are concepts of an object in general so as to include a limitation to the domain of spatial objects in general. The subject might be said to have a derivative location in space by virtue of its body, but the subject is not itself a spatial object.

Kant's thinking about the unity of the subject comes out of his unstated appreciation of the essential difference between inner and outer intuition. It is, one might say, no accident that we do not experience the enduring self as we do outer objects. I have quoted Kant saying that all of the representations that make up the foundation of my knowledge of my existence as a subject of experience presuppose the existence of something permanent other than themselves, namely, enduring outer things. It is inner experience that is mediated. Our inner experiences need an outer permanence, not because they are merely appearances but because, being inner, they are essentially transient. The concept of endurance has no footing here. This brings us again to the idea of things for which *esse* is *percipi*. Berkeley quite consistently applied this slogan universally because he adopted the Cartesian standpoint according to which no outer nonmental thing is an object of immediate consciousness. Thus Berkeley deserved Kant's criticism: he accepts only inner intuition.

The episodes of empirical self-consciousness that Kant contrasts with the transcendental unity of apperception are themselves transient experiences. As such, they stand in need of some conceptual device by means of which they can be understood as the multiple episodic mental contents of one and the same enduring subject. Episodes of self-consciousness are simply more mental items concerning which we must explain how it is that they belong to a subject. We can see the irreducible need for something *outer* here if, in a reductive spirit, we try to collect the mental items that belong to me by identifying *within them* an actual or potential element of self-consciousness. In his explanations of the unity of apperception, Kant seems to suggest such a procedure when he proposes that a common "I think" can accompany all the representations that are mine (B131). Kant does not attempt any reduction here; instead, he immediately identifies the "I think" in question as "an act of spontaneity" and not an element of sensible content. The potentially ubiquitous "I think" is not a common item of empirical content that the subject combines with other materials. It is, rather, a consequence of the "analytic" principle according to which all of my experiences are mine.

In order to feel the merit of Kant's rejection of a synthetic principle here, we might try to suppose that there could be a common element found in all and only *my* representations. Why could not that common element be a foundation for the introduction of the concept of the self, in the spirit of a bundle theory like Hume's? Suppose we think of such an element as somehow a representation of the self that is present along with all of the other representations that are *mine*. The common element, indicating membership in the same bundle, would be something like a musical pedal tone or a brand on cattle. A subject might have the most diverse representations, but along with the varied contents, this qualitatively identical representation of that subject itself would be present:

> Here's my perceptual image of the bridge from my window, and with it, a consciousness of me. Here's a headache, and with it, me again. Here's a hope and me, an inspiration and me, an intention, a fear, a memory, each with the same concomitant representation of myself.

Our experience is not like this. The point is that, if it were, the constant representation of the self would not help with the unity of the self that

Kant calls the "original unity of apperception." The idea that these representations are collectively mine by virtue of a shared element of their content, however described, is simply senseless. A perceptual experience accompanied by a representation "of me" (whatever that accompanying content might be like) is not mine because of this accompaniment. The description of this element of content as a representation "of me" can only be taken seriously (and removed from quotes) if the mental representation is, in any case, *mine*. I can profit only from similarities and differences in representations that are present to me. If representations are present to me, no special content is needed to make them mine, and the absence of a special content cannot prevent them from being mine. As Kant himself says of multiple empirical self-representations, "they exist in separation from one another and without relationship to the identity of the subject"(B133). Generally speaking, all elements of content belong to the domain that presents the problem of the connectedness of mental things as belonging to one subject. No element of content can provide the solution to that problem.

The Refutation of Idealism presents the idea that consciousness of outer things is a necessary condition for the representation of the self as an enduring entity. The gist is that only the experience of enduring non-mental objects in space can provide the conceptual framework within which we can coherently think of ourselves as enduring subjects of experience. The argument is a brilliant stroke. It is the solution to the problem of the unperceived subject of experience, the problem to which Berkeley and Hume drew attention, and at the same time it guarantees the existence of outer spatial things and our direct cognitive contact with them. Kant utilizes this problem of the missing self as an occasion for expressing the fundamental defect of the Cartesian outlook. He shares with Cartesian thinkers the proposition that we are enduring subjects and that we have conscious experience over time. (It is hard to see how anyone could fail to share this view.) We must endure as subjects if it is the case that we experience now this and later that. We do not have, and could not have, an experience of our self now, and then another experience of our self later, on which to ground the notion of an enduring self. But an enduring self is absolutely presupposed by the shared view. Representation of this endurance is secured only through the *existence* of

> a thing outside me and not through the mere *representation* of a thing outside me. In consequence, the determination of my own existence in time is possible only through the existence of actual things that I perceive outside me. (B275)

Kant goes on to say that consciousness of my existence as a temporally determinate subject is conditioned by the existence of outer things, and that

> consciousness of my own existence is at the same time an immediate consciousness of the existence of other things outside me. (B276)

We would not be conscious at all were we not conscious of nonmental enduring things in space, and the real existence, not the mental existence, of such "objects" is presented as a condition for the possibility of consciousness itself. This is as definitive a rejection of the Cartesian outlook in philosophy as one can imagine. Kant himself says in the immediately following note that "the game played by idealism has been turned on idealism itself."

The central connection between this issue of the existence of the enduring subject and the whole Cartesian outlook in philosophy is expressed especially clearly in the second-edition presentation of the Paralogisms:

> [The subject as substance in the rationalist Cartesian system] is not only conscious of itself independently of any external things but is also supposed to be able to determine out of itself the endurance that necessarily belongs to the character of a substance. From this it follows that idealism (at least problematic idealism) is an unavoidable feature of just these rationalist systems. If the existence of external things is not required for the determination of the subject's own existence in time, then it [the existence of external realities] will be merely assumed without ever having any possibility of proof. (B417–418)

Here Kant turns the absence of any experience of the enduring self to surprising advantage. The Cartesian egocentric outlook has to presuppose a subject as the enduring proprietor of diverse mental representations, even though we do not experience any such subject. The representations are given, but the self, though indisputably required, is not given. According to Kant, it is only by recognizing experience as, in the first instance, apprehension of enduring nonmental things in space that we are able to represent the enduring self coherently. The viewpoint of the Cartesian solipsist is incoherent because the subject of experience that it posits is intelligible only as a subject that directly apprehends those nonmental enduring objects whose existence the Cartesian affects to doubt.

This is bold and brilliant, but how good is Kant's "proof"? The best case can be made for Kant by considering the Cartesian alternative that he claims to rule out. Why can we not suppose that we encounter, not outer things, but only our mental representations, many of which purport to be representations of outer things in space? Why can we not adopt, at least for the sake of argument, the skeptical stand that does not assert without qualification that there is a spatial realm of nonmental realities corresponding to our representations? The difficulty to which Kant's Refutation gives prominence is not found in the idea of these mental representations as objects of consciousness but rather in the idea of the subject for whom these are *inner* realities.

I quoted Kant saying, in the Transcendental Deduction, that the "time-determination" of the existence of the subject requires the actual existence of outer objects. This claim is intimately related to the formulation of the Paralogisms, according to which "an objective time order" requires objects in space and cannot be founded on representations of such objects. In order to feel the force of this, we must again remind ourselves that the inner and mental is the realm of transience and only transience. Kant and the idealists are agreed on this point. All of my representations of a moment ago have ceased to exist. It is just not thinkable that any of them have endured at all. We might be confused about this even though we are mindful of the fact that my perceptual experience of the bridge ceases to exist when I close my eyes. Can we not allow inner objects relatively short periods of endurance and illustrate these with the time interval in which I continuously enjoy a view of the bridge before I close my eyes? The answer is that we cannot. Any so-called "enduring experience" has to be regarded as composed of a series of shorter experiences, each of which ends just as another like experience begins. If one of the shorter experiences of the series seems to qualify as a shorter but still *enduring* experience, the same principle will demand its decomposition into a series of still shorter experiences. Experiences will be individuated on the basis of the time at which they exist. An experience at $t + n$ cannot be numerically identical to an experience at t. For it would always be possible for the experience at t to exist and the experience at $t + n$ not to exist. We are in an odd corner of philosophical reflection here, but we all do think this way, and no alternative seems to be at hand. The first part of the experience doesn't still exist at the end of a five-second viewing of a bridge. No one thinks it does, and how could they think such a thing? What is present *now* is the same outer bridge that was present a moment before when I first looked at the bridge. But if we take that outer enduring thing away from the context, there is no residual enduring inner thing. The experience I had of the bridge a moment ago cannot still be present *now*. Nothing endures in this purely mental domain.

The idealists are themselves attentive to this issue, and since they are idealists, they do not appeal to enduring outer things. The destructiveness of the mere passage of time, a destructiveness that we all feel when we confine attention to transient mental experience, tends to affect all reality in idealist thinking. Thus Descartes believes that God must recreate the whole world from moment to moment, else everything would go out of existence by the mere passage of time, and Berkeley invokes an analogous sustaining thought of God to account for the continued existence of things.

When Kant says that an objective time order[7] requires objects and not merely representations, he means that no content of a multiplicity of representations can ground any particular temporal ordering of them. Suppose mental representations were to come with an indication of the time "in the margin," as computer screens do in some programs. Here's the sun setting out the window, and the time is given as 7 P.M.; and here's the window dark, and the time is 10 P.M. A certain narrative bias may incline us to order these things by the represented time, but speaking theoretically, any order is possible for these two representations. A clock is not just a series of representations of times. A clock can ground an objective time order just because it is an object that endures though a series of changes, and we know that the state of the clock that we observe now is a later state of the very same object that existed and was (or could have been) observed before. Here the above point comes into play again. Two observings of a clock, at t and at $t + n$, cannot turn out to be numerically identical observings. But we must have a numerically identical clock observed twice, at t and at $t + n$, if our observings are to establish temporal order. Clocks are reidentifiable objects, while observings are not. Outer objects like clocks are not destroyed by the mere passage of time, as mental states are. A physical object has to fall apart, rot, be dismantled, smashed, or burned up in order that it no longer exist. Even then, its constituents at some level or other will endure. This is the permanence of the perceived outer thing of which Kant speaks. A merely mental object ceases to exist from moment to moment and is replaced by a like mental object, or not replaced, without any question of enduring constituents.

To the extent that this line of thinking is compelling, and I think it is compelling, Kant does refute idealism, and with it the Cartesian stance in philosophy that purports to accept the idea of an enduring subject confronted with its own representations while leaving open the question of the existence of enduring objects in space. This is not a coherent stance, and as soon as we recognize that it is not, we no longer face the familiar schedule of skeptical problems that the Cartesian starting point generates when philosophers mistakenly take it for a feasible or an unavoidable preliminary outlook on things.

Let us review our conclusions concerning Kant's treatment of the subject. The overall point of the principle of the unity of apperception is to show how an undisputed and indispensable conception of the unified and enduring subject enters into our representation of reality in general, and especially how it involves the necessity that consciousness be of real enduring objects and not merely of transient mental things. The discussion is structured by Kant's recognition that at the level of everyday thought, the self, though represented, is *not given*. No intuition or appearance accessible to us corresponds to the enduring subject. Kant does not try to build the presupposed subject out of anything. That is part of the force of calling the affirmation of the unity of the subject the "highest principle in the whole of human knowledge"(B135). The unified subject is not derived from a more basic unity, nor constructed by mental activities applied to materials that are as yet not unified. The transcendental unity of apperception is a condition for the possibility of conscious experience, and the fact that the condition is met, since we do have such experience, presupposes the occurrence of synthesizing activities that also guarantee that our experience will be of enduring outer objects.

No part of the *Critique* has been the focus of more voluminous and more varied critical interpretation than this discussion of the transcendental unity of apperception. One thing is certainly clear enough. The enduring self is not created by mental synthesis. This unity, as Kant says in the opening of the second-edition version of the Deduction, is presupposed for the possibility of the concept of combination.[8] It would be a ludicrous theory that alleged that the unity presupposed in order to combine anything at all should be presented as a product of combinatory activities.

Thus Kant does not argue for the existence of an enduring self. He takes it for granted as an ordinary conception, shared by all philosophers. The existence of the enduring self is presupposed by experience itself, and we do have experience. The philosophical theory addresses not the existence of the subject but the possibility of our representation of the enduring self. The concept of an enduring self is not something introduced by theory. It belongs to ordinary prephilosophical thought, just as the concept of objects of perception belongs to this domain. A special philosophical account of our possession of a representation of the self is needed because, unlike objects of perception, the self is not given in experience. The absolute presumption of the existence of the self is expressed, for example, in §15, where Kant ascribes *all* combination of representations to the combining activity of a subject:

> . . . among all representations, combination is the only one that is not given through the object, it is only achieved, rather, by the subject itself since it is an act of the subject's self-activity. (B130)

That Kant's effort is intended to account for our *representation* of the enduring self is then made clear in §16:

> . . . the empirical consciousness that accompanies various representations is in itself in separation and without relation to the identity of the subject. This relation is not achieved in that I add consciousness to each representation, but only in that I connect one representation with another and am conscious of the synthesis of them. Thus, it is only because I can combine a manifold of representations in one consciousness that it is possible for me to *represent* to myself the identity of the consciousness in these representations. (B133, emphasis added.)

Combination of manifolds of representations makes possible, in the first instance, experience of objects. The accessibility of objects has the desirable by-product of exhibiting consciousness of outer things and their temporal relations as a condition for the possibility of *representation* of the enduring subject. Since the route through outer enduring objects is a necessary condition for self-representation, a conscious subject, Kant finds, is necessarily a subject conscious of enduring outer objects.

I have emphasized that it is the representation of the subject, not the existence of the subject, for which Kant presents a transcendental argument here. This order of thinking is the standard one for Kant. The thesis that consciousness of the subject presupposes consciousness of outer objects is analogous to the impossibility of representing the unity of time except via mentally constructed spatial representations. Let us take a moment to examine Kant's thinking about the unity of time. Kant notes that we must represent the unity of time as a line, and thus represent time spatially.[9] This is unavoidable because time, which in itself is always passing away, does not offer any simultaneously existing parts that might be apprehended together and thus bound into a represented unity. Spatial parts do exist together, so we are able to represent the unity of time by taking parts of space (the parts of a line, for example) to represent parts of time and then synthetically unifying the parts of space.

I introduce this Kantian strand of thought about time not just for its own intrinsic interest but for the light it sheds on Kant's methodology. It is not Kant's view, and no one could sensibly propose that it is, that the unity of time is *constituted* by a synthesis of *spatial* entities that we perform. Of course, time is a unity in itself and *per se*. The metaphysical exposition of time makes this assertion, and it is, in any case, evident. As Kant puts the point, all times are parts of and not instances of time. Things that are collectively temporal are related to one another in time. So a spatialization of time is required only for our *representation* of the unity of time and not for the unity of time *simpliciter*, not for the fact that time is a unity. Although we do not face the same problem of shift in modality in order to represent the unity of space, we should nonetheless respect the need for the same distinction between representation of a unity and the unity thus represented. However we manage to represent the unity of space, that synthetic representation-building procedure will not be understood to create the unity of space, which has to be taken to require no creating.[10] At the level of ordinary *a priori* thinking about the conceptual aspects of space on which the metaphysical exposition of space relies, Kant is able to say that spaces are parts of space and not exemplifications of a discursive concept, and this entails the unity of space, as the parallel point entails the unity of time.

In Kant's elaborate discussion, the synthetic unity of apperception bears the same relationship to the unity of the self as the spatial synthesis of the representation of the unity of time bears to the unity of time. The synthetic unity of apperception accounts for our representation of the unity of the self, but it does not create that unity, which is absolutely presupposed for any mental activity, just as the unity of time is presupposed by the very idea that things are temporal. In both cases, we will go astray if we fail to distinguish the unity of the representation from the unity of what is represented, and if we suppose that Kant is speaking of both when he addresses only the former. Lest the reader be insecure on this point, I stress that the alternative supposition would be the idea that a subject of conscious experience is constituted by its own acts of synthesis. We should not burden Kant with this unpromising opinion.

CHAPTER 13

How Representations Make Objects Possible

We have shown that Kant proposes to account for our possession of a representation of the unity of time and does not aspire to explain the unity of time itself. Can we extend the same pattern of understanding to Kant's account of our experience of objects? Can we say, that is, that Kant means to draw our attention to the spontaneous and creative mental activities by virtue of which we have complex representations of, experience of, and ultimately knowledge of enduring nonmental objects of perception? And can we at the same time deny that Kant presents a reductive account of the things represented, as though they, too, and not merely our representations of them, were constituted by mental synthesizing activities? I will confine myself here to one striking and well-known passage where Kant himself tells us that this is what we should do.

The passage labeled §14 in the second edition of the *Critique* is a preparatory discussion entitled "Transition to the Transcendental Deduction of the Categories." The section contemplates two contrasting patterns of relationship between "synthetic representations" and "their objects."

> Either the object makes the representation possible or the representation alone makes the object possible. In the first case, the relation is only empirical and the representation is never possible *a priori*. And this is the how it is with appearance in regard to that in it which belongs to sensation. In the second case, though *there is no question of the representation generating the*

object with respect to its existence, as though operating via a causality of the will, nonetheless, the representation is determinative with respect to the object if only through the representation is it possible to recognize something as an object. (A92, B124–125, emphasis added.)

Kant means that in the case of an empirical representation like that of warmth, we can have the representation only by encountering something warm.[1] When we feel warmth, the occurrence of the representation is "made possible by" the warmth in the object. As a matter of fact, just this much is rather decisive evidence against any idealist interpretation of Kant's conception of reality. Nonsensuous representation of an object is *a priori.* Sensation comes only from the object, and our mental faculties are powerless to generate a single sensation. But the main point in this context is that the Categories are *a priori* conditions the satisfaction of which makes it possible for us to apprehend objects as such. We do not come to have empirical knowledge that some of the things we experience are objects, as we do apprehend empirically that some of the things we experience are warm. Since the Categories are, as "concepts of an object in general,"[2] imposed rather than perceived features, and since this imposition is a condition for experience, Kant says that the representation (the Category) makes possible the object.

In proposing this contrast of relationships between representations and objects, Kant is himself mindful that the rhetoric of the phrase "makes possible the object" might suggest to readers that there simply wouldn't be any objects without our representations. If representations make objects possible, then categorial representations must create objects, for without our battery of *a priori* representations working on some raw material or other, objects could not exist at all. This would fit with an idealist project and with idealist interpretations of Kant's Copernican revolution. But he does not mean any such thing, and he promptly introduces a parenthetical disclaimer. The representation does not make possible the object *"dem Dasein nach"* (with respect to existence). To think it did would be to invoke a kind of "causality by means of the will." Given the great creative powers Kant ascribes to our synthesizing faculties, such an understanding would require that the mind could engender the things we vulgarly think we merely apprehend. This would be a form of the phenomenalism that is frequently ascribed to Kant. Because, at this point in the first edition, before presenting the Transcendental Deduction of the Categories, it occurs to Kant that some readers might hit on this wild interpretation, he promptly and unambiguously rules it out. The mind does not create the object represented. Its creative activity is limited to the representation of the object, under which it is recognized *as an object.*

This is, indeed, the same contrast between representation and represented that has to be invoked in order to avoid the incoherent idea that Kant takes spatial synthesis to be constitutive of the unity of time. Here, too, it is our representation of the object, not the object itself, for which Kant tries to construct a theoretical account. We no more create objects in synthesizing representations than we create the unity of time by drawing a line. Since we do not create the objects we represent in our perceptual experience, we have to suppose that they are really out there.

CHAPTER 14

Objects and Empirical Realism

If Kant is no idealist, I would like to sum up his view as follows: Kant ascribes enormous creative powers to the understanding, but he does not explain the existence of perceived reality by appeal to such creativity. The reality we perceive, then, would exist even if the human understanding and human experience did not exist at all. The creativity of the understanding explains how it is that our transient, disorganized, and simple elementary representations are developed by our mental powers into representations of stable objects of perception. If we did not impose the Categories on our intuitive input, we would not experience the reality that does exist outside us whether we experience it or not. A plain, naive, realistic account of objects seems to be in the offing here. But the inadequacy of this as an understanding of the Transcendental Analytic is pretty obvious.

What this simple realism omits is an assessment of the ubiquitous subjectivity of our representation of reality according to Kant's doctrines. When this subjectivity is reintroduced, much of the idealistic atmosphere comes back with it. In re-expressing the same view, allowing that we do not create objects *dem Dasein nach,* we will now say, speaking of experience as a whole, only that *something* exists that we subjectively represent as a system of spatiotemporal objects in law-governed relations with one another. The fact that we represent this reality (which we do not create) as a system of objects is tied up with the fact that we have organized intuitive inputs so that they fit laws that come from the structure of our minds and not from the "something" that we represent. The recognition that *existence* comes into this story at all is traced to the something we do not create, but this existent remains permanently at the level of an unarticulated "something." That it is *objects* that we take to exist is traced entirely to our mental powers. In other words, even accepting the account of making objects possible given in the *Critique*, §14, we cannot say that Kant's view is that objects really do exist, but only that something exists that we inevitably represent as a system of objects.

In order to dispel the atmosphere of idealism that Kant's terminology so easily generates, we have emphasized that the contrast between appearances or things considered as they appear to us and things considered as they are in themselves does not indicate two ontologically disjoint sets of things but, instead, two ways of considering the same things. However, when we reflect that the individuation of appearances is determined by subjectively imposed forms and that, as a consequence, we cannot assert that one object of experience is also one thing-in-itself, reliance on the global ontological identity of appearance and reality will seem unsatisfying and inadequate. If we cannot coordinate identity conditions for appearances and things-in-themselves, why should Kant be entitled to say that they are really the same things? Within the domain of appearances, we can say that A is the same object as B, while C is a different object. Since we cannot project the referring terms A, B, and C onto the domain of things-in-themselves at all, the assurance that it is things-in-themselves that appear says very little.

Now this looks quite like the position that we contemplated near the beginning of our investigation. It looks as though Kant is a realist about things as they are in themselves. They have to affect us, and they are not created by the mind. But he is an idealist about appearances. Things-in-themselves are not objects and do not stand in law-governed relationships and are not even spatiotemporal realities. I state this idea plainly because I expect that it will operate in the reader's thinking here. It is not really an option at all. Kant would be an idealist about appearances if he thought that they are really mental realities. He does not.

We cannot summarize Kant by saying that spatiotemporal objects in causal relation to one another exist independently of us, that these objects affect us, and that the original representations that result are concatenated by the active powers of the mind into the representation of a system of spatiotemporal objects in causal relation to one another. Such a realism would be of a degree of naiveté that does no justice to Kant.

Even so, it would be closer to his thinking than any idealistic interpretation.

There is a reality that is not part of our minds, and to have a receptive mind at all is to have the capacity to be affected by this reality. We are sensitive to what exists, and we do not create it. This is the domain of things as they are in themselves. Because of our mental powers, we are not only sensitive to this reality, we also experience it consciously. We have an articulated conception of nature, and we have concepts of the particular spatiotemporal objects that constitute it, and of their interrelations, causal and otherwise. The conscious experience in which all of these concepts are deployed is our everyday experience. It is the experience that contains the grounds for our scientific knowledge. As philosophers, we are asking about the reality of these objects of everyday and scientific experience.

The possibility that objects, conceived as we necessarily do conceive them, are just mental realities is out of the question from Kant's point of view. That would amount to the contention that experience is all illusion, and this is what he finds that idealists erroneously assert. The objects constituting nature are not mental things. They could not be public if they were mental. Mental things could not have mass and attract one another, and thus they could not figure in physical laws. Generally, as I have pointed out repeatedly, spatiality is the mark of nonmental things. Kant says that we represent nonmental reality as a system of spatial, physical, causally interrelated objects. All of these characterizations are subjective. That does not mean that there are no such things. In representing reality in this way, we are taking it *to be this way*. This is not just a mistake that we are disposed to make, as it would be if idealism were correct. It is by virtue of this understanding that Kant is always willing to accept the verbal transition from knowledge of objects to objective knowledge, even though he traces much of the scheme of scientific representation to subjective sources.

There is no doubt that this is Kant's meaning, but there can still be doubt as to the tenability of such an outlook. Kant's account of the subjective source of causal relations, for example, seems to mean that we have to experience things *as if* they are causally related. That's how we are constituted. But this character of our experience ought not to count as a reason for thinking that things really are causally connected. Then the same doubts can be raised as to whether things really are spatial, and whether there really are any objects. Perhaps all of this segmentation of reality is a story that we necessarily cook up, given the kinds of minds we have, but a story for which we have nothing to offer in the way of rationally compelling grounds. Such is the attitude of Hume, but not that of Kant.

In the preliminary discussion of the first-edition version of the Transcendental Deduction, Kant remarks that "if cinnabar were now red, and now black; now light, and now heavy" (A100), and if everything else were to be comparably chaotic in appearance, the empirical imagination that constructs representations of a stable natural world would not have the sort of input that could result in such representations. This illustration is expressed in a realistic vein that sounds puzzling. It seems to presuppose just the naive outlook that we said is obviously inadequate for Kant's conception of things. The impression is given that we are to understand that a stable world in which cinnabar is always red and massive is actually out there, and that the intuitive input from cinnabar and the other stable objects is concatenated by our empirical imagination into a representation that *gets the world right*. In short, this assertion that the affecting reality has to be well-behaved seems to delete the subjectivism and to say that we develop the picture of the world that we do only because a world *just like that* is really out there. This claim, were it made, would violate the principle that we set out earlier: if representing is our only way of knowing the world, then we are not in a position to say that we represent it correctly. Such an assertion would presuppose that we could compare the world itself with all of our representations of it, and thus that we could know what it is like by some means other than representation. We cannot do that, and Kant knows it. But how much of the realist stance can be retained if we give the needed scope to the subjectivity of all of our descriptions of reality?

In order to thread our way through Kant's subtleties here, we have to emphasize the role of ordinary conscious experience and the fact that Kant's philosophy is a vindication of the natural conception of this experience and its objects. At the level of consciousness, we do encounter a world of objects such as specimens of cinnabar. Kant is proposing a theoretical account of our ordinary consciousness and its objects. He knows that we have *attained* this consciousness. It is a complex achievement and not just a question of opening one's eyes. We reach the level of objects on the basis of a mental activity that integrates and aggregates an input (of which we are not conscious).

Of course, this Kantian conception of mental activity operating on a preconscious fund of representations is adapted from Leibniz's theory of apperception. For Leibniz, the mind is unable to process reality on the metaphysically valid level in which each monad represents the states of all of the other monads, of which there are an infinite number. The aggregating of unconscious "*petites perceptions*" is a condition for conscious experience by finite minds such as ours. The salient difference is that Leibniz does not endorse the everyday "phenomenal" viewpoint, although he thinks it is the best we can do, and as a consequence, he is closer to the idealist contention that the whole picture of spatiotemporal existence is a mental fabrication and thus a kind of useful illusion. Although Leibniz does say that phenomenal representation is "well-founded" and provides the subject matter of science, in reality there isn't anything except the unfolding states of the monads. A public reality is traded, in Leibniz's thinking, for the pre-established harmony of the infinity of self-contained unfoldings. Unlike Leibniz, Kant endorses the publicness of space-time and of the spatiotemporal objects that creatures with minds like ours apprehend. This is the rationale for the objectivity Kant finds in the experience that is so pervasively subjective.

If we adopt, in imagination, the perspective of the mind dealing with the original input, we will imagine a subject confronting things that it does *not* characterize as red and massive, or even as spatial or as objects. This is an imaginary and conceptually defective perspective in so far as it is a picture of *experience* of these raw materials. It projects into the workings of the mind conscious experience that precedes the emergence of consciousness. But Kant is definitely imagining this sort of thing when he considers a chaotic input from a chaotic world in which cinnabar and everything else are so unreliable. No experience would arise under the imagined chaotic circumstances. The trouble with this thought experiment, from a theoretical point of view, is that it encourages us to imagine a subject dealing with the world, but prior to the development of the system of concepts that brings consciousness with it. We cannot use the subjectively imposed concepts in characterizing the input for this hypothetical subject, since they have not yet been imposed when the input is still "original." But then it will occur to us that this is just another way of saying that none of the concepts of that system should really be taken to characterize any reality outside the mind. They do not characterize the original input, and they are *imposed by us* in the course of synthesizing activities. These concepts, including objecthood and endurance, are all grounded in the successful working of the mental powers, and original input is not characterizable at all. All descriptive vocabulary presupposes the successfully synthesized manifolds, in Kant's terminology.

This kind of projection of the concept of experience into the first workings of the mind on elementary input is taken at face value in the thinking of reductive phenomenalism. For idealists, there is no conceptual defect here because the phenomenalist has not identified synthesis, as Kant has, as a condition for the possibility of experience. These theorists propose to substitute experience of elementary input such as sense data for everyday experience of the world, which they "bracket." Kant casually, heuristically, and perhaps ill-advisedly, draws on this style of thinking in the cinnabar passage and others like it. But it has no place in his theoretical account. There is no experience of original input. There cannot possibly be. That is the force of the Transcendental Deduction. Experience has to be of objects. We cannot literally project the stance of a subject considering consciously apprehended materials into the theory of mental activity Kant develops. If we were not conscious of objects, we would not be conscious at all.

If we take this to be irrevocable, which we should, then the cinnabar story does not encourage idealism. On the contrary, it alludes to *objective conditions* for the possibility of experience that Kant never excludes and that might be thought to be suitable for investigation by empirical science itself and not by the critical philosophy. I said that a subject constituted so as to meet all of the subjective conditions for the possibility of experience would not necessarily have any experience, for there are also objective conditions. The only obvious allusion to objective conditions in Kant's theory is expressed in the idea that we must be affected by things. The passage about the envisioned unreliability of cinnabar manifests an uncharacteristic willingness to consider objective conditions in much more detail. Because his subjectivism is so very thorough and radical, Kant does not put himself in a position to discuss objective conditions in detail, and this passage is full of tensions created by his seeming to venture on such a discussion. Not every reality could be experienced. The fact that we have experience shows not only that our subjectively imposed Categories have worked up materials into a system of objects; it also shows that the reality that stimulates this creativity meets conditions of regularity that make it possible for it to be represented successfully in this way. Kant describes those conditions in terms of the subjectively characterized reality that is experienced when both subjective and objective conditions are met. These descriptions, like the cinnabar case, are misleading because they pretend to describe elementary input. A more fastidious description would not try to describe the posited chaotic reality that could not be experienced at all. Kant could consistently note that the successful attainment of conscious experience is not guaranteed no matter what the input. But Kant cannot really *describe* inputs that can be worked up into experience or describe contrasting inputs that are too chaotic to yield experience. Describability is conditioned by the success of synthesis. Therefore, success shows that a reality does exist that is sufficiently orderly to make its representation as nature feasible. The law-governed structure of nature then represents that objective orderliness of reality.

This conception is also implicit in Kant's understanding of the difference between illusions and perceptual experience. If the orderliness of nature were entirely a consequence of the imposition of *a priori* Categories on any input whatever, the occurrence of illusions and aberrations would be inexplicable. Why does the mind not just subsume everything under laws? If a law-governed system is just something the mind creates with the materials at hand, as a mason creates a wall from a pile of bricks, then why not use all the materials? Plainly, Kant thinks that the mind does not do this because it cannot be done. The feasibility of representation in a system of laws depends upon objective conditions too. Illusions and hallucinations are seeming perceptions of reality. They are not really a guide to anything at all, while real perceptions fit together in our representations of the world because of the structure of reality. As I have already explained in detail, Kant says that perception involves an input from a source outside the subject, and transient experiences that are not really perceptions of anything are only possible because there are real perceptions. Only perceivers can hallucinate, as I stated in an earlier chapter. The existence of the reality represented in perception is responsible for the fact that elementary intuitions are suitable for organization into perception of stable objects. It is the correlative unrelatedness of aberrant and delusive episodes to any constraining reality that sets them outside the domain of nature.

From another perspective, it is quite legitimate for Kant to speak of the world of ordinary objects of perception as the source of the original representations that are worked up into a representation of precisely that world. This issue belongs to the aspect of Kant's thought that has been called the "theory of double affection" in the scholarly tradition of commentary on Kant. It was expounded by Eric Adickes and others who could not dispel the idea that both things-in-themselves and empirical objects are cast as originating sources of intuitive representation by Kant. On the whole, this theory has seemed troubled if not incoherent to commentators. That reaction is understandable. Kant is continually warning us not to confuse things-in-themselves and empirical realities, and the whole critique of dialectical illusion is a catalog of the defective conceptions by which philosophers are seduced when they have mixed up these two concepts. In much of Kant's discourse, the danger against which we are cautioned seems to be that of conflating things with other things. As Prauss has shown, this is never a satisfactory way of looking at the contrast between things *considered* as they are in themselves and things *considered* as they appear to us. We never get to know anything about things considered as they are in themselves, but it is that realm of things that appears to us as a system of objects connected by laws. In saying that we represent reality as a system of causally interrelated spatiotemporal objects, Kant is saying that we do take reality to be a law-governed system, although we are able to appreciate the irreducible subjective element in all of our thinking about reality.

Among the causal relations that we make out in the world are those that operate in the functioning of our own perceptual apparatus. Empirical science finds out a lot about these relationships. All this characterization is within the framework that Kant calls appearance (but not illusion). As such, it is how we represent the reality of things affecting us. From this point of view, to say that cinnabar is red is to express one case in which being affected by things generates appearance. That is to say, something appears to us as red cinnabar. The only risk in speaking of this event as an occasion that falls under the heading of original affection is the risk of giving the impression that Kant has rescinded his commitment to subjectivism and is ascribing color to things as they are in themselves. He is not doing that except in the admissible sense in which he is using color to describe a way in which things-in-themselves appear. Kant does not use color to describe things-in-themselves considered as they are in themselves.

This strand of Kant's thinking gives us pause, but it is also itself a version of a pattern of thinking about perception that is universal, natural, and acceptable. Consider visual perception. A human perceiver might communicate a visual experience by saying, "I see a red roof down there in the valley." At a nontechnical level of understanding, everyone appreciates that this experience arises out of a very large number of events inside and outside the perceiving subject. Light strikes a roof, and myriad rays are reflected to the eyes of the subject. This complex physical input is "focused" as it passes through the lenses of the eyes. A huge number of things transpire at each retina, and there are further events in vast numbers in the nerves, at the optic chiasm, and in the brain. We understand that many of these events are simultaneous, while there are also sequences of events here that we must think of as causally determined. Events in the optic nerve are consequences of the particular things that happen at the retinas, which are, in turn, a consequence of outer occurrences. There is no question, of course, of experience of these microevents, except in the sense that the perceptual experience reported, the seeing of the "red roof down there," is itself constituted of the aggregate of these occurrences or of some of them. How is it that this multitude of individual events is aggregated and organized as a single experience of which a subject can be conscious and that he can report? We do not have a commonsense answer to this. For one thing, the concept of "a single experience" suggests a principle of individuation that we do not really possess. The question seems to be in part conceptual and in part related to matters where only technical physiological information can help. Nonetheless, we certainly have perceptual experience. That alone requires that we are capable of the required aggregating and organizing.

For our purpose, I want to emphasize that this natural understanding contains the ingredients of Kant's outlook. In describing the multitude of events that go into a visual experience, we make use of concepts like light, eyes, lenses, retinas, and brains. These are all elements of the perceived world. If I tried to rerun the general story of visual perception outlined above as an epistemological story, I would have to redescribe the constituent events so that they did not employ the vocabulary of objects of perception. That vocabulary only gets its footing upon the successful aggregation of those elementary events and others like them. This purification of the story of a perceptual experience is the old phenomenalist project in which we describe reality in sense-data language and effect a reductive analysis of physical-object language. I do not think there are many philosophers left who think this once-prevalent epistemological project is feasible. It is not just a question of running against a wall in trying to devise a truly independent sense-datum language out of a lot of demonstratives and minimalist syntax, or no syntax at all, as in "Red, here, now." There is also a more general recognition that none of this corresponds to anything really experiential. We do not experience anything short of the world. The envisioned reduction does not bring theoretical entities into play by defining them in terms of what is really given. The alleged elements, the sense data, are in fact the theoretical realities, and the ordinary world of objects is what is in fact given. The idea that we *experience* sense data and not objects is just a myth that managed to captivate philosophers for a while. Kant understood this long ago, while empiricists remained captivated for many generations. So Kant does not struggle against the fact that we must describe the conditions for the possibility of experience in terms that have applicability only because those conditions are satisfied and we do have experience of and knowledge of a system of causally related spatiotemporal objects. The feeling that this is epistemologically improper is an expression of the foundationalist impulse that Kant has set aside and that we should all set aside. The view that replaces it is what Kant calls "empirical realism."

Thus Kant says that law-governed connection is the mark of objectivity and of the fact that our experience is experience of objects. But the only laws we know assert relationships between entities that are already conceptualized and objective appearances. In a reductive account, this would not be the case. Readers who are familiar with reductive empiricist epistemological projects are likely to interpret Kant's discussion of law-governed connection as if it is the assertion of such a project. That cannot be right, since the reductive account includes the idea that we really experience not objects but something else such as sense data. Kant is very clear that we cannot have experience of anything short of objects.

CHAPTER 15

The Idealistic Understanding of Kant's Theoretical Philosophy

Nonidealistic reading of the *Critique of Pure Reason* is rare, and what little there is is recent, qualified, and ambiguous. I will discuss salient views of a small selection of idealist commentators here. Then I will turn to a few recent writers on Kant who move away from an idealistic reading, some of whom have had an influence on my own thinking. I want to preface this sketch of the opinions of others about Kant's idealism with a reminder of what I take to be the general explanation for the widespread failure to understand Kant on such a fundamental question.

As we shall see, some writers would like to find a nonidealist doctrine in Kant, but in the end they cannot do so. No doubt the inclination is intelligible in light of Kant's numerous "refutations" of idealism, and his well-known impatient rejection of ascriptions of idealism to him. The inability to decide on a nonidealist interpretation is also intelligible in light of conspicuous passages in Kant. No one can miss the Kantian thesis that all the objects we come to know about are *appearances*. No one can miss Kant's assertion that appearances are merely representations. If "representation" means "mental representation" in this context, then Kant is an idealist and the discussion of that issue is over. Since most readers quite understandably think that Kant means mental representations, they cannot avoid ascribing idealism to him.

After all, what could representations be if not mental representations? There are, of course, nonmental representations such as drawings, diagrams, maps, photographs, and so on. But Kant certainly does not mean to say that appearances are all merely drawings, diagrams, maps, and the like. Is it not just as evident that by "representations" he means things like mental images and mental perceptual impressions? The conviction that this must be right explains why so many modern writers on Kant slip easily into talk about sense data and a Kantian phenomenalism.

I have already devoted a long chapter to the concept of representation and to this issue. I will add only one summary thought here. Kant says appearances are merely representations. Let us not worry for a moment about representations and think a little about appearances. Whatever variety there is among appearances, Kant seems to be talking about all of them. His thesis is certainly not that *some* appearances are merely representations. He is talking about appearances accessible to outer sense, and also about appearances accessible to inner sense. What are inner appearances? At the beginning of the Transcendental Aesthetic, Kant tells us that inner sense intuits "the mind [*Gemüt*]and its states," and then he immediately qualifies this by noting that we do not really get any intuitions of the mind (*Seele*) as an inner *object,* but only inner states of mind (A22–B37). In any case, everything that appears to inner sense is mental, and if mental appearances are representations, they are mental representations. Finally, all the mental things that are apprehended by our inner sense exist in time and are temporally related to everything else that is temporal, because time is the form of inner intuition.

What about outer appearances? This is obviously the crux of the issue of idealism. Does Kant ever say of outer appearances that they are also mental things, or states of the mind, and that as such, they are essentially temporal and related to all other temporal entities? Some passages I have already analyzed certainly *seem* to say that outer is also inner, that outer intuitions reduce to determinations of inner sense, and that though outer things are spatial, they are nonetheless "in us," since space itself is in us. But these passages have all proved to be misleading. Outer sense is definitionally distinguished from inner by the fact that the form of outer sense is space and that what is intuited by means of outer sense exists in space and is locatable with respect to all other spatial existents. Having only mental things in its scope is the distinguishing feature of inner sense. "Outer" means outside the mind of the subject or it doesn't mean anything at all. If outer appearances were said to be merely more mental things, it would be unintelligible for Kant to explain inner sense as that by means of which the mind and its states are intuited. Kant says without any obscurity or ambiguity that time (the temporal) cannot be intuited outwardly, any more than space (the spatial) can be intuited as something in us (A23–B37). So we have explained the confusing passages in such a way as to sustain the view that things that appear to outer sense are not mental things, and if outer appearances are representations, they are not mental representations.

This distinction has to be sustained. It is enunciated at the most elementary level of the *Critique of Pure Reason,* where there isn't much room for differences of opinion. But having found that only inner appearances can be mental representations, we can hardly conclude that outer appearances, as representations, are all things like drawings and maps according to Kant. Therefore, as representations, outer appearances are not mental representations, nor are they nonmental representations (that is, physical objects that represent things as drawings and maps do). But many philosophers, maybe most philosophers (here a ubiquitous Cartesian influence operates) find that the only way to reconcile divergent tendencies in the text is to suppose that Kant does obliterate the fundamental distinction between inner and outer sense, and that, in the last analysis, he reduces so-called outer things to a mere species of the genus of mental representation. This view has the considerable defect that merely mental things cannot conform to the Categories, for the Categories call for enduring objects and no merely mental entities (states of mind) will qualify. Another shortcoming of this resolution is the fact that it has Kant subscribe to the doctrine that there is really only one form of receptivity, the inner, while Kant himself names this view as a basic defect of idealism.

We need some other way of understanding all of the straightforward and fundamental Kantian assertions we have cited here without assigning to him doctrines that obviously conflict with what everyone knows are his core theories and philosophical objectives. We have to understand that by calling appearances "representations," Kant stresses that all our characterizations of them are subjective and none reveal any reality as it is apart from the perspective of our mental powers. Within the scope of this ineliminable subjectivity, inner appearances are mental things and outer appearances are material things, and all of them are accessible to us only as we are able to represent them. *In that sense,* both inner and outer appearances are merely representations. In the first-edition summary of the fourth Paralogism, Kant comes as close as he ever does to making it clear that this is his outlook:

> Neither a material nor a thinking thing lies, as transcendental object, at the foundation of outer appearances or of our inner intuition, but instead an

unknown ground of appearances gives rise to the empirical concept of both the material and the thinking kind of reality.

I am willing to be rather dogmatic about this understanding. In the many passages in the first-edition version of the Transcendental Analytic and in the first-edition version of the fourth Paralogism in the Dialectic where Kant says that appearances are only representations, he means that to describe an appearance is to give an account of a thing under the conditions of our sensibility and thought. Such an account is implicitly contrasted with a kind of description that, were we capable of it, would characterize things independently of us and our cognitive capabilities. Kant is not saying that appearances are mental realities. Inner intuitions (or appearances) are mental as apprehended subjectively. Outer appearances are material as apprehended subjectively. "Mental" and "material" are very general but entirely subjective headings. Absolute reality is neither mental nor material.[1]

Of course, this understanding has to be reinforced with an account of Kant's many puzzling statements about space being in us. I will not repeat the resolution of these matters that has been presented. I turn now to consider the views of some philosophers who, in the absence of this understanding of fundamentals, simply proceed with an idealist interpretation of Kant's philosophy.

———

P. F. Strawson and Dieter Henrich are among the influential modern commentators who base their overall interpretations of Kant on an explicit acceptance of the idea that he is an idealist of some sort. Strawson finds that, in the last analysis, Kant's scheme of things does not differ as much as he thinks it does from Berkeley's paradigmatic subjective idealism.[2] Kant's alleged confinement of consciousness to mental objects, Strawson observes, will generate the traditional problems of skeptical egocentrism:

> Nothing, he [Kant] says, is really given *us* save perceptions. But your perceptions are not given to me nor mine to you. [In consequence,] . . . this version of transcendental idealism must turn into transcendental solipsism or it must be given up.

Strawson notes that the same can be said of Berkeley. In a number of other passages, Strawson says explicitly that Kant's views, in spite of his claims to the contrary, are like Berkeley's subjective idealism. Strawson relies on an idea that seems obvious to him, and to which he devotes no special reflection or investigation, namely, that "us" and "our" have to come down to "me" and "mine" for Kant, and that only "private mental perceptions" are really *given* to us in experience. I have shown here that both of these Cartesian ideas are erroneously imputed to Kant and that the problems of solipsism do not arise from his point of view when it is properly grasped.

Henrich is committed to the thesis that what is, in the first instance, "given" to human subjects of experience is the domain of sense impressions, which are the first foundations of empirical knowledge. He says:

> As everyone knows, Kant considers himself to be justified in the assumption that all immediately given materials for human knowledge, which are presentations, are nothing but simple and isolated qualities. They are not sometimes aspects of complex objects of which we are also conscious. In the domain, and at the level of knowledge, to which the data belong, such objects are never encountered. . . . All objects of our knowledge have to be constructed.[3]

Of course, much of what Henrich says here is indisputable. One could say that the trouble with his reading of Kant lies only in the level of knowledge (*Erkenntnisphase*) to which he assigns "simple and isolated qualities" as "presentations," as opposed to the level at which "objects" are *encountered* as the referents of terms in judgments. I call attention especially to the thought that Henrich does not offer this understanding of Kant as the fruit of his erudition or of his rethinking of a difficult text. On the contrary, Henrich identifies this understanding as part of what "everyone knows" (*wie man weiß*). I think this widely held view from which Henrich starts is incorrect. In contrast, I have sought to establish that what is given in our experience of objects, according to Kant, is always a nonmental object that does not need to be constructed. The simple representations, the items that Henrich calls "presentations," exhaust the realm of the given in Henrich's interpretation. No doubt Kant *seems* to say this clearly and often. But these "givens" figure only in Kant's theoretical explanation of the possibility of our consciousness or experience of nonmental objects in space. Kant's simple representations should not be thought of as embodying "data," if that implies that we are acquainted with them and, in consequence, use them as building blocks or evidence for knowledge of objects. That, of course, is the role of sense data for phenomenalists. Kant's thesis is that when such simple representations are concatenated by the synthesizing powers he ascribes to the mind, complex *representations* of outer objects are constituted. In consequence, we experience not the original simples (Henrich's data) and not our own complex representations, but the outer objects. Both the original simple representations and the synthesizing powers of the mind are theoretically posited items in terms of which Kant explains how it is that outer objects are *given,* that is, immediately—though subjectively—apprehended in experience.

Confusion arises on these matters because Kant's stance allows for two senses of what is "given." In so far as Kant is explaining the possibility of experience, which we have as conscious creatures, the fundamental objects given to us are enduring objects of perception, while elementary, simple, and transient representations are not given but posited for the sake of explaining our capacity to experience objects. From within the theoretical perspective, Kant posits original representations and powers of synthesis, the operation of which culminates in the construction of representations of enduring spatial objects. From a theoretical point of view, the original representations might be said to be what is "given," since they are the raw input for mental synthesis. But they can never be regarded as objects of perception or experience or consciousness. Nor are they evidence on the basis of which we can infer the existence of outer objects. Kant is simply not in the business of gathering evidence for the existence of objects of experience. Since we experience these objects, we do not stand in need of evidence for their existence. One might challenge Kant's theoretical system on the ground that he has inadequate evidence for the existence of the original sense input and the combinatory powers of mind he assigns to us. But one cannot accept the Kantian conception of conscious experience of objects and then ask for evidence for the existence of such objects. Nor can one regard the posited original representations as data supporting assertions about objects. When Kant refers to original representations as data, which he does, he means only that they are the first input for the construction of complex representations, not that they constitute a reservoir of evidence for anything.

A view similar to Henrich's is expressed by Hilary Putnam, who finds that Kant accepts Berkeley's elimination of the contrast of primary and secondary qualities and then takes all qualities to be secondary qualities. Thus Kant deletes any claim, found in Locke and many others, that our representations are in some way similar to their mind-independent objects, and that that resemblance makes it feasible to think of them *as* representations. Putnam still finds a realist stance in Kant, but only in connection with the concepts of judgment and truth. Objects play a role in the Kantian account of human knowledge, as Putnam reads it, in that statements that contain reference to objects can be recognized to be truths:

> There is no correspondence theory of truth in his philosophy. What then is a true judgment? Kant does believe that we have *objective* knowledge: we know laws of mathematics, laws of geometry, laws of physics, and many statements about individual objects. The use of the term "knowledge" and the use of the term "objective" amount to the assertion that there is still a notion of truth. But what is truth if it is not correspondence to the way things are in themselves?

Putnam's response is as follows:

> As I have said, the only answer that one can extract from Kant's writing is this: a piece of knowledge (i.e. "a true statement") is a statement that a rational being would accept on sufficient experience of the kind that it is actually possible for beings of our nature to have.[4]

If this were correct, all of our judgments about *objects* would be grounded on the evidence of experiences that do not involve objects and that belong to an epistemologically more fundamental level (as in Henrich). The level of judgment and truth marks the domain of objects. Putnam's evidential materials that go into "sufficient experience" are confined to a domain of things that do figure directly in experience and are thus *given*. But just as objects are not found at the level of "data" for Henrich's interpretation, so too, Putnam's Kant confines directly apprehended things to secondary qualities that not only are mental but also, following Berkeley, do not resemble any outer nonmental objects. When all is said and done, this is still a form of what Kant calls "problematic idealism." Putnam himself alludes to a passage where Kant says that the enduring viability of skepticism about the existence of things outside the mind is a scandal to philosophy. The passage Putnam mentions is worth quoting:

> Idealism might be considered ever so blameless in regard to the objectives of metaphysics (which in fact it is not), still it remains a scandal of philosophy and of common human reason that the existence of things outside us (from which the whole matter of knowledge even with respect to our inner sense is derived in the first place) must be assumed on the basis of mere belief, and if it occurs to anyone to doubt that existence, no satisfying proof can be raised against him. (Bxxxix)

In the second parenthetical remark in this text, Kant asserts in condensed form the claim of his Refutation of Idealism: inner sense has only representations of "things outside us" for its original input, as far as knowledge of reality is concerned. So we can hardly propose mental materials of inner sense (Putnam's objectless experiences) as the sole evidence for the existence of outer objects. The interpretation of Kant that Putnam advances is thus ruled out by this very passage. I would say that the "common human reason" (*allgemeinen Menschenvernunft*) that is scandalized by the skepticism engendered by idealism refers to the common reason manifested in the conceptions of things ordinarily held by normal human beings whose thinking has not been deformed by metaphysical speculation. Far from being blameless, idealism is precisely what puts the world at a cognitive distance from us and gives entry to a seemingly unanswerable skeptical doubt about ordinary conceptions of the world and our perceptual access to it. The limitation on our experiential evidence for knowledge claims (truths about outer objects) that Putnam reads in Kant conspicuously fails to banish skepticism.

I think Putnam supposes that he is ascribing a form of realism to Kant (he calls it "internal realism") because he invokes a normative or definitional ideal of what a rational being would take to be true. In circumstances where a rational being would take "The cat is on the mat" to be true on the strength of sufficient experience of relevant given data, we can say that "The cat is on the mat" *is true*. It follows that there are certainly cats and mats, and thus an external world, because we know, in those circumstances, that an external cat is on an external mat.

Aspiring to rationality myself, ought I to fall in with this conception? The trouble is that the experiential basis of the proposed truth claim for any rational being is just the "information that is available to a being with our sense organs," and according to Putnam, Kant has confined all that to inner, wholly subjective secondary qualities in conformity with Berkeley's repudiation of the thesis that ideas represent objects by being similar to them. If this were satisfactory, it would not require irrationality to notice, as Descartes and Hume and Berkeley do, that the existence of all of that "information" is compatible with there being no cat, no mat, and no nonmental world. It may be, indeed, that those who have doubts concerning the existence of the nonmental world, including these great philosophers, are all suffering from some philosophical illusions without which skepticism would not appeal to reasonable people. I think this is so, and I would say that Kant thinks so too. But it would be just a kind of strong-arm realism to accept Putnam's limited experiential base, which is not significantly different from that of Descartes, Hume, and Berkeley, and then to call anyone who doubts the leap to *truths* about an external world "irrational."

In sum, like Henrich, Putnam starts by burdening Kant with a conception of simple sensed qualities, and again like Henrich, he finds a

Kantian level of cognition (akin to Henrich's *Erkenntnisphase*) at which we apprehend certain "data" or certain "information" but not objects. The standard idealist view starts from the thought that, constituted as we are, we confront a private domain of "perishing" and objectless data. Putnam seems to go along with this, and then he contributes the idea that, on the basis of such experience, the rational individuals among us find some statements that make reference to objects to be true statements. I say that Kant does not propose this ordering of things, and that, in fact, he thinks it is an impossible and incoherent starting point in epistemology. I have shown that Kant really does dispel the philosophical scandal of unanswered skepticism by arguing that the things we immediately apprehend at the ground-floor level of ordinary experience are nonmental enduring objects. These objects figure in perception, and not merely in judgments, although, of course, one has to make a judgment in order to assert anything about objects—or about secondary qualities, for that matter.[5] In Kant's account of knowledge and objects, objects are encountered and are not theoretical, while private data have either a derived status, as representations of outer things do, or they are theoretical and posited, as elementary simple representations are.

An idealistic and/or phenomenalist understanding of Kant's general outlook is not presented here as a distinguishing achievement by Strawson or Henrich or Putnam. Such understandings do not separate these recent commentators from the preponderance of interpreters in German, English, and other languages. The imposition of an idealist interpretation on Kant among German interpreters goes back to Kant's contemporaries: his philosophical friends, correspondents, first reviewers, and critics. Garve and Feder, Eberhard, Jacobi,[6] Mendelssohn and Lambert[7] are representative. Fichte, Schelling, and Hegel all construe Kant as an idealist who is not idealistic enough. The rise of German idealism following Kant entirely depended on an idealistic interpretation of Kant's conception of objects of experience and a repudiation of his conception of things as they are in themselves. Schopenhauer judges the second edition of the *Critique of Pure Reason* harshly because he thinks it compromises the thoroughgoing idealism that he finds and applauds in the first edition. In a curious combination of admiration and condemnation, Schopenhauer says:

> But let no one imagine that he knows the 'Critique of Pure Reason' and has a distinct conception of Kant's teaching if he has only read the second or one of the later editions. That is altogether impossible, for he has read only a mutilated, spoilt and to a certain extent ungenuine text.[8]

Schopenhauer offers various none-too-flattering explanations for what he takes to be an about-face in the second edition, including a mental weakening in Kant's advancing years, an excessive desire to protect his reputation by changing his doctrine so as to accommodate critics, and generally, a "fear of men."[9]

The most influential English commentaries by Paton[10] and Kemp Smith[11] both present Kant as a "phenomenalist," as does DeVleeschauwer.[12] For the most part, recent writers on Kant in English present the view that Kant is in the tradition of Cartesian thinking in so far as he confines the immediate objects of consciousness to mental representations. Some are a good deal more emphatic than Strawson in urging that Kant's philosophy is like Berkeley's. Colin Turbayne even proposes that Kant had a sound firsthand understanding of Berkeley, and that he actually derived his crucial idealistic conceptions of space and of the empirical realm from Berkeley's writings. Turbayne believes that, "prompted by animus," Kant conceals his debt by "deliberate misinterpretations of Berkeley's doctrine." He explains Kant's hostility in this way:

> The vulgar view of Berkeley, then as now, was of a befooled enthusiast who sought notoriety by his paradoxes. Moreover, Kant abhorred all things mystical and visionary and classified Berkeley's idealism as such. To acknowledge debt to such a man, or even to admit affinity, was quite out of the question for Kant.[13]

But the need for any such explanatory allegation depends entirely on the correctness of Turbayne's finding that Kant replicates Berkeley's idealism. If, in fact, Kant's view is not an idealism at all, then his repudiations of idealism and his denials of kinship to Berkeley are not intentionally deceptive but quite appropriate. Turbayne says that Kant was faced with the danger that his own thought would slide into the very skeptical illusionism he pretends to find in Berkeley:

> The Kantian antidote . . . is not the *a priori* nature of space, but its ideality or subjectivity which assimilates space and its contents into the realm of ideas, and thus *prevents* illusion. (p. 114)

No such antidote is needed, because Kant's subjective epistemology doesn't make space inner and private and does not make spatial objects into mental objects.

Turbayne's interpretation presupposes that Kant's inclination to conceal his idealistic thinking and to offer "refutations" of idealism was occasioned by the fact that readers and reviewers of the *Critique* saw his views as like those of Berkeley. To the extent that Turbayne's scare quotes around "refutations" implies that there must be something drastically qualified and partial about Kant's arguments against idealism, those quotes are quite out of place. Kant's struggle with idealist interpretations of his views is much older than the first reactions to the *Critique of Pure Reason*. In 1770 Kant sent his Inaugural Dissertation to J. H. Lambert, J. G. Sulzer, and Moses Mendelssohn, and all of them responded with doubts about the idealistic and skeptical tendencies they found in his thesis of the subjectivity of space and time.[14] For instance, Lambert urged against Kant's view:

> If time isn't real then no change is real either. It seems to me, however, that even an idealist will have to concede that time really passes and exists, at least in the context of his representations which begin and stop.[15]

Writing about the impact of these criticisms of the Inaugural Dissertation, DeVleeschauwer says Kant

> had to see a misunderstanding in these criticisms. Hadn't he expressly affirmed that he meant to reject idealism? He had declared, in effect, that the cooperation of perception in the elaboration of the phenomenon, inexplicable without the presence of the object, is in itself the refutation of idealism.[16]

DeVleeschauwer notes that the idealistic interpretation of reviewers and readers of the *Critique* ten years later were like a second experience of the same sort for Kant. Just as he rejected the finding of affinity with Berkeley in 1781, so too, a decade earlier, he responded to these reactions to his supposed idealism by trying to clarify his realistic intentions. In this spirit, he turned his attention explicitly to the issue of objects and objectivity, and this eventuated in the theory of the forms of judgment, the Categories, and the Transcendental Deduction.[17] The critics of 1770 are ultimately answered by the conception of empirical objects as enduring realities that cannot be reduced to mental representations because they exist continuously and thus through gaps in the episodes of our representation of them. It is surely not animus toward Berkeley but the misunderstanding of his outlook by these three philosophers, for whom Kant had only respect, that motivated his allusion to charges of idealism in the *Erläuterung* following the exposition of time in the Transcendental Aesthetic (A36, 37). Kant speaks of an objection he has heard from certain "*einsehenden Männern*" who are unanimous in the opinion that time must be real, lest even change in representations be denied. This is, of course, the criticism of Lambert quoted above. Kant concedes the point while disallowing its force against his view. Of course, time is real, time is empirically real, but it is not an existing object. It is the real form of inner sense. Time and space are not objects but forms, and they exist as forms.

Spatial objects, of course, are not forms, and they exist as objects and are not mentalized as Turbayne thinks. I have attempted to establish, contrary to the demands of Turbayne's allegation of deceptiveness, and contrary to all readers who see an idealism like Berkeley's in Kant's "transcendental idealism," that Kant asserts that space is not an object-like container or entity at all, and therefore not a mental object, and that true objects are spatial, and that their spatiality distinguishes precisely the nonmental status of objects of outer sense. Thus empirical objects are certainly not "assimilated into the realm of ideas" by Kant.

A very different form of idealism is ascribed to Kant by Karl Ameriks when he states the aspiration for his study of the Paralogisms. The "most appropriate strategy" for understanding Kant, Ameriks contends,

> retains a kind of mentalistic character in committing Kant to the claim that we should not say that knowledge or reality itself—including one's self—is to be understood materialistically. . . . this modest mentalism . . . appears to be forced on us if we want to be true to the Paralogisms and the full meaning of transcendental idealism.[18]

To be sure, Kant does not present a materialist philosophy of mind. However, the idea that his overall view is any kind of "mentalism" reflects a misunderstanding of the "full meaning of transcendental idealism." There are two lines of thought that might seem to support Ameriks's general outlook. The simpler line would ignore things-in-themselves and rely on the seemingly ineluctable idealism contained in the notion that outer appearances are constituted out of mental raw materials (representations). This idea, that both inner and outer things are really mental, and thus everything we know is mental, is very popular. It has been examined and set aside, especially in chapters 5 and 6. In light of Ameriks's special emphasis on the Paralogisms, and in light of his phrase "the full meaning" of transcendental idealism, it seems probable that he does not invoke this standard support for Kant's alleged mentalism but instead thinks that, for Kant, things-in-themselves are not material things, while the material objects in the empirical world are not fully real because they are only appearances. The trouble with this is that, according to Kant, we know nothing at all about things-in-themselves. Nonetheless, we might decide that we are entitled to conclude that reality—that is, things-in-themselves,—is *not* "to be understood materialistically," as Ameriks says. I concede this point, Ameriks's view still has to be reconciled with Kant's assertion of total ignorance of things-in-themselves. Perhaps it could be reconciled. However, this will be useless for Ameriks's claim to find "a modest mentalism" in Kant because we will have just as good a title to assert that things-in-themselves are not to be understood either materialistically or mentalistically. In his idealistic-sounding first-edition treatment of the fourth Analogy, Kant says that reality, independent of our subjective representation of it, contains the unknown ground for our empirical concepts of both thinking beings and their thoughts (the mental) and spatial objects (the material). But this ground itself is neither mental nor material (A380). Kant surely holds that minds are mental and bodies are material. Since the only true objects of which we have any experience are enduring objects of perception, we might be able to agree that their materiality is only apparent (though not an illusion). But we could never conclude that they are actually mental. It is things outside the mind—that is, nonmental things, and only nonmental things—that are accessible to outer sense.

Kant thinks that all characterizations of reality as it appears to us are subjective, and that means mind-dependent. Were we to accept, mistakenly, the equivalence of "mind-dependent" and "mental," we would think that all appearances are mental. But Kant never deviates from the view that outer objects, the appearances that conform to the Categories, are enduring and thus not mental. However, even if we made the mistake of identifying the domain of appearances with mental reality, we would thereby exclude things-in-themselves from that domain altogether, for things as they are in themselves are by definition not mind-dependent. Therefore, even if that mistake were allowed, it would not support Ameriks when he finds a "mentalist character" in Kant's conception of reality. In this book, I have sought to establish that Kant makes room for nonmental objects and for mental representations, but not for mental objects of knowledge, especially when "object" is used in the sense developed in the doctrine of the Categories. Kant surely believes that there are minds. Minds are not objects of experience, however, for they are not perceived, and only perceived things are objects of experience.

T. E. Wilkerson seems to be attracted by the possibility of a nonidealistic interpretation of Kant's so-called "idealism," but he has to set aside his own realistic proposal in the face of what seem to be too many and too clear general idealistic commitments in the *Critique,* and especially in the face of Kant's unambiguous statements to the effect that we cannot get beyond experience of our own representations.[19] The main body of his book adopts an idealistic line and explains away Kant's refutations of idealism and his other protestations because Wilkerson cannot envision any way around passages in Kant's text that constitute, he thinks, unanswerable reasons for an idealistic reading. Wilkerson finds that things-in-themselves and appearances are "two sets of objects" (p. 27) and then calls that "an absurd philosophical extravagance." He says Kant's effort in the *Prolegomena* to correct idealist interpretations by the first reviewers of the *Critique* merely confirmed those readings; and addressing himself to the section of the second edition that Kant entitled "The Refutation of Idealism," Wilkerson finds Kant's contention

> disingenuous because it is part of Kant's persistent and mistaken attempt to distinguish his own idealism from that of Berkeley. (p. 82)

It is not easy to see how persistence and error merit the charge of disingenuousness but, in any case, Wilkerson clearly thinks not only that transcendental idealism is a form of idealism but also that it is Berkeley's form. The contemplation of a nonidealistic interpretation comes near the end of Wilkerson's volume. He reconsiders the above readings only to reassert them in light of what seems to him to be unmistakable idealism in the Kantian texts. In his reconsideration, Wilkerson presents the possibility that Kant does not mean that things-in-themselves and appearances are two different "sets of objects," and that unlike those of the idealists, Kant's objects of empirical knowledge are always nonmental things while only their formal character is wholly subjective or ideal. Wilkerson thinks that this alternative might be proposed to flesh out what Kant means when he calls his a "formal" and not a "material" idealism. I don't think that his proposal is correct as it stands. For example, Wilkerson includes in it the ascription to Kant of the view that "objects have certain material (as opposed to formal) properties such as color or shape or mass, which are not dependent on our human faculties" (p. 188). This assertion is not compatible with Kant's radical subjectivism. Color, shape, and mass are dependent on our cognitive powers, according to Kant. But Wilkerson's proposal in general is broadly correct and much better than the alternative he decides to endorse, namely, that Kant's stance is simply Berkeley's. What I want to emphasize is the reasoning that induces Wilkerson to give up any such reinterpretation. In spite of the fact that the reading he retains ascribes "silly things" to Kant, it is specific idealistic-sounding passages that exclude a much less silly reading, according to Wilkerson. In explaining his position, Wilkerson quotes some passages whose idealism he takes to be indisputable:

> "By *transcendental idealism* I mean the doctrine that appearances are to be regarded as being, one and all, representations only" (A369), [and] "External objects, bodies . . . are mere appearances, and are therefore nothing but a species of my representations, the objects of which are something only through these representations. Apart from them they are nothing (A370)." Moreover . . . two of Kant's arguments make little sense unless Kant is a Berkeleyan idealist—namely his attack on Descartes' causal theory of perception, in the discussion of the fourth paralogism in the first edition, and the solution of the mathematical antinomies. In short, we should not be confused by Kant's distinction between "formal" and "material" idealism, for his own "formal" idealism is indistinguishable from the "material" idealism of Berkeley. (p. 190)

In the absence of a more satisfactory way of understanding these very passages and many others like them, Wilkerson's reasoning is plausible, while Wilkerson himself seems to appreciate that another way of looking at Kant would be desirable if only he could find it. In this book, I have tried to provide that other way of looking at Kant and of understanding the passages that turned back Wilkerson's promising reconsideration.

Unlike Wilkerson, Paul Guyer does not endorse the "two sets of objects" interpretation of the contrast between appearances and things as they are in themselves. But even though Guyer sees a nonidealistic Kantian ontology, he convicts Kant of idealistic incoherence in characterizing experience:

> . . . it is no help to claim that Kant does not postulate a second set of ghostlike nonspatial and nontemporal objects in addition to the ordinary referents of empirical judgments. Indeed, he does not, except in the special cases of God and the soul. . . . But he does something just as unpleasant—namely, *degrade* ordinary objects to mere representations of themselves, or *identify* objects possessing spatial and temporal properties with mere mental entities.[20]

Guyer's charge here is, in effect, the first and simpler line of thinking by which we sought to understand Ameriks's claim to find a mentalist philosophy in Kant. In comparison with Wilkerson, Guyer makes a much more serious, much better informed, and more penetrating effort to evaluate the possibility that Kant is not an idealist but that he actually endorses a form of direct realism. But, Guyer says,

> Kant appears strongly committed to the view of his times that we are never *directly acquainted* with anything but our own representations. (p. 324)

In this sentence, Guyer identifies the prevailing Cartesian style of thinking of Kant's time and then extends it to Kant himself. In consequence, on the same page, Guyer finds that "the ascription of any form of ontological realism to Kant raises difficult questions." In particular, since Kant rejects causal inference from mental representations to nonmental objects, if he accepts the view of his times confining direct acquaintance to mental representations, there seems to be no feasible route to knowledge of such objects. Further, Guyer argues that the mind-independent status of putative nonmental objects of knowledge would contradict Kant's transcendental idealism. As I understand his reasoning, nonmental objects that are not mind-dependent will not fall under the general heading "things considered as they appear to us," and therefore such objects will be things-in-themselves. But according to this hypothesis, such things would be spatial and known by us. This contradicts a central tenet of transcendental idealism: things-in-themselves are neither spatial nor known. Although Guyer then expounds very interesting and attractive Kantian answers to these puzzles, he finds the residual difficulties of reconciliation of realism with transcendental idealism insurmountable and cannot accept a realistic Kant, much as Wilkerson cannot, because that seems to be definitively ruled out by Kant's irreducible idealist commitments. I have shown that the understanding of acquaintance and the mental that Guyer rightly says was the dominant "view of his [Kant's] times" explains why Kant's contemporaries thought he accepted that view, but it also explains why they were wrong, since Kant does not accept it. Objects of outer sense, in Kant's thinking, are enduring things that are immediately apprehended, and contrary to Guyer, Kant does not reduce them to mental representations or think of them as mental entities.

Other writers think that Kant prefigures a positivistic or verificationist phenomenalism that reduces the physical world to the mental, like the phenomenalist projects of Mach, Carnap, Russell, or Ayer. Ralph Walker, for example, characterizes what he assumes to be a generally shared outlook concerning the existence of enduring objects in space. The shared stance is that of a theorist projecting explanatory hypotheses where what is to be explained is the occurrence and character of our inner experience. I draw particular attention to the fact that this stance is ascribed to Kant because Walker supposes that it is what "*we* think" when speculating about experience. Here Walker assumes that what we think on this point can be assumed to be a generally established opinion and, thus, to be Kant's opinion. Walker embeds the peculiarities of transcendental idealism in the presupposed general Cartesian standpoint:

> Normally, of course, we think that the fact that we have the experiences we do is explained by the way the world is, and we can look upon such ordinary beliefs as the belief in reidentifiable, persisting objects as part of a theory based on our sense-experience and satisfactorily accounting for it. But in the present context this is not good enough. The argument is not transcendental: it does not offer conditions logically necessary for the experience we have, but only conditions empirically required to explain it.[21]

So Walker investigates various improvements on the empirical theory, which, incidentally, sounds very much as if it will turn out to be something like the theory of constancy and coherence of perceptions that Hume examines and properly rejects in the *Treatise of Human Nature*. One improvement Walker thinks promising would be to ascribe to Kant some form of the positivist's Verification Principle (the principle asserts that the meaning of a sentence or statement is the means of verifying it). The invocation of the Verification Principle might help because, under the principle, claims about enduring things would be deemed verifiable by us, if they can be said to be as much as meaningful to us, which no one will deny. Walker's explanation of Kant's conception of knowledge of objects is rather like Putnam's. The sought-for necessity could be provided in that the method of verification would specify the conditions (possible experience) that would establish the truth of a sentence. This turns out to be predictably unsatisfactory, because we have merely shifted our needs to a justification of the Verification Principle. Giving up the search for a transcendental argument, at least for the time being, Walker summarizes the state of his investigation at one point as follows:

> . . . it still seems evident that our beliefs about the world form a theory which goes beyond the evidence. This evidence must come through the senses; for the moment let us suppose it comes in the form of sense-data, more or less as Locke and Hume thought. The theory is constructed on the basis of the evidence, but sense-data can hardly supply the principles we use in theory construction.[22]

There follow further complexities in Walker's search for the *a priori* elements that we do not take in as we take in sense data, and that might yield an articulate understanding of Kant's transcendental idealism. In any case, the important feature here, for our purposes, is the starting point and the presuppositions of Walker's enterprise, not the conclusion. The positivistic motifs Walker introduces make sense here only because he takes it for granted that we do start with transient inner experience and that "persisting objects" play a role in a *theory* to account for experience. It is because he takes this for granted, as more or less common ground in philosophy, that it is easy for Walker to suppose that Kant has also adopted this preliminary perspective. And, of course, this seems to be amply confirmed by the things Kant says about experience and his confinement of experience to mere appearances, which he often seems to identify with mental representations. It is the content of our experience, so conceived (it is constituted of sense data and other mental representations) for which we need an explanation, according to the view Walker takes to be more or less universally accepted, and in any case accepted by Kant.

I have tried to establish that Kant wants to explain not the occurrence of transient sense data and patterns among them, but how it is that we generate representations of enduring objects in space and, in consequence, how we justify the correct opinion from which we all start, namely, that enduring outer objects in space are the immediate objects of our perceptual consciousness. It seems to me that what Walker has Kant posit for the sake of explanation, Kant actually takes as given, and what Walker takes as given for Kant, Kant actually posits for the sake of explanation.

Many think that Kant vacillates between idealistic and realistic views, and perhaps the most common opinion, to which I myself subscribed for a long time, is that Kant is just inconsistent on this fundamental issue. Some contemporary commentators still find, as Schopenhauer did, that the first edition is heavily idealistic, but that Kant tries to mitigate his idealistic commitments in the second edition.[23] Kemp Smith thinks that the second-edition Refutation of Idealism tries to prove "the *direct opposite*" of the first-edition refutation of idealism (found in the fourth Paralogism).[24] The view he finds contradicted in the second edition is that "outer appearances stand on the same level as do our inner experiences." Patricia Kitcher thinks that the "Refutation of Idealism" was put into the second edition, although it contradicts the first edition, only because "Kant was stung by the comparison of his position to Berkeley's."[25] This recurring idea that the second edition moves away from idealistic commitments is only marginally superior to the idea that both editions present an idealist philosophy. The thesis that the first edition is much more idealistic implies, in my opinion, a mistaken interpretation of both editions. Since the first edition does not present an idealist thesis at all, in the second Kant is not trying to distance himself from idealism previously espoused. The charge of inconsistency is very widely leveled at Kant as part of an interpretation that sees an irreducible commitment to idealism combined with anti-idealist aspirations and assertions. So this charge naturally falls away if we dispose of the contention that Kant does adopt fundamental idealist positions much of the time.

The views about Kant's relationship to idealism that I have cited here represent only a tiny portion of the extremely varied response that has been generated by the combination of his expressed rejection of idealism and those of his assertions that are hard to understand at all if they are not expressions of an idealist philosophy. I think it is a fair sample, and that a more extensive survey of scores or hundreds of commentators would confirm the broad pattern of idealistic interpretation exhibited here. I also think that Kant entertained idealistic conceptions of experience before he developed the critical standpoint. It does not make sense to think that he started out in philosophy with his mature anti-idealistic point of view and with the order of thinking that is contained in the *Critique*.[26] I think it is also clear that Kant's concepts of and vocabulary for mental faculties, mental activity, and mental representation are all taken over from idealistic projects of the past, and this contributes heavily to the appearance of idealism in his views, even in contexts where we all understand that he is certainly trying to express a rejection of idealism. I cannot totally exclude the thought that some idealistic-sounding passages may be rightly accounted for as vestiges of earlier idealistic convictions. To this extent, I concede that an idealistic interpretation of particular passages may sometimes be correct. But the overall ascription of idealism to Kant is not correct, and I have tried to make that completely clear. To this end, I have made the central business of the book the examination of the passages in the *Critique* that most clearly seem to demand an idealist reading.

Of course, I do not say that I am the first reader of Kant to whom it has occurred that Kant is not an idealist. As I have stressed from the outset, along with materials that seem to be obvious commitments to idealism, Kant presents various reasoned repudiations of idealism throughout the *Critique* and in other published writings, letters, and the *Nachlaß*. Everyone knows that Kant was irritated by early reactions to the *Critique* that saw an idealist philosophy in it. Although a remarkably large proportion of interpreters go right ahead with the ascription to Kant of the very idealism that they know irritated him and that he rejected himself, there are also some interpreters who try not to repeat this standard reaction. It is this irritation, and not the disingenuousness Wilkerson and

Turbayne think they detect, that led Kant to attempt to correct these mis-readings in a sort of postscript to the *Prolegomena*. When Kant adds the "Refutation of Idealism" to the second edition, and when he asserts the direct apprehension of outer objects in the preface to the second edition, he is correcting misinterpretations. He is certainly not changing his doctrine because its closeness to, or derivation from, Berkeley has been discovered by readers and reviewers, nor is he displaying an elderly weakening of the mind or a craven willingness to change his doctrine at the first appearance of criticism. And lastly, he is explaining and not contradicting what he says in the first edition.

For the most part, and unlike Wilkerson and Turbayne, interpreters of Kant assume that he does mean to reject *some* forms of idealism—perhaps most—while presenting a new form he himself qualifies with the characterization "transcendental." Many contributors to Kant scholarship have tried to make room for his assertions of basic opposition to idealism. Since many of these assertions appear right in the middle of his most idealistic-seeming passages, commentators have assumed that his rejection of idealism is obviously not a complete rejection and that the qualification "transcendental" is supposed to indicate the aspect or form of idealism that Kant retains and shares with other idealists. But I find it quite surprising that this attitude prevails in spite of the fact that Kant never qualifies his criticisms and refutations of idealism as pertaining to defective forms of idealism, or as confined to bad versions of idealism, or as limited in any way. It is the general idea that the reality we directly apprehend is mental—that is, it is the fundamental thesis of all forms of idealism—of which Kant speaks when he says that idealism accepts only one mode of intuition, the inner, and that idealists think of perception as illusion: the illusion of contact with outer nonmental things.

My principal objective in this book has not been to examine in detail what I take to be mistaken understandings of Kant by other commentators. With very few exceptions, beyond the survey in this chapter, I have not discussed the opinions of others, even though many have been very helpful to my understanding of Kant whether or not I agree with them on the issue of idealism. I have used Kant himself as the sole and sufficient source of the idea that he is presenting an idealistic philosophy. I am convinced that this interpretive stance has been popular only because, given the philosophical predispositions of most readers of Kant, idealism is so strongly suggested by his texts. To readers with a broad Cartesian orientation, the appearance of idealism in Kant is so powerful that alternatives to an idealistic reading do not easily come to mind. One of my major goals has been to explain why this is so and then to bring a non-idealistic interpretation into focus.

What seem to be "flat endorsements" of idealistic positions in Kant's writings, and theoretical developments that appear to presuppose idealism, can all be explained away—and they must be explained away if we are to reach a satisfying picture of Kant's achievement. I have not considered all of the passages in the *Critique* and other works of Kant that suggest idealism. I hope it will be conceded that that is both unnecessary and not feasible. I have examined prominent representative passages that seem to demand an overall idealistic interpretation. I believe that my treatment of these passages will suffice to indicate the way in which other passages in Kant's writings are to be understood without ascribing an idealist philosophy to him.

For a long time, I believed that, at best, one must see massive inconsistencies in Kant, and I ascribed these, as I think others have, to Kant's inability to free himself fully from the potent idealist tradition stemming from Descartes. I thought of Kant as susceptible to major and unfortunate lapses into the very Cartesian outlook that he sought to reject and replace. I took Kant's aspiration to repudiate the ubiquitous Cartesian philosophy of mind to be one of the foundations of his greatness as a thinker long before I had any adequate appreciation of his success.

Recently, more writers have been finding their way to a less idealistic Kant. As far as I know, none go nearly as far as I have in showing how the most idealistic-sounding passages can be reconciled with a realistic intention. Furthermore, no other writer seems to flatly state that Kant is just not an idealist at all or of any kind. A few stand out because they do not present an idealistic Kant. I think Henry Allison, Ermanno Bencivenga, Graham Bird, Robert Pippin, Gerold Prauss, and T. D. Weldon[27] are particularly noteworthy. In spite of their very great merit in this respect, none of these writers adequately reconciles a nonidealistic reading with Kant's seeming idealistic commitments. Prauss's solidly developed demonstration of the thesis that appearances and things-in-themselves cannot be considered to be two exclusive ontological domains (not "two sets of things," as Wilkerson supposes) was particularly helpful to me. Once this ontological dualism is collapsed, Kant's alleged idealism will promptly go with it. One of the great temptations in reading Kant is to suppose that he is a realist about things-in-themselves (no one can take these to be merely mental realities or to be in any sense fabricated by our cognitive powers) and at the same time to suppose that he is a more-or-less standard idealist when it comes to appearances. If these ontological domains are one and the same domain, as Prauss shows that they are, a realist stance concerning things-in-themselves and an idealist stance concerning appearances will not be tenable. The reality of things-in-themselves being unimpeachable, appearances, since they are the same *things*, will have to be just as real.

I find support and guidance in the writings of Henry Allison, and his work has done a great deal to call into question the dominant idealist interpretation. The public status of outer objects of experience for Kant is emphasized by Allison. I think this direction of thinking has to be carried further in order to do justice to Kant's philosophy and especially to Kant's conception of the self. For example, in explaining Kant's "empirical sense" of the contrast of idealism and realism, Allison says,

> When Kant claims that he is an empirical realist and denies that he is an empirical idealist, he is really affirming that our experience is not limited to the private domain of our own representations but includes an encounter with "empirically real" spatio-temporal objects.[28]

In my opinion, this is entirely correct but also understated. Allison seems to think that Kant's transcendental idealism is still an idealism of some sort, and he does not hesitate to discuss with apparent approval the alleged "ideality" of various things from the perspective of Kant's philosophy. At the same time, his understanding of the "ideality" of objects, invoking only ineliminable epistemic conditions for our knowledge of them, dilutes the force of "ideality" and "idealism" to virtually nothing. The burden of epistemic conditions yields an irreducible subjectivity. It is more or less standard to assume that a wholly subjective consciousness must be a consciousness of things that exist in the subject's mind. But in fact, subjectivity *per se* has no implications for the mental or non-mental status of the object of consciousness. So Allison's explication of Kant's subjectivism in terms of the imposition of subjective conditions is all to the good. But it is not clear that any of the things that satisfy the epistemic conditions for knowledge of objects are mental things. Allison does not explain why, and to what extent, the terms *idealism* and *ideal* and *ideality* are still apt for characterizing Kant's contentions. Allison appreciates the invitation to traditional idealistic interpretation that is bound up with Kant's often repeated assertion that appearances are "mere representations." However, he does not examine Kant's use of the concept of representations in sufficient depth to relieve the pressure for idealism created by so many and such prominent Kantian assertions that confine our apprehension to representations.[29] When Allison addresses himself to Kant's conception of an intuition as a singular representation that is directly related to its object (A320/B377), one gets the impression that he may retain central aspects of the traditional conception of Kant's idealism that confines acquaintance to mental things (pp. 66–68). In the context, Allison is considering a seeming contradiction in the claim that an intuition "refers immediately to its object."

> The problems is that, according to Kant's theory of sensibility, sensible intuition provides the mind only with the raw data for conceptualization, not with determinate knowledge of objects. Such knowledge requires not only that the data be given in intuition, but also that it be taken under some general description or "recognized in a concept."[30]

No one can deny that Kant speaks this way and very often gives the impression that his thinking is just as Allison represents it. But if this is accepted at face value as Kant's understanding of intuition, Allison will not be able to live up to his contention that experience includes the apprehension of outer public things. The quoted comment on Kant's view of intuition incorporates the idea that we get *raw data* for knowledge of objects only in so far as we are receptive, and that knowledge of objects belongs to another level at which the raw materials have been worked up. Then apprehension of outer objects is not direct. These ideas, familiar from our consideration of the views of Strawson, Henrich, and Putnam, fit in with phenomenalist readings, but not with the contention that spatiotemporal objects and not just representations are "encountered." Allison's discussion of the "resolution of this tension," drawing on W. H. Walsh[31], does not relieve this difficulty.

Let us consider, parenthetically, Walsh's thinking about Kant and the theme of idealism. Walsh seems to think, with a number of others already considered, that the second edition of the *Critique* is more wholehearted in its rejection of idealism than the first, with its "lame attempt to refute idealism."(p. 189). In the relevant lame attempt (at A367 ff.), although Kant urges that nonmental objects are immediately apprehended, they are only representations, so that the nonmental has been assimilated to the mental in the first place. After calling attention to the difference between empirical idealism and his transcendental idealism, Kant says that empirical idealists at best infer outer objects without real security as the cause of inner effects, while, for the transcendental idealist, outer material things are directly (noninferentially) apprehended, just as inner reality is immediately apprehended according to the *cogito*. This is no doubt "a lame attempt" for Walsh. He thinks that Kant achieves his result by arguing that outer things are immediately known since they are actually just more mental representations. I think the crucial text is this one:

> The transcendental idealist can also be an empirical realist, or, as it is called, a dualist, that is, he can accept the existence of matter, without going beyond self-consciousness and without assuming more than the certainty of representations in me, that is, the *cogito ergo sum*. He regards this *matter,* and indeed its inner possibility, as merely appearance, which, if separated from our sensibility, is nothing. Thus, material objects are only a class of representations (intuition), which are called "external," not as though they are related to objects that are external considered in themselves, but just because they relate perceptions to space where all things are located with respect to one another, while space itself is in us. (A370)

I cannot resist a final opportunity to explain how this seemingly idealistic discussion should be understood. When one has become habituated to reading Kant in the setting of Cartesian assumptions, this kind of passage will sound so obviously idealistic that the contention that we immediately apprehend outer objects, and hence can refute idealism, does not sound merely "lame," as Walsh says, it sounds preposterous—simply not to be taken seriously at all. But we cannot lightly assume that Kant has forgotten that outer sense contrasts with inner in that by means of the latter we apprehend the mind and its states, and by means of the former we apprehend, *in contrast to mental things,* objects in space. He has not forgotten that the doctrine of the Categories requires that outer objects endure through alterations, and thus that they exist in intervals during which they are not perceived. Since he has not forgotten these things, we have to dispel the idealistic appearance of this passage. That is not nearly as hard to do as it looks. Kant is emphasizing a parallelism of inner and outer sense, not a reduction of outer to inner. Both generate appearances, that is, apprehension of reality as it appears. Inner sense does not reach the mind as it is in itself, but no one argues, for that reason, that the mental things we apprehend may not exist. They are given in the apprehension of them. The same is true of outer appearances. Our own self-consciousness proves the existence of material things as objects of outer sense, just as much as it proves the existence of our own mental states when we apprehend these via inner sense. This is how Kant is using the *cogito.* He is not saying, as a Cartesian might, that material things are guaranteed by our experience because they are really things we find in our minds. Outer material things are guaranteed by our experience of those outer material things, just as inner mental things are guaranteed by our experience of inner mental things. In both cases, we reach only appearances. Where the empirical idealist thinks we apprehend only inner effects, Kant substitutes the idea that we apprehend only subjective appearances. In both the inner and the outer case, the item apprehended is called a "representation" because it is subjective, it is reality *as represented*. In neither case is an appearance called a representation because it is a mental reality. The subjective appearance of an object in space is not a mental thing in consequence of its subjectivity, and Kant does not say that it is a mental thing. "Space is in us" is not intended to mentalize space, and Kant does not mean that in the last analysis everything we apprehend is mental. That would be a renunciation of the whole of Kant's scheme of things. "Space is in us" is a way of saying that the fact that things are spatially related comes from us and is not a feature of realities as they are in themselves. For this reason, Kant speaks of the "inner possibility" (*innere Möglichkeit*) of matter. Space is the inner possibility because it comes from our cognitive constitution and not from the world independent of us. But the realized possibility, that is, actual spatial objects, are not inner things. Our cognitive constitution spatializes nonmental things in making possible our subjective apprehension of them. Our contribution does not make mental things of outer things, but space is *our* contribution to nonmental appearances that are outside us but not as they are in themselves. Thus everything we know about outer things is qualified by this subjectivity. But it does not tend at all to make the objects we are able to perceive into things inside our minds. That is why it makes sense to say that the transcendental idealist is a dualist. And of course, if he is a dualist, then he is not an idealist and his transcendental idealism is not a form of idealism.

Walsh also thinks that, in the Transcendental Aesthetic, Kant's attempt to avoid a typical idealism like that of Locke and Berkeley is just unsuccessful. The uniqueness of space cannot be affirmed, because we are confronted with private sense data, and in consequence there are "as many spaces as there are perceivers."(p. 32) Considering the wider context that takes in the Transcendental Analytic, Walsh again raises privacy objections that are much like Strawson's. Because of Kant's conception of perceptual experience, he is faced with, and does not satisfactorily overcome, the confinement of each subject to his own domain of mental realities. Walsh contemplates the possibility that Kant means to introduce knowledge of public objects at the level of judgment only. But a lot stands in the way of such an effort:

The sensory content in my mind may well correspond to or resemble the sensory content in yours, but the two cannot be literally identical. But if, as seems reasonable to hold, judgment gets basic material from sensation, will not that mean that judgment too has a purely personal side? Will it not turn out, in fact, that Kant's supposed later position is substantially the same as the view he held at first, according to which knowledge begins with the contemplation of something which is private and advances from that to the grasp of an objective world?[32]

Walsh concludes this theme with the thought that if there is a way of vindicating a Kantian commitment to public objects, it requires that we ascribe to him views about sensation and judgment that he does not state at all. Here again, I want to draw special attention to the thought that Walsh locates Kant's problems and prospects thoroughly within the framework of the Cartesian egocentric stance. Now that I do not look at Kant in this way, it seems to me remarkable that I, like Walsh, Strawson, and so many others, was able to imagine that Kant is confronted by all of the traditional problems of privacy and solipsism although he doesn't seem to notice these enormous problems at all. He never hints at a means of extricating himself from the circle of his own consciousness, which he would have to do on the supposition that he thinks that our experience at the level of the given is confined to things in our own minds. Add to this the fact that Kant does say that the great error of idealism is that it accepts only one mode of receptivity, namely, the inner sense that offers access only to the mind and its modifications. Somehow philosophers, including myself in the past, manage to ignore all that and to ascribe that very error to Kant himself. In contrast, I have argued that Kant's ordering of knowledge, receptivity, and mental states does not raise these problems, and that intentionally outflanking them was the first order of business for Kant.

In contrast to Allison's explanation of empirical realism quoted above, I have argued that directly apprehended real spatiotemporal objects are not merely included along with private representations as objects of immediate experience. Kant reverses the priorities of idealist thought. Public things in space exhaust the objects of experience in the first instance. These are the only true objects of perception. Because there is no scope for the concept of sensation in inner receptivity, "objects" of inner experience, *per se,* have a derivative and/or mediated status. They are never true objects in the sense in which the Categories are "concepts of an object in general." Inner realities are not *perceivable* in any non-metaphorical sense. Sense experiences are not enduring things in which all change must be alteration. For these reasons, our own sense experiences cannot be among the things that are objects for us. Kant's "raw data," to which Allison alludes, has to be understood as part of a theoretical account of experience and not as the actual given in experience at all. Outer sense is our receptivity relative to nonmental things, and inner sense, considered as a second source of empirical knowledge, is merely our receptivity to our representations of outer sense. That we have a certain consciousness of ourselves and of our inner mental states is entirely dependent upon our apprehension of nonmental outer things. The idealist picture of the starting point in epistemology—that is, the subject of experience initially contemplating a domain of what is "given" limited to the mental realities that constitute its own conscious experience—is turned upside down by Kant. Kant finds that the very idea of such a starting point is not coherent. Our consciousness itself, with all of our empirical knowledge, including self-knowledge, rests on the encounters with the public, nonmental, spatiotemporal objects that Allison merely includes among Kant's objects of experience.

Robert Pippin's work also embodies an admirable nonidealistic understanding of Kant's views. Pippin is particularly lucid against the supposition that Kant is a phenomenalist:

> Kant is not claiming that transcendental idealism means to "reduce" all claims about material objects to claims about sense experience.[33]

and

> We do have knowledge of external objects, but we can only understand such objects in terms of rule-governed synthesis of representations, that is, in terms of judgment and intuition.[34]

This seems to me to be just right. We have knowledge of external objects. The concepts of rule-governed synthesis, and representations, and even the enforcement of rigorous distinction between our faculties of judgment and intuition, all belong to the project of understanding how we are able to have this knowledge. It is not as though one has to be attentive to one's representations and apply the right rules while synthesizing them in order to know external things. Knowledge of external objects is what sense experience is, at least when appearances are not misleading. The representations, and synthesis and forms imposed by intuition and understanding, figure only in our explanation of the possibility of such knowledge. The synthesis and the representations are not manifest in knowledge of external things. They must be present as Kant says they are, and they must play the roles that Kant says they do, if his theoretical account of our knowledge is correct. The *a priori* necessity of Kant's theses derives from the claim that they are necessary conditions for the knowledge of the world that we do attain. That we do have such knowledge is a premise for Kant. It is the given to be accounted for, the given against which Kant's theory involving space and time, the synthesis of raw materials, and the unity of apperception can be judged to be adequate or inadequate.

I cannot say that this is certainly what Pippin intends in the above citation, although something like this is suggested by his formulation. In urging us to understand that Kant does not think of us as hopelessly separated from reality behind a "veil of appearances," Pippin makes use of Kant's expression "objects as they are in themselves." Although we never get to know reality apart from the conditions imposed by our own forms of receptivity and judgment, "we do know the empirical world as *it* is in itself."[35] In the long run, I think this bold thesis about empirical knowledge does more harm than good in Pippin's exegesis of Kant. He proposes that this understanding of Kant's seeming willingness to say things about things-in-themselves is responsible for the widespread rejection of his concept of such things:

> If we can know all experienceable objects as *they* are in themselves, subject to our forms of experience, why go on to insist that we cannot know how things "really" are in themselves? Almost everyone initially sympathetic to Kant, from Solomon Maimon, the German Idealists, and neo-Kantians, to Strawsonian austere reconstructions. has tried to eliminate this noumenal dimension to Kant's theory.[36]

If Pippin were right about the reasoning of all these philosophers in their repudiation of the doctrine of permanent ignorance of things-in-themselves, that repudiation would be based on a realist reading of Kant. Pippin is saying that others reject Kant's *ignorabimus* because Kant claims that we do have knowledge of things outside the mind, namely, empirical objects in space, and that, knowing empirical objects *as such*— that is, as subject to formal conditions we impose—we know them as they are in themselves.[37] But although it is quite true that all those philosophers reject the doctrine of things-in-themselves, it is not true that they interpret Kant as a realist. On the contrary, all or almost all of them are initially in sympathy with Kant interpreted as an idealist. Either, like the German Idealists, they approve of the idealism and do not want it to be qualified by the assertion of a reality independent of mind or, like

Strawson, they disapprove of the idealism and do not want to have us permanently out of reach of knowledge of mind-independent reality.

There is something wrong with the very idea of knowledge of empirical objects (that is, of appearances) as they are in themselves. Kant uses this phrase himself. But I believe it is only in contexts where he wants to distinguish between misleading appearances, such as optical illusions, and appearances that are not misleading. In no case will it be correct to speak as Pippin does, that is, as though Kant agrees that sometimes we do have knowledge of things as they are in themselves, namely, knowledge of empirical things when we recognize that they are appearances and thus known as conforming to conditions imposed by our minds.

We cannot speak this way because things considered in themselves and things considered as they appear to us are the same things. It is things-in-themselves that "appear," as Kant likes to say. Things-in-themselves are the things that affect us and thus engender experience. Therefore, to know an empirical things *is* to know things as they appear. If we were to allow Pippin's locution, we would have to say both (1) that knowledge of empirical things is knowledge of things as they appear to us and (2) that knowledge of empirical things is knowledge of things-in-themselves. If we are clear about what we mean, we may assert either of these. But when we are thinking in terms of one, we are excluding the other. If we want to stress that experience of things in space is our way of knowing reality, we will assert (2). If we want to remind ourselves that encounters with spatial things afford only subjective descriptions of things, we will assert (1). Appearances get their standing in the context of knowledge from the fact that they are appearances of reality. If they were not appearances of things-in-themselves, then there would be no empirical knowledge. This is the reason for the ineliminability of things-in-themselves. Were it not for their relation to things-in-themselves, empirical things would be, using a Kantian phrase from another context, less even than a dream. So even in the work of an anti-idealist reader of Kant as acute as Robert Pippin, there may be a residue of the standard idealist line of thinking when he says that our knowledge of empirical objects as empirical objects is knowledge of them as they are in themselves.

In spite of the work of opponents of traditional idealistic interpretations, the notion that Kant denies that we directly apprehend a public and physical world continues to dominate the thinking of most students of Kant, and for that matter, most teachers of Kant. When we survey the assertions and developed arguments in the *Critique of Pure Reason* and

Notes

PREFACE

1. See, for example, Jonathan Bennett, *Locke, Berkeley, Hume* (Oxford: Oxford University Press, 1971) pp. 136–137. Bennett is also among those who interpret Kant's transcendental idealism as a form of phenomenalism, and hence as a form of idealism. Thus, in *Kant's Analytic* (Cambridge: Cambridge University Press, 1966), p. 24, Bennett says, "The transcendental idealist takes 'There are nonmental things' to say something about actual and possible experiences."

2. Simon Blackburn, *Oxford Dictionary of Philosophy* (Oxford: Oxford University Press, 1994), p. 184. This definition, bringing transcendental idealism under idealism in general, would be satisfactory were an exception made for Kant's transcendental idealism. Schelling, for example, calls his philosophy, which certainly is idealistic, "transcendental idealism." But such an exception would itself be perverse, and the definition quoted is surely, though mistakenly, intended to cover Kant.

CHAPTER 1. KANT AND THE CARTESIAN PHILOSOPHY OF MIND

1. The conceptual priority of empirical objects asserted here is a general guideline for Kant's thinking in the *Critique*. I am not merely calling attention to a result endorsed by Kant in the context of his account of *empirical* knowledge. The expression of this guideline is Kant's idea that the conclusions of the "critical" philosophy have no application to anything other than experience and the objects of experience. The shared empirical world *is* the world.

2. Bxxxix. These words are to be inserted at B275, in the Refutation of Idealism, according to Kant's instructions in the preface to the second edition.

3. "Allein hier wird bewiesen, daß äußere Erfahrung eigentlich unmittlebar sei . . ." (B276–277); and ". . . innere Erfahrung selbst nur mittelbar und nur durch äußere möglich ist" (B277).

4. "Mein sogenannter (eigentlich kritischer) Idealism ist also von ganz eigentümlicher Art, nämlich so, daß er den gewöhnlichen [Idealism] umstürzt, daß durch ihn alle Erkenntniß a priori, selbst die der Geometrie, zuerst objektive Realität bekommt, welche ohne diese meine bewiesene Idealität des Raumes und der Zeit, selbst von dem eifrigsten Realisten nicht behaupten werden könnte. Bei solcher Bewandtniß der Sachen wünschte ich, um allen Mißverstand zu verhüten, daß ich diesen meinen Begriff anders benennen könnte." (*Prolegomena*, Anhang, *Werke*, Akad., IV, p. 375). In short, transcendental idealism is essentially a critical doctrine, and it overthrows what is commonly called "idealism." Kant here appreciates that it would have been a good idea not to use a title that suggests that his is a version of idealism. As we shall see, the point to which Kant alludes in saying that his idealism is "critical" is that it exposes the error of empirical idealists who think that introspection acquaints us not with a realm of inner appearance but with absolute reality, or with things as they are in themselves. Thus, transcendental idealism exposes an illusion to which ordinary ("*den gewöhnlichen*") idealism is susceptible. It is an essentially negative view, and Kant does not put forward any positive idealist thesis at all. In a footnote at the same point in the text, Kant says that the goal of his critical idealism is exhausted in showing how *a priori* knowledge of objects of experience is possible.

5. Ibid., p. 374. It is often said that Kant does not really know Berkeley's work and misrepresents it. This seems to me to be very likely. Berkeley does not think that what is ordinarily taken for knowledge of outer objects is an illusion. On his principles, it is quite feasible to distinguish between illusions and perceptions. In the quoted passage, Kant does not ascribe to Berkeley the view that what passes for empirical knowledge is illusion but only the view that "all knowledge of things out of pure understanding or pure reason" is illusion. As far as I know, Berkeley never addresses the status of knowledge fitting this very Kantian characterization.

6. See H. J. DeVleeschauwer, *La déduction transcendentale dans l'oeuvre de Kant* (1934; reprint, 3 vols., New York: Garland Publishing, 1976). Vol. II, p. 334. DeVleeschauwer refers this idea to Natorp and Windelband. A somewhat similar idea is developed by Schelling in the identification of the transcendental subject with a universal "*Geist.*"

7. P. F. Strawson, *The Bounds of Sense* (London: Methuen, 1966), p. 196. Strawson's understanding of Kant is discussed in the last chapter of the present study.

8. Most contemporary materialists accept the broad characterization of *inner* mental phenomena offered by Descartes and differ essentially only in allocating these phenomena to the brain and the nervous system rather than to a nonphysical status and to events taking place even further "inside" the subject, as we might put it. The behaviorists, too, accept the Cartesian contention that psychological discourse such as ascription of belief refers to facts about subjects that have to be constituted in them somehow and, in the spirit of this assumption,

they offer complex dispositions as making up what it is about a subject by virtue of which we can ascribe mental states to him. For a detailed critique of these Cartesian assumptions and a presentation of a non-Cartesian way of thinking about mental concepts, see my book *The Nature of Mental Things* (Notre Dame, Ind.: University of Notre Dame Press, 1987).

9. David Hume, A *Treatise of Human Nature* (London: J. M. Dent & Sons, 1911) I, ii, 4.

10. Bertrand Russell, *The Problems of Philosophy* (London: Williams and Norgate, 1912), chap. 2.

CHAPTER 2. SUBJECTIVISM VERSUS IDEALISM

1. The "patchwork theory" of the composition of the *Critique*, developed in great detail by Erich Adickes and promoted by Norman Kemp Smith, testifies to this complex of difficulties facing the reader. In particular, Kant's liking for unannounced recapitulations and fresh starts makes such a radical hypothesis plausible. To a considerable extent, the patchwork conception depends upon finding inconsistencies in Kant's doctrines that I believe are only apparent. When the notion that Kant is presenting an idealist philosophy and a "phenomenalism" is set aside, the seeming inconsistencies are dispelled for the most part, and the occasion for an hypothesis as extreme as the patchwork theory goes with them. See Norman Kemp Smith, *A Commentary to Kant's 'Critique of Pure Reason,'* 2d ed. (New York: Humanities Press, 1962), pp. xx–xxi.

2. Descartes's *Regulae* provide a good example of a speculative account in which the physical features of bodies that induce conscious perception of colors are identified with various patterns in the stimulus which do not involve color at all. This account prefigures and may be the source of Locke's contention that secondary qualities of which the ideas are experienced as colors are, in themselves, merely fine-grained structures of primary qualities. See René Descartes, *Regulae*, Adam and Tannery eds., *Ouvres de Descartes*, 11 vols. (Paris: J. Vrin, 1974), p. 413; and John Locke, *Essay Concerning Human Understanding* (Oxford: Oxford University Press, 1975), bk. II, §viii.

3. For a discussion of subjectivity and secondary qualities compatible with the view that I propose here, see C. McGinn, *The Subjective View* (Oxford: Oxford University Press, 1983), chaps. 3, 8.

CHAPTER 3. IDEALISM AND TRANSCENDENTAL IDEALISM

1. "Denn der äußere Sinn ist schon an sich Beziehung der Anschauung auf etwas Wirkliches außer mir" (Bxl). This draws on Kant's account of the distinction between inner and outer sense presented prominently at the opening of the Transcendental Aesthetic, A22–23, B37.

2. B278. Kant sums up, "Es hat hier, nur, bewiesen werden sollen daß innere Erfahrung überhaupt nur durch äußere Erfahrung überhaupt möglich sei" (Here we only have to prove that inner experience in general is only possible through outer experience). The point is that the general dependence of inner on outer

experience is not compromised by aberrant cases where, only on the basis of past normal perception, a subject can seem to make out an outer reality when there is no such reality present.

3. Of course, idealists do not always or even for the most part use the term *idea* as a general expression for any mental reality. Perhaps Berkeley comes close to this usage, apart from his thesis that, in addition to ideas, we have a "notion" of spirits or subjects that have ideas. The familiar expression "the way of ideas," characterizing the philosophical turning that engendered all the traditional versions of idealism, does use "idea" as a general term for a mental reality in the same spirit as the discussion here.

4. As I will show in chapters 11 and 12, the assertion of parallelism between inner and outer receptivity contains serious difficulties that I do not believe can be explained away. In any case, those difficulties do not indicate that some kind of overall idealistic interpretation of Kant is feasible after all, or that Kant has to accept some kind of apprehension of things considered as they are in themselves.

5. A369. See also A491, B519. Kant's identification of appearances as "*bloße Vorstellungen*" is an example of his ambiguous use of the concept of representation. As applied to space and time themselves, either as the forms of outer and inner sense respectively, or as formal intuitions, Kant's explicit assertion that they are empirically real and transcendentally ideal needs to be appropriately unpacked. Space and time are not empirical objects, as the metaphysical expositions make clear. Nor are they things-in-themselves. But the intent of empirical realism and transcendental idealism is not mysterious in its application to space and time. They are empirically real because it is only in the empirical domain that spatiality or temporality are exemplified. They are transcendentally ideal in that there are no transcendental realities that correspond to our ideas of space and time.

6. "Der Idealismus (ich verstehe den Materialen) . . ." (B274).

7. For example, at B147, Kant explains that mathematical propositions are true only by virtue of their potential application to objects of experience. Although Kant speaks of the construction of objects of mathematics in pure intuition in explicating the *a priori* character of mathematics, such pure objects are not ontological competitors of the objects of which the Categories are concepts precisely because constructions in pure intuition are at best mental things, which objects of experience are not. This shows itself in the fact that a geometrical figure constructed in pure intuition is not spatially locatable with respect to the furniture of the outer world. It is at best a quasispatial object, since it is not to be found in the unique all-embracing matrix of public spatial existence.

8. F. H. Jacobi, *Werke* (Leipzig, 1812–1825), vol. 2, p. 301, quoted in G. Martin, *Kant: Ontologie und Wissenschaftstheorie* (Berlin: Walter de Gruyter & Co., 1969), p. 159 (my translation). Jacobi's rejection of both the empirical object and the "transcendental object" for the role of the "object that affects us" is understandable if we read Kant as asserting that spatial objects reduce to complexes of representations that are concatenated by our own mental activity. But I am saying that we have to read Kant so that enduring nonmental, empirical

objects can and do stimulate our sense organs. To the extent that there is a Kantian thesis that must be *explained away,* it is the thesis that empirical objects exist only "in us," and in particular, in our faculty of representations.

9. Ibid., p. 160.

CHAPTER 4. ARE THINGS-IN-THEMSELVES NOUMENA?

1. All these terms are applied to noumena in the chapter at the end of the Analytic entitled "Von dem Grunde der Unterscheidung aller Gegenstände überhaupt in Phaenomena und Noumena."

2. No doubt, in the setting of his moral writings, Kant does not give prominence to any such qualifications about the existence of noumena. Nonetheless, the globally hypothetical structure of the *Groundwork,* for example, implies that, for all the scope given to the idea of a noumenal self, Kant's doctrine is strictly compatible with the cautious exposition from the *Critique of Pure Reason* that I have summarized. The theory of the free, rational, noumenal self appears as the culmination of Kant's exploration of the metaphysical presuppositions of the reality of duty. According to Kant, we all—understandably—believe that not all actions can be seen as the satisfaction of inclinations. Thus we believe that there are or can be human actions that are motivated by a sense of duty. Kant even argues that we must understand our action under the assumption of freedom, which entails a noumenal realm. He does not purport to prove that these universal beliefs are correct. Thus the theoretical conclusions of the *Groundwork* are valid only within the scope of an undischarged hypothesis of the reality of duty.

3. "Damit aber ein Noumenon einen wahren, von allen Phänomenen zu unterscheidenden Gegenstand bedeute, so ist es nicht genug: daß meinen Gedanken von allen Bedingungen sinnlicher Anschauung befreie, ich muß noch überdem Grund dazu haben, eine andere Art der Anschauung als diese sinnliche ist, anzunehmen, unter der ein solcher Gegenstand gegeben werden könne, denn sonst ist mein Gedanke doch leer, obzwar ohne Widerspruch" (A252). In the absence of this "positive" characterization, Kant speaks of a negative concept of noumena, but such a concept is not properly a characterization of any kind of object at all. The merely negative concept collapses into that of things considered as they are in themselves (B308). But in this context, too, Kant makes clear that if the concept is to function in the schema "phenomena vs. noumena" by means of which existing entities might be classified, the idea of a suitable form of intuition cannot be omitted from the concept of a noumenon.

4. Kant's thinking about noumena in the context of God's mental powers has just the same logical relation to a commitment to the reality of noumena as does his moral thinking as summarized in note 2. He believes that there is a God who apprehends all reality without being affected by things. Thus he *believes* that all things-in-themselves are noumena. But this a matter of faith. The existence of things-in-themselves is not a matter of faith but an ineliminable commitment of Kant's philosophy. If there were nothing that might affect us and thus give rise to appearances in the first place, there could be no empirical objects and no consciousness, according to Kant. No comparably definitive argument given by Kant

guarantees the existence of God, the reality of moral judgment, or the existence
of a single exemplification of the concept of noumena.

CHAPTER 5. THE CONCEPT OF REPRESENTATION

1. "Dieses ist nun der Grund einer dreifachen Synthesis, die notwendigerweise
in allem Erkenntnis vorkommt: nämlich, der *Apprehension* der Vorstellungen,
als Modifikation des Gemüts in der Anschauung, der *Reproduktion* derselben in
der Einbildung, und ihrer *Rekognition* im Begriffe" (A97, Kant's emphasis).

2. The idea behind these forbidding Kantian terms is that inner representations are essentially transient, so that past representations, even those in the
immediate past, are not accessible to be taken up together with any *present* representation for the purpose of mental combination (synthesis) or construction.
Imagination, which is for Kant the thought of what is not actually present, comes
into play in order to reproduce the past representations, engendering something
that, since it is present, can be combined with other present representations.

3. Just this shift from an idealistic A-edition to a much more realistic B-edi-
tion has been detected by large numbers of readers of Kant from Schopenhauer
to P. F. Strawson and Paul Guyer. Although it is easy to see explicit realist claims
in the second edition, the idea of such a shift is not at all convincing to me. Unless
we are able to understand the first edition without the idealism, the explicitly
realistic passages added will seem to be incoherently tacked on to a work that is
too profoundly committed to idealism to accept such revisions. In fact, this is
pretty much what Schopenhauer thought, as did numerous other readers of
Kant.

4. In the first few lines of his account of space and time, Kant says expressly,
"Time cannot be intuited as something outer, any more than space as something
in us" (A23, B37).

5. The passage is intended to clarify what "an *object* of representation"
means. Kant says that such objects are "sensible representations that must not
be regarded as objects apart from the power of representation" (*außer der
Vorstellungskraft*). Then he says that the thought of something corresponding
to such an object is merely "something in general = X, since we have nothing
apart from our knowledge [*außer unserer Erkenntnis*] that we might set over
against that knowledge." Notice that *außer* cannot literally mean "outside" in
a spatial sense here, since "our knowledge" does not define or occupy a spatial
region. In other words, Kant says that we do not have a way of apprehending
things not subject to the conditions of our receptivity by virtue of which we could
compare the object as represented, that is, the appearance, with the object as it
is apart from our conditions of representation.

6. "Weil indessen der Ausdruck: *außer uns,* eine nicht zu vermeidende Zwei-
deutigkeit bei sich führt, indem er bald etwas bedeutet, was als Dinge an sich
selbst von uns unterschieden existiert, bald was bloß zur äußeren Erscheinung
gehört, so wollen wir um diesen Begriff in der lezteren Bedeutung, als in welcher
eigentlich die psychologische Frage, wegen der Realität unserer äußeren
Anschauung, genommen wird, außer Unsicherheit zu setzten, empirisch äußer-
liche Gegenstände dadurch von denen, die sie so im transzendentalen Sinne

heißen möchten, unterscheiden, daß wir sie geradezu Dinge nennen, die *im Raume anzutreffen sind*" (A373, emphasis Kant's). In sum, Kant does not assert that we apprehend and have knowledge of anything "outside us," where that means "apart from our subjective spatiotemporal receptive faculties," but he certainly does assert that we do apprehend things "outside us" when that means "things that are to be met with in space," and in fact, his aim is to reject definitively the claim of idealists that the existence of such objects in space outside the mind is uncertain or false.

7. For example, see A38, B55; and B276.

8. *Nouveaux essais de l'entendement par l'auteur du système de l'harmonie préetablie*, II, xxiii, 2 (my translation, italics added).

9. Ibid., II, xxiii, 4.

10. I take this opportunity to draw attention to another Leibnizian idea that suggests Kant's views, whether or not it was a direct influence. In the preceding chapter of the *Nouveaux essais*, where Locke's chapter "On Power" is under discussion, Leibniz envisions an analysis that will be deeper than, and stand as explanation of, Locke's account of primary and secondary qualities. In the course of his remarks, he tells us that our consciousness of our own thoughts is conditioned by our consciousness of other things, and outer perceived things in particular: "Les sens nous fournissent la matière aux reflexions et nous ne penserions pas même à la pensée, si nous ne pensions à quelque autre chose, c'est à dire aux particularités que les sens fournissent" (II, xxi, 73).

The passage prefigures, whether or not it influences, Kant's assertion, already cited above, that the understanding must be given materials from sensible intuition in order to attain knowledge, as well as the Kantian doctrine that thought about thought itself is conditioned by thought about sensible objects.

11. Following Erdmann.

12. An explicit assertion of this ordering of the relationship between, on the one hand, illusions, dreams, and imaginings and, on the other, actual apprehension of outer realities is found in the discussion of the fourth Paralogism at A375. This passage is discussed in some detail in the next chapter.

13. This equation involves the usage that collapses representation and represented into the outer, as discussed above.

14. Whether or not this is a correct characterization of Berkeley's view, it is the view that Kant ascribes to Berkeley in making his philosophy the paradigm for dogmatic idealism, just as Descartes is Kant's paradigm for problematic idealism.

15. Kant says that the appearance of paradox is dispelled by attention to the difference between apperception and inner sense, but his discussion accepts the underlying assumption that the affecting reality that generates the empirical representation of the subject is the subject as it is in itself. As in the case of outer objects, only an empirical reality comes to be known. Thus, "die Bestimmungen des inneren Sinnes gerade als dieselbe Art als Erscheinungen in der Zeit ordnen müssen, wie wir die der äußeren Sinne im Raume ordnen, mithin, wenn wir von den letzteren einräumen, daß wir dadurch Objekte nur sofern erkennen, als wir äußerlich affiziert werden, wir auch vom inneren Sinne zugestehen müssen, daß wir dadurch uns selbst nur so anschauen, wie wir innerlich von uns selbst affiziert

werden, d.i., was die innere Anschauung betrifft, unser eigenes Subjekt nur als Erscheinung, nicht aber nach dem, was es an sich selbst ist, erkennen" (B156).

16. In the first chapter of *Kant und das Problem der Dinge an sich*" (Bonn: Bouvier, 1976), Prauss makes an exhaustive survey of Kant's use of *Ding an sich*, *Ding an sich betrachtet*, and related expressions. In discourse about Kant's philosophy, the prevalence of *Ding an sich*, used as a designation for a distinctive reality other than the reality exemplified by appearances is shown by Prauss to be an artifact of commentators, starting from the first generation of readers of Kant. Attention to the exact words in the great preponderance of cases in which Kant makes or appeals to the relevant distinction does not at all support this traditional and prevailing attitude toward the concept of things as they are in themselves.

CHAPTER 6. "SPACE IS *IN* US"

1. See *Prolegomena*, §13. For the gist of the problem of incongruent counterparts see p. 70 and note 10 in this chapter.

2. This conception appears in several passages, for example, A240, B299 and A713–14, B741–42.

3. Such *wirkliche Wesen* would be things-in-themselves, on Kant's understanding. Newton's account of space and time fails because it makes things of forms. Forms represent only the possibility of objects, and all of these possible objects are empirical objects since they are spatiotemporal.

4. A37–39.

5. What about the thesis of uniqueness? Does it apply to time as it does to space, and how shall we understand the privacy of inner representations if everyone's representations are located in one and the same time to which we all have access, as we all have access to the same space? Kant's stand on these issues reinforces our contentions about the publicness of space. He does assert a parallel uniqueness of time. This will mean that all temporal things, all mental events, in the first instance, stand in temporal relations to one another. A thought in my mind has to be before or after or simultaneous with any mental reality in your mind. But Kant recognizes that the temporal relation between my mental contents and yours presents a problem. Even the temporal order of my own mental states needs something external to them to ground what Kant calls an "objective time order." Ultimately it is the endurance of outer spatial realities that serves as a foundation for such a time order. An objective time order is one that is rooted in *objects* that exist in our shared perceptual world. The temporal relations among my mental states and between mine and yours are established through relations to enduring spatial realities. Only the material world can furnish a clock within which the ordering of our transient private representations can be conceptually stabilized. This theme appears in scattered pieces in the Transcendental Deduction, the Refutation of Idealism, and the Paralogisms. I return to these matters in chapters 11 and 12.

6. Suppose we take Kant to be positing pure triangles as things that we can construct in our own visual space. Perhaps he thinks that we can then, in some sense, read off mathematical truths from these spatial objects of our own man-

ufacture, truths such as the fact that any two sides of a triangle must always be longer than the third. This way of thinking faces the familiar problem of the generality of conclusions drawn upon consideration of a particular mental triangle. Apart from this, the idea of contemplation of an entity constructed in the mind generates special problems of interpersonal generality, as well as problems of spatial relations with outer spatial things that are not mental at all. For example, if I construct a mental triangle, I cannot say that this constructed object is "in this very room" or "more than one hundred miles from the Caspian Sea." Thus, mutual locatability, which is part of the very point of the spatial form of objects, cannot be extended to pure objects. Figures constructed in the mind will not be of any particular dimension, although the area of a mental semicircle will be half that of the mental circle. Along with the privacy of pure spatial objects, we will lose reidentifiability. The contrast between contemplating the very same isosceles triangle constructed in pure intuition *again* and contemplating a *different* but exactly similar isosceles triangle constructed in pure intuition will have no significance. To the extent that Kant is appealing to the immediate access that a subject has to his own mental constructs, that person would have to worry lest the truths he might enunciate fail to conform to constructs others make of spatial objects accessible only to those others. Worst of all, if Kant's thinking is moving along these lines, the idea of immediate access to inner spatial things conflicts with his healthy insistence that outer intuition is *immediate* apprehension of outer spatial things, and his general confinement of spatiality to things that are not mental at all. All in all, the thought that we might be able to explicate geometrical truth in terms of access to private constructions is full of grave problems and little promise.

7. See Leibniz's fifth paper, §29.

8. Leibniz's relational theory of space is, one might say, *too objective* according to Kant, even though Leibniz does not make space a system of relations between things-in-themselves but, in a sense that is certainly not wholly different from that of Kant, confines spatiality to *phenomena*.

9. The grammatical clue to the meaning of the third option is even more prominent in Kant's German. The first, Newtonian, alternative is expressed in the question "Sind es wirkliche Wesen?" The second, Leibnizian, alternative asks "Sind es zwar nur Bestimmungen oder auch Verhältnisse der Dinge, aber doch *solche* welche ihnen auch an sich zukommen würden, wenn sie auch nicht angeschaut würden," and the third possibility, continuing the same sentence, is framed, with the help of the Leibnizian doctrine just expressed, in the question ". . . oder sind *sie solche* die nur an der Form der Anschauung allein haften. . . ?" I have added the emphases to call attention to the fact that the expression of the final option incorporates the Leibnizian feature that identifies space and time as systems of relations among things rather than entities and differs only in substituting Kant's subjective origin of the systems of relations for Leibniz's objective conception. Both Leibniz's view and Kant's take space and time to be "determinations or relations of things." For Leibniz, these determinations or relations would apply to things even if we did not intuit those things, and for Kant, the determinations or relations apply only to the form of intuition and would not fit anything were it not for such intuition of things.

10. This whole discussion of incongruent counterparts requires a hypothetical framework, since it seems very doubtful that we should think that counterparts must fill different regions of absolute space. We know that such counterparts in a plane do not really fill different regions, in that one counterpart can occupy the space of the other if rotated in the third dimension. This reflection has to deflate the intuitive feeling that there really is an intrinsic difference between a left and a right glove so that, if the only spatial thing in existence was one glove, it would still make sense to say that it is a left-hand glove. If there really is no intrinsic difference between incongruent counterparts, then the example of such figures would not seem to support a theory of absolute space. If there is a difference, a subjective relational theory ought to explain it as well as an absolute theory. If we take space to be the system of possible outer (non-mental) objects, Kant's solution to the problem of incongruent counterparts will be the claim that the possibility of existence of a right-hand glove differs intrinsically from the possibility of existence of a left-hand glove. If this claim is false, it is false because the counterparts in question are not really incongruent. Just as two-dimensional incongruent counterparts can be shown to be congruent after all, so too could three-dimensional counterparts be shown to be congruent by rotating one of them in a fourth dimension.

CHAPTER 7. OUTER CAUSES OF PERCEPTION

1. Note that "sensible relations" presumably refers to space and time here. Sensation provides a manifold of representations that determine an object when represented elements are related to one another spatially and temporally so as to produce an entity with spatiotemporal integrity. If this is correct, the passage contains a more or less explicit assertion that space and time can be thought of as systems of relations, in the manner of Leibniz, as long as one adds the subjective source of the relations in question.

2. The parenthetical disclaimer concerning the objects constituting this outer reality, "*ohne diesen zu bestimmen*," may express the idea that, in experience, we do not find out anything about things-in-themselves. The predicates that we ascribe to objects on the basis of perception do not fit the mind-independent something that appears to us. They all fit only the appearance, which is, at the same time, an appearance of that reality that remains uncharacterizable considered as it is in itself.

3. I would like to draw attention to this confirmation of the essential Leibnizian strands prominent in Kant's conception of space as not itself a reality.

4. This passage articulates the faults to which I have drawn attention in the conception of judgments of perception that Kant proposes so atypically and rashly in the *Prolegomena*. See the discussion on pages 52–53.

5. "Die Anschauung eines Dinges als außer mir setzt das Bewußtsein einer Bestimmbarkeit meines Subjekt voraus, bei welchem ich nicht selbst bestimmend bin, die also nicht zur Spontaneität gehört, weil das Bestimmende nicht in mir ist. Und in der Tat kann ich mir keinen Raum als in mir denken. Also ist die Möglichkeit [einen] Dinge in Raum [als] in der Anschauung vorzustellen [bloß] auf dem Bewußtsein einer Bestimmung durch andere Dinge gegründet, welches

nichts weiter als die ursprüngliche Passivität von mir bedeutet, bei der ich gar nicht tätig bin. Daß der Traum [eben dergleichen] Täuschung hervorbringe von Existenzen außer mir, beweiset nichts dawider; denn es mußten allemal äußere Wahrnehmungen vorhergehen. Ursprünglich eine Vorstellung von etwas als außer mir zu bekommen, ohne in der Tat passiv zu sein, ist unmöglich . . ." (Akad., XVIII, p. 307).

CHAPTER 8. KANT NOT A FOUNDATIONALIST

1. Gottfried W. Leibniz, *Philosophical Papers and Letters*, 2d ed., ed. L. Loemker (Chicago: University of Chicago Press, 1976), p. 385. Leibniz never fails to advert to the coherence of our philosophical and mathematical assertions with the great body of our everyday experience. Comparing Descartes's procedure with the effort of geometers to prove their axioms, he says, "We accept these [axioms] both because they satisfy the mind and because they are proved by countless experiences . . ." (ibid., p. 383). In discussing Leibniz's method, Loemker contrasts his efforts to formulate an explicit philosophical methodology (which is not a foundationalism in the Cartesian sense, in any case) with his much broader and more liberal practice in philosophical reasoning. Loemker cites Leibniz's "own recognition that in the analysis of existence his own efforts to arrive at finality are blocked by man's finiteness." He says, "To anticipate Kant, we may say that such efforts finally confront the antinomies which mark our knowledge of existence—those of finiteness and infinity, plurality and unity, activity and passivity, change and permanence. Leibniz's failure to apply his own method perfectly illustrates this . . . [and] except for his logical studies, his approach to philosophical problems was relative to experience and applied the method only within empirically applicable limits" (ibid., p. 22). For the relationship of Kant's conception of antinomies to Leibniz's thought, and to the Leibniz-Clarke Correspondence in particular, see also Al Azm, *The Origins of Kant's Thinking in the Antinomies* (Oxford: Oxford University Press, 1972).

2. I have in mind especially Louis Couturat and Bertrand Russell, both of whom claimed that all of Leibniz's major views are supposed to be derivable from his logic, and who jointly have exerted an overwhelming influence on thinking about Leibniz in the twentieth century. See Louis Couturat, *La logique de Leibniz* (Paris: 1901; reprinted Hildesheim, Olms, 1961); and Bertrand Russell, "Recent Work on the Philosophy of Leibniz," *Mind* vol. 12, 1903, reprinted in Harry Frankfurt, ed., *Leibniz: A Collection of Critical Essays* (Garden City, N.Y.: Doubleday, 1972).

3. When Leibniz does appeal to self-knowledge, the appeal has a quite different orientation from that of Descartes's solipsistic foundationalism. In the first place, Leibniz gives a kind of priority to apprehension of outer things, which was standard until the Cartesian reorganization of epistemology, and he presses for the acceptance of self-consciousness as a further source of insight. Secondly, self-consciousness serves Leibniz as a source of metaphors and hints for his metaphysics of monads and not as a reservoir of incorrigible premises: "In whatever sense they are taken, it is always false to say that all of our notions come from the senses, which are called external; for the notions which I have of myself and

of my thoughts, and, consequently of being, of substance, of action, of identity, and of many others, come from an internal experience" (*Philosophical Papers,* p. 321). In my opinion, this appeal to self-consciousness contains suggestions that may have operated in Kant's thinking in so far as Leibniz (1) contrasts inner and outer sense; (2) finds a subjective foundation for the Categories; (3) gives great importance to apperception in the transcendental deduction of the Categories; and (4) places our ordinary knowledge of our own judgments and their logical form in a determinative role with respect to the discovery of the Categories. Be this as it may, in Leibniz's thought, as Loemker concludes, "the nature of the scientist himself, as given in immediate experience, throws a more concrete light upon the metaphysical implications of his work" (ibid., p. 23). I want to emphasize that it is the everyday experience of oneself, and not a purified base of absolutely secure premises, to which Leibniz makes analogical appeal.

4. *Prolegomena,* Akad., IV, p. 366.

5. Ibid., p. 327.

6. Ibid., p. 353. This passage is quite suggestive of Hume's contention that when it comes to metaphysical objectives, philosophy is impotent, while nature has not left things to chance but has irrevocably instilled in each of us the beliefs that philosophy is powerless to establish.

7. Ibid., p. 365.

8. See *Prolegomena,* §38.

CHAPTER 9. THE "HOW-POSSIBLE" QUESTIONS

1. Philosophers are tempted to develop hypotheses out of the phenomena of dreams, which do involve spatial things and are private and thus separate spaces. A table in my dream is not anywhere with respect to the table in my kitchen, although it may be to the left of the dream window. Such conceptions, however elaborately developed, will not flesh out the conception of multiple spaces for Kant because, in the framework of his thought, dreams belong to the class of illusions of apprehended things and do not offer a second space in which real things might be located. The spatial structure of an illusion is either ordinary outer space, which is the locus of hallucinations like Macbeth's dagger (not a real object but located in the ordinary space in front of Macbeth's hand), or it is merely the illusion of space with the illusion of objects in it, as in dreams.

CHAPTER 10. THE "CLUE" FOR FINDING THE CATEGORIES

1. Not all judgments are of the subject-predicate form. A more general picture of judgment as essentially combinatorial is no less appropriate for the expression of Kant's perspective.

2. It has to be conceded that the combinatory powers that Kant discerns in the forms of judgment operate at different levels and do not make a natural list. In particular, the forms of compound judgments and of modal judgments are constructed in very different ways, taking complete subject-predicate judgments as proper parts.

3. See René Descartes, *Dioptrique,* Adam and Tannery, eds., *Oeuvres de Descartes* (Paris: J. Vrin, 1974), vol. 6, p. 84.

CHAPTER 11. THE PARALLELISM OF INNER AND
          OUTER SENSE

1. B66–68. Henry Allison discusses parts of this passage in his *Kant's Transcendental Idealism;* see chap. 12 and especially p. 264. I am indebted to Allison for my appreciation of the importance of this passage.

2. Ibid., p. 261.

3. "So sage ich nicht, die Körper *scheinen* bloß außer mir zu sein, oder meine Seele *scheint* nur in meinem Selbstbewußtsein gegeben zu sein" (B69).

4. According to Kant, it is only the failure to appreciate the parallel status of space and time that enables philosophers to put forward skeptical idealist views. No philosopher has advanced the absurd view that the existence of the subject is pure illusion. The Kantian parallelism makes the contention that objects in space may not exist equally absurd.

5. "Mit der inneren Anschauung ist es eben so bewandt" (B67).

6. This corresponds to familiar conceptions of the "transparency" of the mental. There is no procedure for apprehending one's own mental states, and for that reason, it has seemed to many philosophers that there is no gap though which error could enter our assessment of the contents of our own minds.

CHAPTER 12. THE SUBJECT OF EXPERIENCE

1. See A106–107 for the ascription of both of these characterizations to this unity.

2. "Das Bewußtsein seiner selbst, nach den Bestimmungen unseres Zustandes, bei der inneren Wahrnehmungen ist bloß empirisch, jederzeit wandelbar, es kann kein stehendes oder bleibendes Selbst in diesem Flusse innerer Erscheinungen geben" (A107).

3. The correct characterization of "conscious perceptual experiences" is a topic that cannot be addressed in this context. Although I think Kant is himself a captive of traditional and indefensible conceptions of mental realities, this defect, if I am right about it, does not vitiate the overall wisdom of his work and his conception of ordinary experience.

4. Kant endorses the traditional concept of substance as a preliminary example of the *a priori* in the introduction, B5–6.

5. Hume, "*Treatise of Human Nature,*" appendix.

6. This is an immediate consequence of the first analogy and is stated as such at the beginning of the proof of the second analogy, the burden of which is to show that the changes in appearances, all of which are alterations, fall under universal causal laws. See B232.

7. See B156 and B277.

8. "Die Vorstellung dieser Einheit kann also nicht aus der Verbindung entstehen, sie macht vielmehr dadurch, daß sie zur Vorstellung des Mannigfaltigen

hinzukommt, den Begriff der Verbindung allererst möglich" (Thus the representation of this unity [of consciousness] cannot develop out of combination, rather, the fact that the representation of unity attaches to the manifold makes the concept of combination possible in the first place) (B131).

9. §24, B154.

10. See §26, B161.

CHAPTER 13. HOW REPRESENTATIONS MAKE OBJECTS POSSIBLE

1. Here again, one must bear in mind that aberrant perceptual experiences in which there is no object or in which the object does not have the perceived sensuous feature are dependent, in Kant's understanding, on prior *perception,* that is, direct apprehension of outer objects.

2. By "concepts of an object in general," Kant means just "concept of an object, irrespective of any further specification or characterization of the object of experience."

CHAPTER 15. THE IDEALISTIC UNDERSTANDING OF KANT'S THEORETICAL PHILOSOPHY

1. There is, of course, a fundamental connection of the inner and the outer, the temporal and the spatial. Theoretically posited outer representations, which are not themselves temporal, are the input for inner sense. The resulting inner representations of outer representations are temporal representations of spatial representations. The synthesis of these engenders complex representations of enduring objects that are both spatial and temporal. From the perspective of consciousness, these objects are immediately given, and the theoretical apparatus is offered in explanation of the possibility of our conscious experience of enduring, and thus temporal, outer objects.

2. P. F. Strawson, *The Bounds of Sense* (London: Methuen, 1996), p. 196.

3. Dieter Henrich, *Identität und Objektivität* (Heidelberg: Carl Winter, Universitätsverlag, 1976), p. 42 (my translation). I share in the general admiration for this insightful book. At the same time, on the issue of Kant's idealism, passages like this one provide good illustrations of the understanding of Kant I take to be fundamentally misguided.

4. Hilary Putnam, *Reason, Truth and History* (Cambridge: Cambridge University Press, 1981), p. 64.

5. Although it may be an undesirable interpolation into his epistemology, Kant seems to allow for judgments at the level of sense qualities in his conception of "judgments of perception" in the *Prolegomena,* §20. See the discussion in chapter 5 above.

6. C. Garve's review of the *Critique,* edited by J. Feder, *Göttinger Anzeigen von gelehrten Sachen,* 1782, annoyed Kant with the charge that his view was akin to Berkeley's. This criticism is widely, and in my view wrongly, thought to have induced Kant to move to a less idealistic position in the *Prolegomena* and the second edition of the *Critique.* For Eberhard's views, see Henry Allison, *The*

Kant-Eberhard Controversy (Baltimore: Johns Hopkins University Press, 1973). Allison quotes Eberhard: "For in the theory of critical idealism synthetic judgments can have no objects outside of the representations; for they cannot relate to anything which is actual apart from the representations, and their logical truth thus consists merely in the agreement of representations in us with the same representations in us" (p. 41.) Quoted from *Philosophisches Magazin*, 1788, vol. I, pp. 321–322. J. H. Jacobi, *David Hume über den Glauben, oder Idealismus und Realismus* (Leipzig: Gerhard Fleischer, 1815).

7. See pages 163–164.

8. Arthur Schopenhauer, *The World as Will and Idea*, trans. R. B. Haldane and J. Kemp (London: Routledge and Kegan Paul, 1883), vol. 2, p. 30.

9. See Gerhard Lehmann, *Beiträge zur Geschichte und Interpretation der Philosophie Kant's* (Berlin: Walter de Gruyter, 1969), p. 173.

10. H. J.Paton, *Kant's Metaphysic of Experience*, 2 vols. (New York: The Humanities Press, 1936).

11. Kemp Smith, *Commentary*.

12. DeVleeschauwer, *La déduction transcendentale*. DeVleeschauwer and Paton do not present an exclusively idealist picture of Kant. For one thing, both writers reject an ontological distinction between appearances and things in themselves. It ought to follow that, if an entity or existing thing is not a mental entity when considered as it is in itself, then it will not be a mental entity when considered as it appears to us, for the appearance and the thing in itself are one and the same entity. I think this is the correct understanding. In spite of his generally realist interpretation, Paton seems to present the more common idealist conception of phenomenalism, for example, in saying, "Kant . . . [holds] that we are given only ideas, and that nothing else is given which can correspond to our ideas and so be their objects" (vol. 1, p. 383) and ". . . to know an object is to recognize the presence of necessary synthetic unity in our ideas" (vol. 1, p. 385). DeVleeschauwer, in turn, seems to be solidly in the phenomenalist-idealist camp when he says things like "The subjective function [in the forms of judgment] precipitated in the pure concepts of the understanding has an objective value because they make the object possible, for they constitute it" (vol. l, p. 179, my translation).

13. C. M. Turbayne, "Kant's Relation to Berkeley," *Philosophical Quarterly*, vol. 5, 1955; quoted as reprinted in Lewis White Beck, *Kant Studies Today* (Lasalle, Ill.: Open Court, 1969), p. 115.

14. For the letters from these three contemporaries of Kant, see Akad., vol. 10, pp. 103–116. The letters from Lambert and Mendelssohn are included in Arnulf Zweig, *Kant's Philosophical Correspondence, 1759–1799* (Chicago: University of Chicago Press, 1967), pp. 60–70. This correspondence is often discussed; see Paul Guyer, *Kant and the Problem of Knowledge* (Cambridge: Cambridge University Press, 1987), p. 345; Paton, *Kant's Metaphysic*, vol. 1, p. 182; W. H. Walsh, *Kant's Critique of Metaphysics* (Edinburgh: University of Edinburgh Press, 1975), p. 30; and especially, DeVleeschauwer, *La déduction*, vol. 1, pp. 164–167.

15. See the letter from Lambert to Kant, October 13, 1770, Akad. vol. 10, p. 107 (my translation).

16. DeVleeschauwer, *La déduction*, vol. 1, p. 166 (my translation).

17. Ibid., vol. 1, pp. 164–167. Kant got much the same critical reaction from his friend Johann Schulz.

18. Karl Ameriks, *Kant's Theory of Mind* (Oxford: Oxford University Press), 1982, p. 8.

19. T. E. Wilkerson, *Kant's Critique of Pure Reason* (Oxford: Oxford University Press, 1976).

20. Paul Guyer, *Kant and the Claims of Knowledge* (Cambridge: Cambridge University Press, 1987), pp. 334–335.

21. Ralph Walker, *Kant* (London: Routledge and Kegan Paul, 1978), p. 123.

22. Ibid., p. 127. Walker might well have added Descartes as the historical originator of the standpoint of Locke and Hume.

23. Of course, I do not claim that there are no inconsistencies in Kant, but only that this particular charge of inconsistency springs from mistaken ascription of idealism, which indeed contradicts Kant's many denials that he espouses any such view.

24. Kemp Smith, *A Commentary*, p. 312.

25. Patricia Kitcher, *Kant's Transcendental Psychology* (New York: Oxford University Press, 1990), p. 93.

26. I do think it makes good sense to think that Kant is already persuaded that idealism is a dead end by the time he writes the Inaugural Dissertation, and that the first edition of the *Critique* argues against idealism and for the view that we encounter nonmental enduring objects in ordinary experience.

27. Henry Allison, *Kant's Transcendental Idealism* (New Haven: Yale University Press, 1983), p. 7; Ermanno Bencivenga, *Kant's Copernican Revolution* (New York: Oxford University Press, 1987); Graham Bird, *Kant's Theory of Knowledge* (London: Routledge and Kegan Paul, 1962); Robert Pippin, *Kant's Theory of Form: An Essay on the Critique of Pure Reason* (New Haven: Yale University Press, 1982); Gerold Prauss, *Kant und der Problem der Dinge an sich*, 3d ed. (Bonn: Bouvier Verlag, 1989); and T. D. Weldon, *Kant's Critique of Pure Reason*, 2d ed. (Oxford: Oxford University Press, 1958). Along with interpretations that do not make Kant an idealist, I find that even these writers, for the most part, persevere in speaking of the transcendental ideality of space and time and empirical objects as if this does have something to do with idealistic philosophy as traditionally understood.

28. Allison, *Kant's Transcendental Idealism,* p. 7.

29. See Allison's brief discussion of this matter. *Kant's Transcendental Idealism*, pp. 26–27.

30. Ibid., p. 67.

31. Walsh, *Kant's Criticism*.

32. Ibid., p. 94.

33. Pippin, *Kant's Theory of Form*, p. 191.

34. Ibid., p. 192.

35. Ibid., p. 190.

36. Ibid., p. 193.

37. This is the very conception that Kant sets aside on the ground that it contradicts transcendental idealism.

Index

Compositor: Braun-Brumfiield, Inc.
Text: 10/13 Sabon
Display: Sabon
Printer: Braun-Brumfield, Inc.
Binder: Braun-Brumfield, Inc.